OTHER BOOKS BY JEANNE AVERY

The Rising Sign: Your Astrological Mask
Astrological Aspects: Your Inner Dialogues

Astrology
and
Your Past Lives

JEANNE AVERY

A FIRESIDE BOOK
Published by Simon & Schuster, New York

Copyright © 1987 by Jeanne Avery
All rights reserved
including the right of reproduction
in whole or in part in any form.

A Fireside Book
Published by Simon & Schuster, Inc.

Rockefeller Center
1230 Avenue of the Americas
New York, NY 10020

FIRESIDE and colophon are registered trademarks of
Simon & Schuster, Inc.

Designed by Karolina Harris
Manufactured in the United States of America

11   13   15   17   19   20   18   16   14   12

Library of Congress Cataloging in Publication Data
Avery, Jeanne.
Astrology and your past lives.

"A Fireside book."
1.   Astrology and reincarnation.   2.   Saturn
(Planet)—Miscellanea.   I.   Title.
BF1729.R37A83   1987   133.5'81339013   87-7520
ISBN 0-671-63294-9

Acknowledgments

To Lama Lopsang Tsultrim,
a friend and teacher returned to help me on my path

Writing a book is indeed a group effort, for it is impossible to accomplish such a task without the good will and active support of many people. The author receives the accolades, if the book is successful, but the unsung heroes are the editor and the people working alongside who combine efforts to bring about the safe delivery. The birth of a book should include a moment when all concerned could come onstage and take a bow.

It is difficult to name everyone who gave aid or comfort during the year of birth struggle, but I would be remiss if I didn't give thanks to some special people. First, thanks must go to my clients who shared their very personal experiences so that others might gain a new perspective on the riddle of life. Next, to my agents, Lynn Nesbit and Suzanne Gluck, for exuding enthusiasm and support, the very breath necessary to do the job. Finally, but not least, I give thanks to Barbara Gess, my editor, who worked with me under very tight deadlines and whose expertise was invaluable.

I am eternally grateful for the synchronous events that dropped me into the warm lap of Ibiza, Spain, where friends give the gift of true freedom, "Do what you need to do." My special thanks go to the Hotel Hacienda, where I held my conferences, and to Ernesto Fajarnes, "El Jefe." Then to my wonderful neighbors Antonio and Catalina, who cared about my eating properly, and to Eulalia Guasch and her lovely family. I am grateful to Estela Bence and Jackie Riley, who held the fort in my absence. Loving thanks go to Xhico and Daniel Siegel, who took responsibility for my contact with the outside world, and to Freda Birchnall, who did secretarial work on her vacation. Special gratitude goes to Lola and Paul Tanner, Anna, Jean Claude, and Harold for bringing

Lama Tsultrim into my life at the very moment I was writing a book on reincarnation and needed him most.

On this side of the ocean, friends have been no less caring in giving me comfort and shelter during my sojourns in New York. I especially thank my long-time friends Marilyn Rothkopf and Sandra Sherrard. Also Marily and John Whitney, Ellen Nagler, Jane Nichols, Dale Haddon, and Isobel and Ron Konecky. Glen Janss deserves a huge hug for being a warm, loving, and enthusiastic friend. Very special gratitude goes to Peter Cooper for finding special reference material and to Douglas Sissons for his perceptions about the book and what was needed, and to Charles Harvey for thinking about me.

As always, I count myself a lucky person to have attracted such wonderful children into my life. Here's to Sharon and Tony, Charles and Stephanie, Diane and Lee, Berit, and David and Lori.

Preface

Twenty years ago when I conducted my first regression sessions, I was absolutely amazed at the information that poured forth from the people I worked with. Apparently, memory lies closer to the surface of our minds than we care to believe. With only a small amount of permission and guidance, the subconscious appears eager to unload the burden that has been carried around for centuries, perhaps eons. The profound relief that most people experience after such a session is reason enough to delve within, but there are even more valuable reasons for the exploration of the subconscious.

Perhaps the most important revelation, beyond the personal ones which give such an exciting new perspective on life, is the sense of continuity. With a review of several lifetimes or states of existence, the fear of death can be conquered once and for all. It becomes clear that there is a thread of consciousness that is never broken. Death is simply the birth into a new state of existence, just as birth into this earth plane is the death of an old condition. We actually experience death in a thousand ways during one lifetime. There are temporary deaths of relationships, cycles and events that continue to prepare us for the possibility of rebirth. Without that clearing away of old conditions, we could not go on to allow growth and continuing expansion into our lives. There is a constant housecleaning that goes on when we decide to discontinue certain habits, associations or proclivities, making room for the new.

Each night is a kind of death. We need to complete a certain segment of time, take a break and be prepared for the coming dawn. If we have conquered the fear of giving up and going to sleep at night with the thought, "Tomorrow is another day," we can apply the analogy to lifetimes. A child is consoled with the suggestion that he get some rest because the activities of the coming day will be even more exciting than those of the last one. And so it is with the coming life.

We have dreams at night that can be interpreted to guide us through our daytime decision-making process. A regression session can do the same on a broader scale. Many people have described the peace and sense of oneness, like a floating feeling that comes in between lives, like sleep, that give us a breather and a chance to review our actions and interactions on earth.

If a child has had a nightmare, he needs to talk about it and see it in the light of day so that he doesn't fear going to sleep again at night. The nightmare somewhat mars the pleasure of his daily fun. But with some hugs from Mom and reassurance, he is able to create activities and plan his day in spite of his bad dreams. If he doesn't tell anyone what he experienced, he may be panicked at the thought of another frightening experience during sleep. If we can clean out the karmic garbage pail with a review in the light of day, we see clearly that we have options and responsibilities to create what we need and want to enable us to live more productively. If we are not willing to take a look and share the nightmare, we carry unnecessary burdens around, mitigating the joy of present existence.

Even more important, we don't neglect the responsibilities we've set in motion on one day just because we know there will be another dawn, but at the same time, if we cannot accomplish everything we set out to do, we can carry over the remaining list of activities to the next day. In a review of past life experiences, it is important to forgive ourselves for omissions and commissions, but it is also important to realize there is no easy out. We are fully accountable for our actions. At bottom line, however, no one suffers more than we do ourselves for our errors.

Not only can we see more clearly how to achieve a better balance in life, but we can actually begin to create the conditions of a future life by making plans, such as making a list of activities for the new day ahead. This takes away all the judgments and sadness about not accomplishing our dreams in the present existence. There is always a second chance, a new day dawning.

In one esoteric school, the instruction is given to start the day with meditation and to end it with a review of the day's activities.

The meditation creates the aura within which we can function and the review enables us to reevaluate, forgive and transmute the events into more tolerable memories before going to sleep. In this way, we clean up our act on a daily basis. A lot of future karmic pain can be avoided by this process.

In the final analysis, this book is neither about astrology or reincarnation. It is an attempt to share another process in the continuing search to understand life and the human condition. My greatest frustration in writing the book was having to choose from among hundreds of regression sessions to find those that might be more universally meaningful. My hope is that through whatever means available, we can all develop more compassion and caring for ourselves and for others.

Foreword

Throughout my years of formal psychiatric training at Columbia and Yale universities, I knew something was missing. Later on, as a professor of Psychiatry at two prestigious medical schools and as chairman of the Department of Psychiatry at a major teaching hospital, I still had the feeling that something vital was missing from my education. I just couldn't put my finger on what.

I discovered astrology, studied the subject thoroughly and carefully, and found that I had new insights into character analysis. Some years later, a patient of mine spontaneously regressed to past-life experiences while under hypnosis. Her symptoms, which had been lifelong, severe, and unresponsive to traditional therapy, disappeared. She has remained permanently cured. This has since occurred with a dozen more patients Finally, I knew what was missing.

In this gem of a book, Jeanne Avery clearly and brilliantly documents the benefits of past-life therapy and sets the stage for a major therapeutic tool of the future. Laced with fascinating case histories, the book echoes the writings of Edgar Cayce, Dr. Edith Fiore, Dr. Joel Whitton, and others. But this book goes beyond the others. The astrological influences, especially the location and aspects of Saturn in the natal chart, are examined with clarity and used as a map and indicator of the directions to take in therapy. This is new, innovative, and extremely practical knowledge. She has succeeded in synthesizing astrology and past-life experiences to produce a powerful technique for swiftly and accurately understanding and resolving emotional conflicts, which may have been tormenting patients for many, many years and which may have been resistant to the techniques of traditional psychotherapy.

No prior knowledge of astrology is needed. All the astrology you need to know is contained in these pages. No hypnotic techniques are used. Her method is even simpler. Whether you are a therapist who wishes to know more, or someone who wants to get rid of unwanted symptoms or remove blocks and grow toward happiness and self-fulfillment, the answers lie within this book.

Jeanne Avery has written the most important therapy book of the eighties. She may not realize this yet. But the knowledge is so important and the techniques so powerful and practical that the very foundation for the therapies of the nineties is now being set.

Brian L. Weiss, M.D.
Chairman, Department of Psychiatry
Mount Sinai Medical Center
Miami, Florida

Contents

There are two ways of entering this world . . .
one of them is through the female body. . . .
Anonymous

God created man because he loves good stories. . . .
—ELIE WIESEL (courtesy of Ellen Nagler)

I
Karmic Reckoning

CHAPTER ONE

The Case for Reincarnation and Regression

hakespeare said, "All the world's a stage, And all the men and women merely players." According to metaphysical principles, life is indeed a drama of our creation. Carl Jung said, "Any unrealized energy or potential exteriorizes as fate or destiny." All that might be interpreted to mean that we consciously, or unconsciously, set in motion the specific circumstances and conditions around us. Theoretically, then, we are not victims of our environment but rather the creators of it. If that is so, why are we not all successful, healthy, happy and constantly on top of any situation? Who would deliberately pick illness, physical disability, poverty, isolation, loneliness or despair? Yet all we have to do is look around to see heartrending difficulties in people's lives.

The doctrine of the power of positive thinking may or may not always work. Many advocates of that philosophy seem just as plagued with heartaches and problems as anyone else. Although that philosophy can be very important for a cheerful outlook and a better view of life, when real tragedy or trying times hit, that attitude may seem like trying to pour a cupful of oil on a raging, torrential tidal wave. Even the most successful, dynamic and intelligent people have cycles and patterns that can turn their lives around at a moment's notice. Optimism falls desperately short of effectiveness in the face of suicides, death or tragic accidents. Modern therapy seems to have found some answers, yet the road to fulfillment can seem like a long one. Attempts to change lifelong habits and patterns can seem like a slow and painstaking trip to the top of Mount Everest. How can we discover a surefire formula to achieve a different perspective? Does one exist? Is there some magic answer to it all?

The attempt to understand the human condition is not a new one. For centuries, philosophical man has explored the workings of the human mind, taking a variety of approaches to delving within the subconscious, hoping to find the key to more successful living. Descartes decided that existence was directly related to thought processes when he said "I think, therefore I am." Freud was convinced that abnormalities, demons and unexplained behavior, producing unhappiness, were connected to the experience of early childhood sexual fantasies. He made inroads into the understanding of the unconscious mind, and Carl Jung went a step further and described what he termed the collective unconscious. His theory was that man not only had his own subconscious memories but could also tap a universal memory bank, containing the genetic codes and thought forms of mankind as a whole. Dr. J.B. Rhine conducted experiments into still another facet of mind by looking at psychic phenomena and the paranormal.

As we prepare to enter the Aquarian Age, subjects that were once considered taboo or frightening are being accepted by science, medicine, psychology and even big business. Meditation, once considered a subject only for mystics, is being taught to businessmen to help relieve the stress of daily corporate life; housewives are becoming involved in yoga classes and learning about holistic healing; scientists use such tools as biofeedback to measure the effects of thought processes on bodily functions, and the medical profession is beginning to seriously investigate and work with people who are natural healers.

Seminars are readily available all over the world to acquaint everyone with healing of body, mind and soul, and the practice of holistic medicine is no longer mysterious. Awareness of right-brain and left-brain functions enable many individuals to tap more creative potential. Smokers' and weight-loss clinics are now big moneymakers in the self-help field, using techniques such as hypnosis and affirmations, phrases to reaffirm positive decisions, to break the chain of dependency on cigarettes and food. Neurolinguistic training programs seek to teach three distinct facets of the mind process—kinesthetic, auditory and visual—in hopes of bettering communications. Group therapy workshops form support systems for those who wish to explore painful subjects or nonproductive behavior in expectation of reaching a better understanding of themselves and their patterns.

How can all this information be integrated? Do all the new techniques really help, or do they merely distract us? Why do new problems arise as one set seems resolved? If we are really creating the circumstances of our daily life scripts, where does religion enter, and who is the real mastermind of our drama? How can we possibly progress at our own rate? Why do we still have conflicts and personality clashes if we are becoming more aware of action and interaction, cause and effect, and our acting as a mirror for the people we encounter in relationships? What about health conditions that are beyond our control? What about luck?

Transactional Analysis says, among other things, that we have a life script. The rising sign, or ascendant, in the astrological chart describes early survival decisions, thereby relating to the life script. Some of those survival decisions are productive but some are nonproductive. That script, or drama, may be chosen for us by our parents before birth or some time after that event, or the child may pick his own script at some early point in his life. Sometimes the script can be simple, but at other times, the individual can seem caught in an intricate web of his own convolution. The aim of prolonged therapy in the discipline of Transactional Analysis is to break the script. In terms of astrological awareness an aim is to drop the mask and tap inner richness that may be hidden. Medical science is making great strides with research into prenatal conditions as a possible answer to the perplexity of subconscious patterning.

But as advanced as research into prenatal conditioning can be, it may not explain some of the more complex and conflicting dialogues that exist within the human framework. For instance, why are we attracted to one person and not another? Why do we fall in love when the mind clearly tells us that caution should be the watchword? Why are we effective or talented in some areas and not in others? Why do we fear success if we have been programmed to be successful? Why do accidents occur? Why does a child born into a family of average intelligence show genius potential at an early age or talent that has never emerged in the family lineage? Why are some children born with exceptional good taste when the environment may not have fostered that quality? On a broader philosophical level, why are some people born with everything while some have to struggle throughout their lives? Children born into the same family, with similar environmental conditioning and what might appear to be the same parental messages, can have incredibly varying abilities, qualities and predispositions.

Astrology can give a different insight into the mysteries of life and cycles. It has been recognized throughout the ages as a tool for understanding. That tool can be utilized on levels that penetrate and go beyond surface appearances and conditions, for it shows the bare skeleton of an individual, his masks, inner dialogues, conditioning, and predispositions or talents. It is a language that crosses all barriers erected by social conditions, color, race and nationality. The symbology is universal in cutting to the core of a problem or situation. It can make headway in answering some of the questions that continue to mystify mankind. If nothing else, the astrological chart can point the way and help stimulate man to answer his own questions. For all the answers lie within. A lifetime of searching the far corners of the earth for answers to these puzzling philosophical matters eventually leads to the awareness that man is a universe within himself. Struggles to overcome limitations can be successful at times and fruitless at others, yet man survives, to go on to new conditions and different sets of problems, for he is basically a problem-solving mechanism. Astrology describes how he goes about solving those problems.

KARMIC ATTRACTIONS

The final answer may lie with the theory of reincarnation. For it is only from the perspective of a continuation of existence that the inequalities of life can be explained. "What ye sow shall ye reap." "An eye for an eye, a tooth for a tooth." Biblical references to reincarnation abound and make sense of mysterious phrases otherwise almost incomprehensible. Eastern religions accept the theory of reincarnation without question; in Tibet, prior to the Chinese invasion, the whole governmental system was based on the discovery of the reincarnation of the Dalai Lama. The Western world is beginning to open its eyes to the possibility of such a concept. Much of this is due to the advent of a new age, approximately three hundred years away. But with the approach of the Aquarian epoch, old conditions, philosophies and activities must give way to a more humanitarian earthly experience.

There are always forerunners who pave the way for enlightenment. One very special man was Edgar Cayce, called the Sleeping Prophet because of his ability to diagnose physical illness while he was in a trance state. He was able to tap what might be called a universal data bank by putting himself to sleep. The information he brought forth staggered and awed him, in particular because of his traditional religious upbringing. He reluctantly came to accept the theory of reincarnation after hundreds of cases poured forth from his subconscious. He was aware of the miraculous cures that were effected as a result of his diagnosis of physical conditions of people miles away from him at the time of his readings, but he struggled with the horrifying thought that perhaps what he revealed was the work of the devil. He agreed to a special session with professors who wanted to ask him philosophical questions, and explained the reincarnation doctrine in trance, responding to some tough interrogation. He was especially horrified, when he was once again in a waking state, that he had satisfied such erudite men with his answers. Edgar Cayce had only a rudimentary education at best, and certainly in his conscious mind he felt he was not equipped intellectually to know anything about such a strange philosophy. Eventually he came to accept the theory of reincarnation as truth, but only when it was clear that the material he was revealing had a positive effect on the lives of his subjects.

It was stressed in his readings that a practical approach to the idea of many lives was very necessary. Memories of a previous existence were unimportant and could even be detrimental unless the individual applied that knowledge to present life conditions. On no account were these memories to be used as an ego builder or a rationale for conduct. To let the glamour of a memory of a previous high position, for instance, obscure the lesson that was to be learned in the present life could actually delay spiritual growth. To take one life memory away from the whole cloth might also obscure the overall picture, for indeed the thread running from life to life could have woven around it a gamut of experiences. Lives could run from high to low, exciting to routine, productive to static, as was required for soul development. The central theme running through all those existences might indicate that present-day circumstances were not so very different from past life conditions, no matter what the outer trappings. It seems we take centuries upon centuries to learn some lessons. In her book *Many Lives, Many Loves*, Gina Cerminara clearly states, "It is significant I think, that the theory of reincarnation and karma is one of uncompromising accountability and responsibility."

Lifetime to lifetime is like yesterday to today. Death is like sleep between days and rebirth like getting up and putting on a new body or suit of clothes. The memories linger like a continuous thread on a subconscious level. Nonproductive decisions or those born of fear and trauma continue to haunt long after the event is forgotten. Behavior characteristics can stem from seemingly unimportant events that were never resolved, and very real life problems, physical disabilities and psychological blocks may have a past-life traumatic situation at the core of the matter.

We seem to have not only individual karma, or lessons, to be resolved, but there is also an interplay of characters from lifetime to lifetime. Ruth Montgomery says in her book *The World Before*, "Human beings, like Cervantes' birds of a feather who flock together, tend to reincarnate in cycles with those they have known in previous earthly sojourns. By some curious law of karmic attraction we return again and again with these perennial companions to work out mutual problems left unresolved, or enjoy each other's company.... But since each of us earthlings, once caught up in the wheel of karma, must experience physical life in all major creeds and geographical areas, we do not always return to the same race or locale." To carry that a step further, we do not always return as the same sex. The memories of life spent on another stage can explain attractions, relationships, sexual leanings, physical health, talent, intellect and problems.

Astrological Significator

The individual astrological chart is a dynamic indicator of just what that past life conditioning might be and just how it manifests itself in present life. One key to the understanding of the karma or major lesson to be resolved in present-day existence is connected to the planet Saturn and its placement and aspects in the natal chart. Although other points, such as the moon's nodes, also give some clues, the placement of Saturn in the natal chart is a major indication of just how that lesson is to be resolved and through which department of life we may expect to have the greatest level of responsibility and the greatest level of stress.

The description of Saturn's placement, aspects and rulerships in the horoscope is most important in the process of uncovering past life experiences. It can be likened to a knot in the thread of consciousness that must be untied at some point, to avoid a continuous repetition of the same old mistakes. But first it is important to understand just what Saturn symbolizes in personal behavior characteristics. For centuries, Saturn has symbolized hardship, toil, drudgery, limitation and something to fear. The correlation of astrology and psychology has revealed a more positive concept of this energy, for Saturn can be related to the parent ego state, which can be judgmental but is also highly responsible. Saturn represents gravity. Without gravity, we cannot remain on earth. Without Saturn in the chart, there is no reason to be here in a physical form in the school of life. It seems we pick our own particular type of gravity to hold us to the Earth plane, in the form of outer conditions, much like finding sandbags to hold down a helium-filled balloon. The trick is to learn how to operate the balloon, using the sandbags as a grounding agent only as long as we need them for stabilization. Gaining more control over our lives can be accomplished by taking on the right quality of responsibility and letting go of negative conditions.

The awareness of past life conditioning gives one permission to let go of negative programming and situations by clearly revealing what they may be. We may have used safe but nonfulfilling situations to provide a perverse kind of comfort. Centuries of clinging to safe but limiting concepts or conditioning may have become very tedious, heavy and burdensome, but until we're ready to fly, we can't walk away from what is familiar. Guilt is familiar comfort that can prevent all efforts to leave stagnant and limiting circumstances behind.

The roots of these patterns go very deep into the subconscious, like the submarine depths of an iceberg. The patterns may lie at the very beginning of time itself, when mankind first began to cut away from the one force or God consciousness. Edgar Cayce's explanation of creation describes the need for expansion of consciousness through new experiences. The comfort and security of oneness in the very beginning gave way to a need for individuation. Sparks of the spiritual consciousness looked for experiences and became trapped in earthly pleasures. Then came a need for a better physical form for mankind. With the soul as a dividing line between man and animal, God gave mankind the gift of free will. So it is free will that enables man to evolve back to the oneness of all, at his own rate of speed. He is free to take centuries to miss that divine comfort and perfect harmony. This concept of original sin is quite different from that held by traditional religion. The word *sin* in Spanish means "without." In the approaching Aquarian Age, that separation of man from the God force within (man without Soul consciousness) is the real sin. It is ultimately the soul that is the connecting link between God and mankind on the highest level. After enough struggles on the earth plane, or in the school of life, man begins to long for that divine connection again. It may be that all his struggles on earth are connected to his sorrow and inability to forgive himself for breaking the all-important connection in the first place.

In the book *Ponder On This*, based on the writings of Alice Bailey and the Tibetan Master Djwhal Khul, a discussion of karma goes a step further. "The law of karma is the most stupendous law of the system and one which is impossible for the average man in any way to comprehend, for, if traced back along its central root and its many ramifications, one eventually reaches the position where causes antedating the solar system have to be dealt with. . . . This law really concerns, or is based on causes which are inherent in the constitution of matter itself and on the interaction between atomic units, whether we use this expression in connection with an atom of substance, a human being, a planetary atom, or a solar atom." In this book, however, we will only deal with the simplest analysis of the effect of karmic law on a person's life. In doing so, it is important to stress the positive as well as the negative concept of karma. It seems we focus on the continual retribution that is part of this concept and punish ourselves unmercifully, eons into eons. This is somewhat like trying to dig the golf ball out of the sand trap with an inappropriate club. The ball goes deeper and deeper. It is possible to forfeit points and start again with a new ball. In life, we seem to overlook that possibility and continue to hack away nonproductively.

The word *karma* simply means "the law." It is the term that describes the biblical phrase, An eye for an eye, a tooth for a tooth. We all know that in one lifetime, this ancient law simply doesn't work. People get away with many actions, even murder, without any obvious punishment. In the light of reincarnation, no one gets away with anything! Everything must be balanced, reconciled, the slate wiped clean. Outer circumstances may teach us many lessons, but true enlightenment comes with full awareness of what it is that must be reconciled from the past. The first step is to acknowledge what we may have done. Guilt seems to be the forging link to future troubles.

REGRESSION THERAPY

It is possible to tap memories or concepts of past life experiences without the use of drugs, hypnosis or any other artificial means. We have easier access to our unconscious than we may imagine. After hundreds of regression sessions conducted with the subject's mind fully open, conscious and aware, I have encountered perhaps two people who were unable to get to an important past life memory. These sessions have taken place over a period of twenty years and have been conducted with people of all races and nationalities and in all locations. The information that is within the human mind is staggering, not only to me as the leader of the sessions but also to the person experiencing a new part of his inner being for the first time. Even after years of psychoanalysis, one subject expressed amazement that she had touched on matters that had never been hinted at in her sessions of analysis.

The most important part of the regression process is learning to trust your ability to have a dialogue between your conscious and unconscious mind. This trust is established by first learning to ask the right kinds of questions and then being willing to accept the answers that come to mind. It is necessary to put the skeptical part of the mind aside and allow oneself to listen to the answer within. It is not necessary to believe in reincarnation to tap these memories, for whether these memories are real or fancied does not really matter. If they emerge from within, they belong to us and may clearly give an explanation to present-day problems or circumstances. The willingness to avoid making judgments about whether those answers are correct seems the only prerequisite to a successful regression session.

The conscious mind seems to allow specific memories to come forth only when we are ready for them. Other details may emerge over a period of time when we least expect them, but the resulting feeling of "aha" shows that they are meaningful, even years after the original regression session. The incredible wealth of storytelling that lurks in the mind of almost everyone is astounding. In a regression session, those experiences, memories or fantasies emerge backward, as it were. Imagine photographing an automobile involved in an explosion. When the film is run backward, all the pieces of that car fly through the air from the wrong direction, floating into place easily to produce the original outline of the automobile in its entirety. So it is with a regression session. The story emerges line by line, scene by scene, but in reverse order, only to be connected to experiences in this life after the session is complete.

These experiences usually come forth from the subconscious with accompanying deep emotion. If indeed the person is not living a real moment from his past, he is a genius of an actor as well as a writer. He never knows the final outcome of the plot until he reaches the dropped stitch of his trauma. Many times the subject of such a session asks, "Do you think I made that up?" My reply is, "What do you think?" He or she usually says, after a moment's pause, "I couldn't have. It was just so real." I am always just as amazed at what comes forth as the person undergoing the regression, for neither of us has an idea of just where these sessions will lead. Although the astrological chart is the key to the structure, or bare bones, of the situation, what is finally revealed cannot be predicted.

Subjects of these sessions have seen themselves as kings and commoners, beggars and thieves, saints and sages. But invariably, a deep sense of relief comes with the memory, no matter what kind of experience is uncovered from the past. The residual effect is positive, almost like relief from a mental burden that has been carried too long. The process of recollection seems to resolve the issue on a major level. Little by little, the experience of that memory begins to be integrated into present-day existence quite naturally. After a period of time, the individual becomes aware of having a different perspective about a particular situation or relationship that seems to heal the present. Sometimes a third person, unaware of the session and the information that has come forth, can also be healed. The power of the mind is formidable. With a new perspective, we make new decisions almost automatically and begin to rewrite our script of life.

REGRESSIONS THROUGH HYPNOSIS

Regression into past lives is not new. When Morey Bernstein regressed housewife Virginia Tighe to a past life as Bridey Murphy, living in Ireland in the last century, it triggered the public's imagination about reincarnation and regression through hypnosis. That session took place in 1954. The book recounting her experience in that Irish lifetime seemed to inaugurate and stimulate interest not only in reincarnation but also in the whole spectrum of spiritual awareness. A great deal of material began to emerge on the subject of past-life memory and the untapped areas of the subconscious.

One of the pioneers in the revelation of metaphysical material was Jess Stearn, a former reporter for *Newsweek* magazine, who began writing about spirituality and reincarnation. His nononsense reporter's style presented information about the occult that enabled many fearful or skeptical people to overcome psychological or religious blocks for the purpose of investigation. Jess rarely drew conclusions for his public. Instead he allowed people to make up their own minds about the information he had revealed in his books.

After writing the best-sellers *Edgar Cayce, The Sleeping Prophet* and *Yoga, Youth and Reincarnation*, Jess began to utilize hypnotherapists who regressed subjects into past lives. One of his most compelling books was about Taylor Caldwell, who felt that the incredible richness of details she wrote about in her novels were mainly fed by her own past-life memories. The results of Jess's exploration through hypnosis into Caldwell's past life is contained in a fascinating book entitled *The Search for a Soul*. Jess's latest book, *Soulmates*, continues with regression sessions but this time focuses on relationships that seem to be a continuation of past-life experiences.

Another pioneer in the area of hypnotic regression was Dick Sutphen, who not only regressed thousands of people into the past but taught others to regress themselves. Dick wrote about his work in *Past Lives, Future Loves* and *You Were Born to Be Together*

Again. He encouraged couples to look to past-life situations for explanations and solutions to present-life difficulties. As more and more research emerged in connection with this process, it appeared that the reconciliation of many problems might be attained through investigation of past-life situations.

Traditionally trained therapists discovered value in this procedure, many times quite by accident. Hypnotherapist Dr. Edith Fiore discussed her findings in the book *You Have Been Here Before*. Dr. Fiore first became interested in hypnotherapy after a weekend seminar at the Esalen Institute in Big Sur, California. After an introduction to the technique, she discovered that the therapeutic process was greatly speeded up by using hypnosis in her practice. She soon realized that many patterns and symptoms could be traced to birth experience. A turning point occurred, however, when a male patient suffering from sexual dysfunction came to her for help. She instructed the patient under hypnosis to go back to the origin of his problem. To her surprise, he went to a lifetime in seventeenth-century Italy where he was a priest. Dr. Fiore discounted to some degree the validity of the findings because she knew the gentleman believed in reincarnation. After several such cases of spontaneous regression under hypnosis with people who had expressed such belief, she used the regression technique with a patient whom she later realized had no belief in reincarnation. The patient was actually distressed to realize that she had described a past-life situation. However, her phobia about snakes disappeared with the memory of a past life as an Aztec girl who was traumatized watching priests dance with poisonous snakes in their mouths.

Carl Schlotterbeck founded the Atlantic Guild for Past-Life Awareness after discovering the value of past-life regression therapy with his patients. Again, his professional training and career nad been traditional until he discovered an exciting breakthrough based on the unorthodox treatment which he cautiously termed "regression imagery." Eventually, he went public and discovered favorable reaction from his colleagues. He talks about his work in his book *Living Your Past Lives*. Mr. Schlotterbeck departed from the usual hypnotic technique for regression by using a system devised by a Los Angeles psychologist, Morris Netherton, Ph.D., who developed a different procedure. Dr. Netherton discovered that by careful interviewing over a period of time, the patient was able to focus his attention on his subjective and emotional reaction to his predicament, allowing the emotions to rise closer to the surface of the conscious mind. A trained therapist was then able to recognize obvious patterns and bring the patient to recall of the past-life trauma in that way.

Dr. Brian Weiss, Chairman of the Department of Psychiatry at Mt. Sinai Hospital in Miami, Florida, also with traditional medical training at only the most prestigious schools, discovered the technique of regression therapy almost by accident when a patient went into spontaneous past-life memory while under hypnosis. Dr. Weiss has stated that many phobias seemingly untouched by traditional methods have been released after the awareness of the origin of the patterns from previous times. Dr. Weiss said that he had always felt something was missing in therapeutic techniques. His upcoming book, *Many Lives, Many Masters*, reveals fascinating information gleaned through his pioneering work with one patient in particular. Dr. Weiss is perhaps the first psychiatrist to "go public," presenting his findings to the medical profession as well as to a variety of interested professionals and nonprofessionals.

REGRESSION WITHOUT HYPNOSIS

No matter what technique is utilized to regress people to past lives, all the practitioners agree on one thing: the purpose and benefits of a regression session. That purpose is not for titillation of the ego, but to clarify and bring forth the fears, restrictions, guilts and sometimes malicious events of the past in order to make more appropriate choices in the here and now. One such situation that becomes crystalline with a new perspective is a rather common *flirtation* with suicide. There are several reasons it simply doesn't do any good. It solves no problems because the problems do not go away. We may encounter a new life in which the same problems are more difficult because of our own past decision to self-destruct. There are several cases that I will discuss in later chapters in which the individuals saw no other way out of their loneliness and sense of frustration than to kill themselves. The result is that they come back feeling an even more intense loneliness, with the added karma of having deprived others of their companionship, associations or love. It is also my understanding that these individuals are not released from the confines of the earth plane until the natural time of death anyway. They must wander, trapped, on the earth plane without the protective shield of a body. It is like deliberately driving an automobile over a cliff and then having to walk everywhere without the benefit of a new car, for no good reason at all. Better to have the use of the present automobile, which can facilitate getting around to solve the current problems.

I have a strong feeling about doing a regression session without hypnosis. I am concerned about the possibility of putting something into the subconscious mind through hypnosis that is inaccurate or simply didn't exist for the individual prior to the session. When the person is fully conscious, awake and aware, he sees everything from the perspective of the here and now. He sees time in a different way and learns how to have a dialogue with his own inner mind. The procedure activates a part of the thinking process that may have been dormant before and reveals an ability to pull forth answers from within that the subject may not have known were available to him. I have been on the receiving end of a formal regression session only once, yet the doors to intuition seemed to be blasted open rather quickly. I have also experienced past life memories through sessions with a Reichian therapist, for instance, that were profound and very real. In one instance, I relived a moment of terror from a past life that I know could never happen again in the present. As a result, I have never been afraid since that time. Reich's theory that all memories of pain or trauma are encapsulated in the muscular structure certainly can apply to past lives. In a moment of pressure, worry or fear, we tend to tense some part of the body to hold on for survival. We can therefore release a lot of energy by knowing where that tension resides in the body and how it began. Regression sessions eliminate a lot of hard work, for the releases, physically, mentally and emotionally, are spontaneous and continue to have benefit long after the session is over.

As a result of my own session, I have also had spontaneous flashes of previous existences when traveling in strange territory. I recall going over the Pyrenees for the first time and seeing a Spanish village in the distance. I had already sensed a time spent in Spain as a temperamental, volatile young lady, running down a narrow street that was quite steep. As I passed that village, I felt it was similar to our own village, but this one was flat. In a few moments, the train sped past another fifteenth century village that was on a hill, and with the confirmation of the hair standing up on the back of my neck, I felt it was the same one where I had lived before. Arnall Bloxham cites many such experiences in his own life. That view and sensation, taken alone, were not so important in my life except to provide an extraordinary memory. It was not until many years later that two people totally unrelated to each other also saw themselves, *and me*, in that same time frame and place. The details emerging from their regression filled in spaces that were incredibly valuable in my own life.

Shirley MacLaine describes regression sessions she experienced through the aid of acupuncture in her book *Dancing in the Light*. She said, "The acupuncture pressure points opened up the paths to the intuitive right brain area (yin). The left brain (yang) must not be permitted to close those paths. And when I dispensed with the objections of my finite mind and got out of my own way, the pictures became more specific. They were rich in texture regarding clothing, body movement, sound, emotional attitudes, but, more than anything else, and increasingly, the images that came up were imbued with a conscious understanding on my part of why I was remembering them today."

In the beginning of her sessions, Shirley had protested that she wasn't consciously aware of having created those images that came to her mind. She continued, "I protested to Chris that I *was* creating the images in a free-associative way. She agreed. But she said I was creating the images because they had come out of my own experience. That was imagination."

The images come forth from the subject with incredible detail, even when the individual is not aware of a conscious recollection or memory of a particular event. I vividly recall a session with a man who lived in an industrial area. He was retired, after having worked very hard all his life. He was of a practical nature and might not be expected to be interested in exploring what might be only a fantasy. However, the pictures emerged very easily. He saw himself at two, dressed in a white dress, as was the custom in his youth. But he was quite surprised to discover that he could actually *see* the texture of the lace used to decorate that dress, worn many years before and never consciously recalled earlier in his life. He then saw himself at about eight months, expressing curiosity about a can of paint. He knew he was wearing only diapers, and knew that the color of the paint was green. He knew the exact shade of green and felt himself putting that delicious color all over his body. He also felt the pain of being cleaned up. He was stripped of his diapers, put in a tub and liberally soaked with turpentine to remove the paint from his body. His screams still rang in his ears. This man had no problem accepting the reality of that experience in his youth, even though the incident had never been discussed before. He similarly accepted readily the experiences that poured forth about his past lives. No matter how much time elapses, the exact details and memories do not fade.

Arnall Bloxham discussed a vitally important issue in connection with regressions. He decided during a particular session that he would experiment a bit. "I wanted to see how reliable the regression was. I wanted to know if I could encourage the man to tell me a lie." Bloxham suggested to the hypochondriac he was working with that he might have been a highwayman. "There was uncertainty for a minute and the man said, 'That question you asked me. I was never a highwayman, but when I was a lad we used to go to the forest and pretend to hold up people. But we didn't ever do it.'"

I have also discovered that it is impossible to influence or lead people to something that doesn't jibe with their own feelings. I might suggest, for instance, that perhaps an individual would respond to a certain situation in a particular manner. If such is not the case, the person always says, "No, that isn't the way I feel about it." If I'm on the right track, he or she may correct my perceptions just slightly to clarify exactly how it is that he or she experiences a particular situation. Since so much information and awareness emerges from the individual without drugs, hypnosis or any artificial means, I feel it is extraneous and very unnecessary to use other methods. It seems that in this manner, an individual can continue to have new awareness floating into his consciousness from time to time, especially when he is preoccupied with matters unrelated to past life existence. In fact, after the sessions are over and the pressure of the experience has abated somewhat, even more information is free to float into the conscious mind.

During the sessions themselves, I encourage people to describe in as much detail as possible the information that comes to them. If they can focus on a specific date, time and place, even more description seems to be clear. The process is somewhat like focusing a camera. Millimeters of light coming from the wrong direction can distort the picture, yet with the right aperture, direction and film speed, the resulting picture is very much in focus. During the process of seeing the lace on a dress or visualizing the placement of furniture in a room, more important information has a chance to crystallize. The balance of work between right hemisphere and left hemisphere centers the mind and allows the information to pour forth.

These sessions take about two hours. In a later chapter, I will describe not only this process but also other techniques that can help you begin to release this vital information into your own experience.

The most important instruction I give when conducting regression sessions is that the individual must be willing to trust his fantasy. Even if he feels he is making up a story, he must follow that line of instinct. He can change the story as many times as necessary to get it right. His "feelings" have much to do with whether the story sits well with him or not. If, indeed, the whole process is simply fantasy, the fantasy *belongs* to the person. He imagines situations that are very different from what another person might conjure. I suggest many times that the individual see the scene before him as if it were his own movie. In that movie, since he is the writer, director and actor, he can clothe the "star" of the film in whatever he wishes. He can create the scenery he feels appropriate and combine the cast of characters in any way he wishes. His *choices* are important. He chooses a particular situation, scenery and costume quite by accident, yet it is no accident when the session is all over. The subject then realizes that those details are very unimportant to the truth of the ultimate fact that emerges from such a session. However, those choices enable him to get past what might otherwise be stumbling blocks. "Did I really fall out of my crib when I was two months old?" He becomes aware, at the end, that indeed he most likely did fall out of the crib, yet that was not the important issue at all.

Edgar Cayce, Arnall Bloxham and I share the same feeling that such memories are only important when they have meaning in present times. If those emerging details clarify actions, choices and attractions, or focus and release fears that are debilitating in this life, the process is a very valuable one indeed. It is not so important, for instance, that a person recognize his power in another lifetime, or his position or prestige. It is what he did with his position and power that is essential for the here and now. The review of specific cases will illustrate that more fully. The review of a past life can help an individual see where and how he developed particular judgments that limit him in the present.

These memories are very subjective. It is possible that they are only meaningful to the person reliving them. The fact remains that the extracted memories bring not only a profound sense of relief but a life-changing attitude.

Bloxham expressed it this way: "Most people who have been regressed find it helps them a great deal. If you can remember doing things in a previous life, well, you can probably do them in this one. The past is very important—after all, if you couldn't remember living yesterday, you wouldn't know very much today. And if you can't remember your previous lives, well, you won't know as much as you might. I think all great musicians and great artists of the past, they've perhaps been aware of having lived before and that's why they become prodigies at a very early age."

For me, the remembrance of a great talent is not as essential as the negative associations that block progress. I feel that if a great talent has been developed, it is clearly expressed again today, *unless* a very traumatic condition developed in connection with the expression of that talent previously. Regressions have seemed to be especially helpful in working with recovering alcoholics, for instance. Among the recovering alcoholics with whom I've conducted regression sessions, it seems to be a consensus of opinion that alcoholism didn't just happen in the present life, even if there is a genetic cause, but has been developed over many lifetimes of using alcohol as a way of blotting out pain. That perspective seems to give the alcoholic the ability to forgive himself as well as to deal with the resulting problem of addiction. In most cases, it is clear that there is no time like the present to solve the problems that may have taken centuries to develop.

Shirley MacLaine pointed this out very clearly. "The purpose of getting in touch with past-life experience, then, is to isolate the areas of emotional discord so that the conflict in relation to today's incarnation can be understood. All of life is based on the *totality* of the soul experience.... Thus the Buddhist theory of 'bless your enemy, he enables you to grow' suddenly makes sense.

With that new perspective, it becomes very clear that the external conditions we may not like are actually the creative scenarios of our imagination—and we have chosen the *exact* external circumstance necessary to force us to learn what we haven't been able to learn in an easier way. We have picked the precise mothers and fathers, sisters and brothers, and life-styles that help rather than hinder our progress along the path. Sometimes hardships are the only way we can reconcile the karmic balance. Unfortunately, we seem to do our learning through pain, restriction, limitations and difficulties. However, we rarely acknowledge or take responsibility for having created a given condition. Instead we project blame onto other people or conditions. When we can begin to ask ourselves what it is we are to learn from a given situation, instead of defensively saying, "They made me do it," or "I did it because . . ." we are on the way to being home free.

Forgiveness follows responsibility. After a regression session, forgiveness can take place more easily when we see the perspective of lifetime to lifetime. The healing of difficult relationships often comes as a result of understanding *why* we had to come into a situation in which someone can do us harm. Usually there is a debt to be repaid or a lesson to be learned. Finally, self-forgiveness acts as the most powerful healing agent of all. That self-forgiveness is born from a position of responsibility, not from rejecting our role in an interaction with a person or situation.

In selecting the examples to share in this book, I have culled about two hundred tapes from among about five or six hundred regression sessions. I still find the information overwhelming and the stories so wonderfully fantastic that each one might become a novel in itself. One young film producer has, in fact, used her own regression as the basis of a film. A whole book could be written dealing only with mother-daughter issues. In the light of reincarnation, it is no wonder that all such relationships are full of situations to be resolved. For whether it is mother-daughter, father-daughter, mother-son, father-son, sibling rivalry or any other interfamily situation, those relationships are there for a purpose. Many times the purpose of an especially close relationship is to give oneself a bonus and support system that will help one to get through. The beauty of the tapestry of these interwoven lives almost defies imagination. In each session, even when what seem to be negative or fearful memories emerge, the result is a feeling of lightness and joy that seems to come in no other way.

CHAPTER TWO

Spontaneous Past-Life Memories

I n Eastern countries, reincarnation is accepted as a fact, a truth and a philosophy. Western civilizations see this belief system as an excuse for the people of the East to develop a very passive attitude toward life. In fact, East and West are different for a very good reason. In the search for food, Easterners had to develop patience, whereas Westerners had to become aggressive. Rice and grain cannot be forced to grow any faster than nature dictates, and animals won't stand still to be killed. However, the two cultures have much to learn from each other.

When Western civilizations began to explore the East Indies, they did so with a superior attitude. They said, in effect, "We know what is best for you. We will Westernize you and then you will be happy." That approach is bound to cause problems, because it is basically a "rescue" situation. (In psychological terms, when a rescuer rescues a victim, the victim becomes the persecutor and persecutes the rescuer. It is an "I'm okay, you're not okay" situation.)

In all interpersonal relationships, if one person assumes the role of knowing what is best for the other, he is actually saying, "I have access to all the answers, but you don't." Resentments easily occur with this kind of outlook. If, for example, explorers in the

East or in the New World of the Americas had approached the natives with an attitude of "What can we learn from you and what do you want to learn from us?" relationships between East and West might have developed in a very different way. In interpersonal relationships, the same can be true.

What we might have learned, earlier and more easily, is that there are many ways of approaching the truths of life and nature, and that we are all viewing the world through individual eyes— the eyes of our personal accumulated experiences. To acknowledge that those experiences might encompass more than one lifetime opens a profound new approach to the present, like looking at a light through a prism that reflects many refractions of that same light. Greater tolerance can exist when we realize the kinds of accumulated baggage each person or race must work with. In particular, the theory of reincarnation can enable man to understand more fully that each person must work out his individual life path as best he can. Fortunately, with the approach of the Aquarian Age, or the Age of Enlightenment, mankind is beginning to recognize the right of individual choice. Tolerance, acceptance, compassion and the *right kind* of assistance are becoming keynotes for the development of man in the coming new age. To restore the cultural balance between East and West, we can indeed respect the basic qualities of life while allowing an exchange of perspectives.

Because of the necessity to wait for food, the Eastern world had more time for reflection, meditation and introspection. We in the Western world are trying to learn those techniques to calm our hectic pace. In the East, the doctrine of reincarnation had a chance to take root in all areas of life, including government. Tibet, for instance, was a monarchy established solely on the basis of reincarnation. There are many instances of spontaneous past life recall among children in Tibet. (Although there may be just as many in the West, we are prone to think a child simply has a vivid imagination rather than to take him seriously when he talks about his memories.) Perhaps the most profound illustration of the efficacy of those memories of lifetime to lifetime is documented with the discovery of each Incarnation of the Dalai Lama.

The Story of the Dalai Lama

The choice of His Holiness, the Dalai Lama, is based solely on reincarnation. The office and line of incarnations of the Dalai Lama were established after the death of Tsong-kha-pa in 1417, who was viewed as an avatar of Buddha and was a great reformer of Lamaism in Tibet. Tibet had a history as a seat of mysticism and occult learning in Asia, but the pure Buddhist philosophy had been desecrated. To correct misconceptions, a prominent feature of Tibetan Buddhism was introduced—the belief in the successive incarnations of the Dalai Lama, with some others, into the same high role or office previously held. The Dalai Lama represents in his person the return to earth of Chenrezi, the god of grace, one of the thousand Living Buddhas, who have renounced Nirvana in order to help mankind. Chenrezi was the patron god of Tibet, and his reincarnations were always the kings of Tibet. (The title of *Dalai Lama* had been designated by Altan Khan, a Mongolian ruler who embraced Buddhism.) The people of Tibet pray to the Dalai Lama as a Living Buddha rather than as a king, yet he is the ruler of the land.

The present Dalai Lama is the fourteenth incarnation. An ancient prophecy foretold that the fourteenth Dalai Lama would not rule in Tibet. With the imminent threat of the invasion of China, the Dalai Lama came to the throne when he was only fifteen, but his coronation in November, 1950, was too late to prevent the takeover of Tibet by the Chinese. He was allowed to rule until March, 1959, when he was forced to flee for his life in disguise, thereby fulfilling the prophecy. Since that time, he has been in exile, traveling around the world to further the cause of world Buddhism.

The discovery of the correct incarnation of the present, fourteenth Dalai Lama constitutes quite a story. Heinrich Harrer, who wrote about his life in Tibet and his eventual position as the tutor of the Dalai Lama, was fortunate enough to hear the story firsthand from one of the few living eyewitnesses to the event, Commander in Chief of the Army Dzasa Künsangtse. He says in his book *Seven Years in Tibet* (published by Jeremy P. Tarcher, Inc.):

Some time before his death in 1933, the thirteenth Dalai Lama had given intimations regarding the manner of his rebirth. After his death, the body sat in state in the Potala in traditional Buddha posture, looking toward the south. One morning it was noticed that his head was turned to the east. The State Oracle was straightway consulted, and while in his trance the monk oracle threw a white scarf in the direction of the rising sun, that is, toward the east. But for two years nothing more definite was indicated. Then the regent went on a pilgrimage to a famous lake to ask for counsel. When the regent, after long prayers, came to the water and looked in its mirror, he had a vision of a three-storied monastery with golden roofs, near which stood a little Chinese peasant house with carved gables.... (With us it is generally, but mistakenly, believed that each rebirth takes place at the moment of the predecessor's death.... Buddhist philosophy declares that years may pass before the god once more leaves the fields of Heaven and resumes the form of a man.) Search groups set out to explore in the year 1937.... Following the signs, they journeyed eastward in quest of the Holy Child. The members of these groups were monks and in each group... they carried with them objects that had belonged to the thirteenth Dalai Lama.

The group to which my informant belonged journeyed... until they reached the district of Amdo in the Chinese province of Chingnai. In this region there are many monasteries, as the great reformer, Tsong Kapa, was born here.... They began to fear that they would fail in their mission. At last after long wanderings they encountered a three-storied monastery with golden roofs. With a flash of enlightenment, they remembered the regent's vision, and then their eyes fell on the cottage with carved gables. Full of excitement, they dressed themselves in the clothes of their servants. This maneuver is customary during these searches, for persons dressed as high officials attract too much attention and find it hard to get in touch with the people. The servants, dressed in the garments of their masters, were taken to the best room, while the disguised monks went into the kitchen, where it was likely they would find the children of the house.

As soon as they entered the house, they felt sure that they would find the Holy Child in it, and they waited tensely to see what would happen. And, sure enough, a two-year-old boy came running to meet them and seized the skirts of the lama, who wore around his neck the rosary of the thirteenth Dalai Lama. Unabashed the child cried, "Sera Lama, Sera Lama!" It was already a matter for wonder that the infant recognized a lama in the garb of a servant and that he said he came from the Cloister of Sera, which was the case. Then the boy grasped the rosary and tugged at it till the lama gave it to him; thereupon he hung it around his own neck. The noble searchers found it hard not to throw themselves on the ground before the child, as they had no longer any doubt. They had found the Incarnation. But they had to proceed in the prescribed manner.

They bade farewell to the peasant family, and again returned a few days later—this time not disguised. They first negotiated with the parents, who had already given one of their sons as an Incarnation to the church, and then the little boy was awakened from his sleep, and the four delegates withdrew with him to the altar room. Here the child was subjected to the prescribed examination. He was shown four different rosaries, one of which—the most worn—had belonged to the thirteenth Dalai Lama. The boy, who was quite unconstrained and not the least bit shy, chose the right one without hesitation and danced around the room with it. He also selected out of several drums one which the last Incarnation had used to call his servants. Then he took an old walking stick, which had also belonged to him, not deigning to bestow a glance on one which had a handle of ivory and silver. When they examined his body they found all the marks which an Incarnation of Chenrezi ought to bear; large, outstanding ears, and moles on the trunk which are supposed to be traces of the four-armed god's second pair of arms.

In the late summer of 1939 the four delegates, together with their servants, the merchants, the Holy Child and his family, started for Lhasa, the capital of Tibet. As soon as they crossed the border between China and Tibet, a cabinet minister gave the boy a letter from the regent confirming the official recognition. For the first time, the lamas accompanying him were able to pay homage to him as the Dalai Lama. His parents now learned that he was no less than the future ruler of Tibet.

From this day the little Dalai Lama distributed blessings as naturally as if he had never done anything else. He has still a clear recollection of being borne into Lhasa in his golden palanquin. He had never seen so many people. The whole town was there to greet the new embodiment of Chenrezi, who at last after so many years returned to the Potala and his orphaned people. Six years had passed since the death of the 'Previous Body' and of these nearly two had elapsed before the god reentered a human body.... Everyone was astonished at the unbelievable dignity of the child and the gravity with which he followed ceremonies which lasted for hours. With his predecessor's servants, who had charge of him, he was as trusting and affectionate as if he had always known them. I was very glad to have heard this account at firsthand. During the lapse of time many legends had collected around these extraordinary events and I had already heard several garbled versions.... I knew how much the young king desired to lead his people one day out of the fog of gloomy superstition. We dreamed and talked endlessly about enlightenment and future reforms.

It was not easy for the young king to satisfy the demands made on him. He knew that he was expected to give divine judgments and that what he ordered and what he did were regarded as infallible and would become a part of historical tradition. He was already striving by means of week-long meditation and profound religious study to prepare himself for the heavy duties of his office. He was much less self-assured than the thirteenth Incarnation. Tsarong once gave me a typical example showing the dominating character of the late ruler. He wished to enact new laws but met with bitter opposition from his conservative entourage, who quoted the utterances of the fifth Dalai Lama on the same context. To which the thirteenth Dalai Lama replied, "And who was the fifth former body?" The monks, thereupon, prostrated themselves before him, for his answer had left them speechless. As an Incarnation he was, of course, not only the thirteenth but also the fifth and all the other Dalai Lamas as well.

The personality difficulties and changes described in the account of the Dalai Lama and his successive incarnations can illustrate exactly what happens to lesser evolved people when they come into life with a different set of circumstances and personality characteristics. Inwardly, with each life, we are the same soul, developing and growing toward our sainthood and reconnection with God, but outwardly, we may have different qualities imprinted on the "mask" or personality. (In the astrological chart, the positions of the planets describe the inner qualities that constitute development of character, talent and moral codes, whereas the outer wheel, determined by the time of birth, as distinctive from the date of birth, indicates the new body or suit of clothes put on for this particular incarnation and sojourn through life. It may be likened to trading in an old car for a newer, more streamlined and efficient vehicle.)

It is interesting to note that birthdays are not celebrated in Tibet. Harrer commented, "I already knew that he [the Dalai Lama] was born on June 6, 1935, in the neighborhood of Lake Kuku-Nor, but when I congratulated him on his birthday, I was the only person who did so. Birthdays are unimportant dates in Tibet.... For the people the date of their king's birth is quite without interest." Perhaps the focus on the inner life, that of the god presence of Chenrezi in the case of the Dalai Lama, makes the timing of the return to life entirely unimportant.

It is interesting to speculate that astrology may be more valuable to us in the West, simply because it enables us to look past the outer mask or facade of personality into the inner qualities of a person. We tend to ignore, by and large, the observation of soul qualities in favor of the blinding exhibition of the personality. The focus on the "illusion" of the body obfuscates the realization of the true identity of an individual. Western civilization continues to be impressed by station in life, appearance, material well-being and social status rather than venerating the level of evolution sometimes painfully attained. It is through eventual transformational experiences that we begin to take a deeper look at the inner light of another being. With metaphysical practices and the acknowledgment that we are merely mirrors for each other, we may develop more acceptance of the variety of qualities of self-expression on the earth plane.

FORMER FRIEND RETURNED

Westerners are accustomed to thinking of all Tibetan monks as *lamas*. This title, however, is formally allowed only to high-ranking Incarnations and to monks who have lived very saintly lives.

I was extremely fortunate to have a visit from a Tibetan lama. Lama Tsultrim came to Ibiza, Spain, to teach a group of us and stayed in my house for four days. Coincidentally, I had recently found the house, C'an Tirurit, after much searching for the right place to live and moved there in order to write this book on reincarnation. I had only a cursory knowledge of the rich heritage of the house. After the group sessions, Lama Tsultrim and I walked in the garden and, with the help of his translators, talked of many things. When he learned that I was writing a book about reincarnation he agreed to share some of his own experiences with me. He told me about the reincarnation of a former classmate and friend who had died at about thirty-five years of age. Lama Tsultrim had entered the Monastery of Gaden-Pelgye-Ling when he was only thirteen to begin the studies that would qualify him for his life's work. After graduation from Sera-je College, he lived there permanently until 1959, teaching and using his debating skills. His expertise in epistemology as well as an in-depth knowledge of the Tibetan texts he had translated seemed the basis for his future in the monastery. Yet with the Chinese invasion of Tibet, a particular way of life changed drastically. Many lamas traveled to parts of the world they might never have visited if they had not been forced to flee for their lives.

One of the lamas from Lama Tsultrim's monastery visited Canada. One day he was stopped by a five-year-old Canadian boy, who had obviously never seen a Tibetan lama before. He asked why the lama was wearing the robes of his (the boy's) Master. When the lama asked the young boy the name of his master, the boy gave the correct name. The child then revealed his Tibetan name while he had lived and studied at the monastery. When Lama Tsultrim was in Paris a few years later, to his great surprise, an eleven-year-old boy (the same Canadian child) came over and introduced himself as his former friend, this time born with an Occidental face.

Ibiza had been honored by visits from two other lamas before I was fortunate enough to meet Lama Tsultrim. In fact, my house had been a former Tibetan meditation center. One identifying mark of the house is a Tibetan "hat" on one of the chimneys, always painted yellow and blue since the time of the lamas' residence in the house. Lama Sopa and Lama Yesha were a team, and they became favorite friends to many of the island's residents and visitors. Lama Yesha had been told that he had a bad heart and wouldn't live a very long life in this incarnation. However, he lived about fifteen years longer than expected. When he died in 1982, an autopsy was performed on his body. It was discovered that he had grown an extra loop of skin around the damaged heart that allowed the blood to flow freely. When Lama Yesha died, his former students and friends who loved him very much, waited with excitement to discover where and when he would be incarnated again. There were reports of possibilities of that special birth, but such reports are carefully checked for accuracy. It became Lama Sopa's special task to be on the lookout for the child who would be the reincarnation of Lama Yesha.

Lama Sopa felt that Lama Yesha wouldn't be out of the body for very long. One night he had a dream. He saw a big dome, the dome that had been used in Ibiza in front of my house, for large conferences and was now used for retreats in Granada, Spain. Inside the dome, he saw a baby crawling on all fours. He felt that was an omen and portent telling him of the birth of Lama Yesha. Some time later, Lama Sopa was in Granada and saw a child crawling on all fours inside the big dome. He remembered his dream and asked the name of the child. The parents, Maria and Paco, had decided to call him Osel, which means "clear light." Maria and Paco had met while Paco was living in C'an Tirurit (now my house in Ibiza). Paco was part of the group that sponsored the early teaching sessions conducted by Lama Sopa and Lama Yesha. Maria was also closely associated with the two lamas since she was a participant in the conferences. They became very active in the Buddhist community that eventually held retreats on the Spanish mainland near Granada.

After the discovery of the baby in the dome, Lama Sopa felt it was time to ask the Dalai Lama for confirmation of his feelings that this child was the reincarnation of his friend Lama Yesha. He put ten names on slips of paper. (There had been several reports of the birth of children who might have been the Incarnation.)

The Dalai Lama picked the slip of paper with the name Osel on it. Lama Sopa then began the real investigation to verify the identification. He asked Maria to bring the child to India to the Buddhist Center, where he was then living. He had some articles of clothing that had belonged to Lama Yesha. One of them was a robe. He placed that particular robe among many robes, all of different colors, some very bright and pretty that might attract a child's attention. The baby Osel went immediately to the robe that had belonged to Lama Yesha. Other objects were placed in front of Osel in the same way, but the baby always chose the objects that had been Lama Yesha's. Finally the parents and the baby were brought into the presence of the Dalai Lama. Osel was crawling on the ground while the Dalai Lama was talking to his parents. He crawled over to a patch of flowers growing nearby, picked some, and then crawled over to lay them at the feet of the Dalai Lama. The confirmation of this child as the true Incarnation has now been completed, and he has once again assumed his role as a high Lama. At the age of two years, he wears his robes and crown with ease, and gives blessings. He participates in ceremonies with all the knowledge, dedication and dignity developed in his former life as Lama Yesha.

OUT OF THE MOUTHS OF BABES

My friend Ann was a Protestant minister's wife. She had no knowledge of the theory of reincarnation. When her first son was born, her labor was extremely difficult. It took three days and there was nothing the doctors could do to hasten the delivery.

We were both so dehydrated when he was finally born, we almost died. On top of that, when they brought him to me, he took one look and screamed in fury. I wasn't so sure I was going to like this child, because it was a terrible rejection. All the other babies were peaceful and sweet, but for a week he was so angry at me, it was terribly embarrassing. Finally he got very sick and was forced to stay in the hospital. I visited him every day, but I wasn't allowed to hold him. I wasn't sure he was going to make it, but the doctors refused to let him die.

When he was three months old, we moved to the West Indies. The rectory was his only frame of reference as he grew up. We had West Indian servants, and of course people came in and out of the rectory, but he never saw television, or heard a radio or saw a movie. He also had no picture books. One day when he was about three years old, he came into the kitchen and said, "Mommy, do you remember that time when we had to ride down that mountain on the same horse? We were in such a hurry because we had to catch that boat. It was so hot because we were wearing those heavy, heavy clothes." He got very angry with me when I didn't remember. I had no idea what he was talking about. He persisted, "Mother, you must remember!" I finally said I did, just to pacify him. I asked him what the clothes were like. He described in perfect detail uniforms such as Spanish gentlemen of the first century wore... breast plates and full mutton sleeves. He talked about all my clothes that kept getting in the way, although he didn't know the word for skirts. When I said I remembered, he said, "Well, I thought you would." Then within seconds he said, "I had a terrible time finding you, Mommy, because Papa God let me off in the wrong place. It took me so long to find you and I was so tired when I finally got there." I now know why he was so angry when he was born.

He slept very little as a baby. In fact, if I hadn't been lucky enough to have help I'm not sure I would have survived. He slept from 10:30 P.M. to 1:30 A.M. and that was all, except for another hour between 5:00 and 6:00 A.M. It was like he didn't want to let me out of his sight. When he was an adolescent, he had a burst appendix and I was told I must take him to Switzerland for recuperation. The danger of infection was too great, and in London, where we then lived, it was cold and damp.

We arrived very late at night in pitch darkness and we went right to our rooms. The next morning, in a half sleep, he said, "We came in the wrong door last night." I said, "What do you mean?" He said, "When I used to come here with my father, we'd come in the drive in a carriage. He would get out and go in the house and I would go play with the rabbits." I said, "Who would your father come to see?" He replied, "He came to see the bishop. I wonder if they still have rabbits here. I had such fun with them." He didn't mention it again, but when we went downstairs for the first time in daylight, there was a carriage drive around the other side of the little hotel, and they still raised rabbits. The hotel had been the house of the Protestant bishop of Zurich, but had been used as a hotel since 1890! He knew Zurich like the back of his hand. He would be so disgusted with me when I didn't know my way around. He would constantly tell me what to expect to see just around the corner. He was really amazing when he was a small boy, especially in his comments about me. He had the distinct memory of being my husband in another life. Our relationship was not typical of parent-child until he was much older. Then, fortunately, it stabilized into a quite normal mother-son interaction.

Another friend, Marie, had a similar story to recount. When he was only two years old, her son started talking about his other daddy. My friend said, "What do you mean?" Marie was already acquainted with the concept of reincarnation and sensed that he was talking about another lifetime. Her son said he'd been talking to his other daddy. Marie questioned him about that other person and asked him what his other daddy looked like. The child said, "He had real dark hair and a beard." Marie continued, "What does he do?" Her son replied, "He works in a factory, so I cut the wood." Marie asked what his other mommy looked like. The boy continued, "My other mother had real dark hair too. I had lots of brothers and sisters." Marie said that in the middle of other conversations, quite unrelated, he would talk about that other family. I finally asked him where they lived. The only information he could give me was, "It was far, far away."

A psychic friend named Dorothy told similar stories about her daughter. She said, "My daughter was born with Cancer rising. Of course, I didn't know then what I know now, and I must admit she had good reason to feel the abandonment that goes with that rising sign. For one thing, she was not getting enough milk. My mother kept telling me she was hungry. She was my first child and I didn't know the milk wasn't flowing through the nipple easily enough. All I had to do was make the holes in the nipple a little larger and she wouldn't have had to work so hard for the milk. In my state of unawareness I also told my mother, in response to her suggestions, "I don't want her to be fat." So my child, now grown up, cannot stop eating. She is potentially a very beautiful young lady, but she's very angry, talks incessantly and can be quite mean at times. I couldn't nurse her and I didn't know enough to talk to her and explain what was happening. She remembered starving to death in another life during the holy wars.

INSTANT RECOGNITION

Many people have cited examples of past life memories from dreams. Some of those individuals, who have recurring dreams, may not think to acknowledge the possibility that glimpses of past lives may be trying to filter through for an important reason. There are other examples of fragmentary information that comes on a conscious level and seems to have no meaning at all. Yet later on, at an unexpected moment, a chance meeting or a view of a particular bit of scenery will trigger more information to complete the whole picture. Some people have described the uncanny sensation of seeing themselves as one thing, inwardly, and being aware of a new physical form.

I remember quite vividly standing in front of a mirror when I was four years old, wondering who that stranger was who was staring back at me. I knew "I" was inside me, but it seemed impossible to recognize myself in my present form. It was a most peculiar sensation. I finally just accepted that reflection as my own exterior. Another instant recognition occurred when a special friend of mine asked me to do an astrological reading for her mother, who was visiting from out of town. When I met the woman with my friend, I found myself staring at her. I apologized and explained that she somehow reminded me of my own mother, even though their physical characteristics were quite different. As I was preparing her horoscope in my home later that evening, I suddenly sat bolt upright in my chair, with chills running down my back. I was shocked at the thought that had just occurred to me. I saw in my mind's eye a lovely young woman bending over, grasping her stomach, obviously in great pain. She seemed to be alone, in the evening, suffering the ordeal of a miscarriage. Her husband finally arrived home to help her. I saw quite clearly the bedroom and bathroom of her apartment. She seemed quite saddened but resigned to the loss of her first child. Her husband, on the other hand, seemed rather relieved.

The shocking thought that had occurred to me was that I was the baby she lost. I wanted to see, through her astrological chart, if it was possible for her to have had a marriage and a miscarriage at least nine months before I was born to my family. The position of the planets indicated that the timing coincided, making it a possibility. I shook myself back to reality and realized there was no way that I could tell this near-stranger my fantasy, and I completed the work of setting up her chart.

The next day, when she arrived for her appointment, I was very startled to hear the words that simply popped out of my mouth before I had even taken her coat. I said, "Did you have a miscarriage before your first daughter was born?" She said, with great surprise, "Why, yes. It was very early in the pregnancy, and of course my husband was still in school, so it was just as well." I replied, "I think that was me." Her reaction was especially amazing, considering she had only met me the evening before. She said, "I've always said I was supposed to have a red-haired child. Where's my red-haired child? You can ask my best friend in my hometown and she'll confirm that." Needless to say, a strong bond was formed immediately. My friend, far from being upset with me or feeling that I was encroaching on her relationship with her mother said, "Why of course. Just look at the two of you. You look more alike than my Mother and I do. I've always had a sisterly feeling toward you, with all the sibling implications." Her mother and I remained friends until she died. When I heard the sad news, I felt a deep loss of my own, far beyond that of the loss of a friend's mother.

There is no way to prove that these fantasies are real. In psychological terms, a fantasy belongs to an individual just as much as a real, provable experience. An explanation that is quite valid is that possibly we are tapping into a universal mind. When two or more people come up with the same information, at different times and from a different perspective, the similarity of the stories makes that explanation quite plausible. The mystery remains, however, of why certain people would simply happen to tune in to the same fantasy, whereas two other people would not.

Just as reading a good book can stimulate the mind, these fantasies can work their magic as well. It is possible to approach any results from an investigation into past lives on several levels. From a practical, mundane point of view, fantasy can act like an exercise for stiff muscles. We know so little about the workings of the human brain (even geniuses utilize only about 5 or 6 percent of their potential brain power), so any investigation or exploration into the mind can only be beneficial. Studies have proved that there is a higher mind connected to the pituitary gland. Dr. Dwight Pollack, a mathematician doing research at California Institute of Technology in Pasadena, California, confirmed that studies prove brain function to be directly connected to body coordination. If a baby skips the crawling stage in his development, he may have a greater tendency toward learning disability. If an individual loses a thumb by accident, paralysis or amputation, his brain waves go askew. He may even exhibit schizophrenic tendencies. From a physical standpoint, exercises such as the cross crawl, a simulation of a baby's crawl, will charge up the brain coordination and enhance learning ability. Stimulation of a specific point on the thumb increases activity of the pituitary gland, connected to higher brain wave function.

A regression session may be another exercise to stimulate an opening of unused portions of the mind. Many people report that after an initial regression session, they begin to have experiences that are especially positive. Not only do they feel a sense of release, but many individuals have spontaneous regression and recognitions after only one session. In my own case, I felt a distinct difference in my ability to tap creative energy more easily. I felt more able to focus my attention and push away distractions. On a psychological level, the memories gave me an explanation of some of the situations in my life that seemed truly mysterious and without any logical explanation.

From a metaphysical point of view, there may be an even greater value. In her book *The World Before*, Ruth Montgomery gives an urgent message. She said, "The guides now take us a giant step forward by asserting that between lives it is also necessary to experience the vibrations of other planets before completing our spiritual development and reuniting with the Creator." She continues by describing particular experiences one might have on specific planets. For instance, "In Mars, we pit ourselves against the dislikes others have for us, and if we return this in kind, it becomes a test of all that is worst in human nature since the beginning of homo sapiens on earth." Then the admonition comes. "Best to mend one's fences while in physical life." She describes Mercury as "a good place to recast and reframe motivation and to find something of value in each incarnation on which to build for a supreme effort to erase all bad karma in a single lifetime." She continues, "Don't view this as an easy Rest Shop, for to face oneself and review all the mistakes and sins of an entire evolutionary process is rather torturous. *Stop now* to review everything you've done in this particular lifetime of which you are not proud, and which you would not wish another to know.... Face oneself while in physical life. Why not take time now to begin this process of cleansing the akashic record? ...

Regression not only allows us the possibility to review guilts, fears and injustices done to us or by us in this life, but in past lives as well. With a review of several lives, an individual becomes aware of a thread of similarity, like habit patterns that wind through each life. People and situations come back with great regularity again and again in different guises and situations. When many lives are reviewed, it is clear to see that we have an eternity to resolve all conflicts and karma. The universe has infinite patience. However, with centuries of running into the same old obstacles, it also becomes clear that there is nothing like the present to get on with things.

CHAPTER THREE

Birth Trauma and Birth Defects Revisited

When I first began doing regression sessions for some of my astrological clients, my purpose was to enable them to experience for themselves what I saw in the astrological chart. I sometimes felt an inadequacy to explain exactly why certain limitations were in effect from the moment of birth. In certain charts, there was an obvious sense of rejection from one or both parents that seemed to predetermine the present life circumstances in a very harsh vein. Usually the sense of rejection was not what it appeared to be at all. For instance, with the expectation of a new baby, a parent may have momentarily said to himself or herself, "Oh no." That coming event may have made necessary a more practical but limited career change for the father, yet the child seemed to take on a dreadful burden and sense of guilt because of that change. The overreaction to that momentary rejecting thought of the parent can cause an overdeveloped sense of responsibility throughout life and set in motion an unwarranted sense of rejection. Many times there was no intentional rejection at all.

One of my earliest experiences pointed this out in a verifiable way. A young woman asked for a regression session because she had continuous pains in her arms and legs. She had confirmed that there was no medical reason for such anguish and had been working with body therapy to try to relieve these blocks of energy. In the regression session, she saw herself as a two-month-old baby in her crib. She was first aware that her movement was restricted and then realized that her arms and legs were tied to her crib so that she couldn't move. Her fear was coupled with extreme anger and feelings of helplessness. She then looked to see how this could have happened. She knew that a nurse had tied her down, but even as a two-month-old baby, she blamed her mother for the action. Her parents had evidently chosen to go out for the evening, leaving her with someone they trusted to be responsible. This made her very angry and she had kicked up a big fuss about being left behind. The nurse had resorted to tying her to the crib. When her parents returned and discovered what had happened, they were quite upset and fired the nurse, but the damage had already been done.

During the first part of the regression session, the young woman had observed herself being very cold toward her mother. She commented several times that it was unreasonable on her part, and that although she really loved her mother very much, she wouldn't accept any demonstration of affection from her. She said, "I don't know why I reject her so much. She is warm and loving to me and I really want to respond to her, but I just won't let myself." She was shocked that she had held those feelings of revenge for such a long time. The next day she called her brother to tell him what had transpired. Her brother's response was, "How did you find out? Mother never wanted you to know. She was afraid you'd blame her for what the nurse did to you."

Although this young woman did not go to a past life for an explanation of her physical symptoms on her relationship with her mother, no doubt deeper meaning would have emerged from that larger perspective. She did comment, after the regression session, that her attitude toward her mother was quite different. She understood from her adult position that since her mother had not rejected or abandoned her intentionally, she didn't deserve the unconscious resentment and punishment she had been subjected to. The daughter automatically began to relate to her mother in a very different way.

PRENATAL CONDITIONING

Among the things that the ascendant, or rising, sign in the horoscope describes are birth survival issues. I describe it as a mask in my book *The Rising Sign, Your Astrological Mask*, because the sign on the horizon at the time of birth is indicative of the personality development of the individual. It is not necessarily what the person is like *inside*. In the study of acting, all the exercises and techniques are designed to rid the person of the so-called phoniness or facade he has developed in his habit patterns. A bad actor immediately whips into his "personality," which covers an essence much more interesting to observe. If he can let down that mask, he reveals sensitivity, poignancy and *real* responses. It is very difficult to let go or to drop the mask.

The reason that the mask sticks to one like glue is that it goes so far back into the development of the individual and is connected to basic issues such as survival, life or death and raison d'être. In my reading of astrological charts, it became clear to me that dropping the mask is like defying gravity, for it hides what is most frightening to reveal. The twelfth house in a chart describes the quality that eventually can be brought forth into the daylight of expression, but only when the individual is in a safe situation. Otherwise that mask, or personality mechanism, rises up like a drawbridge over a moat to defend or protect the vulnerable inner being.

Transactional Analysis theory talks about a life script that is indicative of the major drama in a person's life. The rising sign, or ascendant, in the astrological chart describes survival issues usually developed at birth or even before that time that are clearly related to the life script. During the therapeutic process, that script is reexamined and eventually broken to reveal the rich being inside. When nonproductive survival issues are released, more productive decisions can emerge that will act as a true protective agent. During regression sessions, the subject sees quite clearly what his particular formula for life might be. That formula seems to preclude all the decisions down the line until, at last, the individual understands that it prevents truly enlightened behavior. In some cases, that formula or life script is developed prenatally. Investigation of the birth trauma itself through regression sessions has pointed out how important it is to create ideal conditions at the time of birth so that the entrance into life is as welcoming and safe as possible. For it is that special moment that sets up patterns that can exist for the entire lifetime.

Parents may unwittingly keep a child in a life script to fulfill their own needs. If, indeed, unspoken and often unconscious parental fantasy can actually shape or mold a child's emotional life, it would seem especially important to become more cognizant of that influence. Parents might spend much more time consciously planning their expectations and programming for their child. Perhaps much of parent-child conflict begins even earlier than we suspect. Dr. Thomas Verny's pioneering work in prenatal psychology strongly indicates sentience in the womb. In his book *The Secret Life of the Unborn Child*, he describes some dramatic and fascinating case studies. In one case, a woman played particular cello pieces quite often during her pregnancy. Her son, Boris Brott, became conductor of the Hamilton (Ontario) Philharmonic Symphony. He said, "I was mystified by an unusual ability to play certain pieces sight unseen. I'd be conducting a score for the first time and suddenly the cello line would jump out at me. I'd know the flow of the piece even before I turned the page of the score." The mystery was solved when he told his mother of the unusual occurrence—all the scores he knew by sight were for pieces she had played during her pregnancy. In a less happy vein, Dr. Verny quotes the research done by Dr. Michael Lieberman that showed an unborn child becoming emotionally agitated each time his mother even *thought* about having a cigarette. The physical sensation caused by the lowering of the oxygen supply would thrust the fetus into a state of chronic uncertainty and fear. That may be all that is necessary to cause a later predisposition toward deep-seated conditioned anxiety.

One practical example that illustrates the relief that can result from a look at the birth experience is that of a beautiful, talented young woman who was adopted as an infant. Gloria did not go past the birth memory in her session because the information that came forth flooded her consciousness with a profound sense of awe. To go further at that moment would have been to overload her and mitigate vital new awareness. She saw, in her mind's eye, exactly what her real mother looked like and knew exactly why her mother gave her up. Usually people ask, after such a session is over, "Did I make that up?" Gloria had no need to ask me if what she saw was real because the tears that poured forth came from a very real emotional experience. She saw her mother in her early twenties, pregnant and very sad at the prospect of giving up her child. She had an opportunity to marry the father of the unborn Gloria but knew that she would be compromising her principles to such a degree that she would make everyone unhappy. After a great deal of thought, she made her decision and entered a home for unwed mothers to wait out the pregnancy.

Gloria's most important realization was that she fully agreed with her mother's decision. It was as if they had made a pact that each would go a separate way. Gloria had no feeling of rejection from her mother. She was also aware that her mother asked not to see her after the birth because she was afraid she would be tempted to change her mind. So Gloria was handed over to a nurse who was very warm and mothering. The nurse seemed to be a frustrated mother herself, and devoted herself to Gloria's care. Gloria relished such attention and responded with great affection for this woman. The shock of rejection came when the nurse handed her over to a stranger without so much as an explanation.

In almost every session, I find that great hurt and bewilderment accompany the lack of communication between parents and infant. The newborn soul feels tremendously ignored, as if his or her feelings about what was taking place really didn't matter. The person frequently expresses such bewilderment by saying, "If they had only told me." The mother's lack of acknowledgment that the fetus is a *real person* is more insulting and debilitating than almost anything else. Yet how many pregnant mothers would even think about having a deep, adult conversation with the child they carry?

In Gloria's case, evidently her mother was attuned enough to explain to her how she felt and why she had made her decision and to ask Gloria to forgive her and have a happier life than she herself would be able to provide. Gloria responded in a noble manner and actually agreed with her mother's decision. Before the session, Gloria's sense of abandonment had been damaging her life, even though she was adopted by a very caring, loving person and even though the abandonment had come from the nurse, not the real mother. But after the session was over, Gloria had new respect and admiration for a mother who had had the courage to live up to her convictions.

Another woman, adopted at birth, had a different reaction altogether through her regression session. Although Mary knew that her parents were not her natural parents, she felt loved and wanted by them. She was particularly close to her adoptive mother, but the stigma of having been abandoned at birth by some other woman made her very sensitive about her status. During her session, it became clear to her that the woman who adopted her was actually her *real* mother, even though she had not delivered her into this world. The other woman merely acted as an instrument for bringing her into the world so that she could be with the mother who was unable to have her by natural means. She clearly saw that she was selected before her birth on two different levels. Her adoptive parents had enough material resources to investigate the background, genetic lines and level of intelligence of the prospective mother and make a conscious choice to adopt Mary. Yet it was also clear that the choice was made on a soul level as well. The magnetic pull to her adoptive parents was exceptionally strong, enough so that they were led to find Mary even before her actual existence on the earth plane.

The new parents took extreme precautions to hide the birth records legally so that Mary would never be able to trace her background. No expense was spared to assure the comfort of the expectant mother. Mary knew she was wanted, adored and eagerly awaited before her birth. The separation from her natural mother was apparently not much of a shock. Her excitement came from already knowing who and what would be waiting for her at the other end. She had been told absolutely nothing throughout her life about her prenatal situation, nor anything about her natural parents. It was a subject that was a closed book in her family. However, in the regression session, she clearly saw in her mind's eye what had transpired. She knew that she was of another nationality than that of her adoptive parents. She had felt throughout her life that she had an Italian heritage and was not of the nationality of her family. In the session, she was aware that her father was indeed Italian and somewhat well known in his country as an artist. She reveled in her newfound heritage and developed an artistic ability as a result of her new awareness. The arts had always lured her, yet her parents were not of an artistic temperament and had not encouraged the exploration of her talent.

When she explored another past life situation, that artistry was even more pronounced. In this particular case, she saw herself as a member of a very prominent Italian Renaissance family and a most important patron of the arts. Much of the luxury and opulence surrounding her in this previous existence had been brought back in her current life, but in very different circumstances. Mary felt that she now had permission to continue to develop the potential that she had begun using in another time frame. Mary's sense of welcome into this life and ease and comfort in another existence gave her a different sense of security and new permission to express a latent talent.

MEMORY OF BIRTH

Sometimes the interpretation of a person's astrological chart is difficult because the client may be totally unaware of subtle forces within himself that I can see clearly in the chart. When a client has been exposed to some form of therapy and is more aware of his patterns, he can understand more of his horoscope's subtle messages. If I describe what was true about his birth process and his relationship with his parents, for instance, he may vigorously deny any such interaction or birth survival decisions. If he subsequently goes through a regression session, those "facts" become quite clear. He is usually left with a profound sense of wonderment at his own early but forgotten conscious choices. In many cases, a strong Saturn pattern is apparent, which indicates to me that denial is a quality of his survival and that there is an even stronger need to uncover the truth through a regression session.

The most tragic of these cases often has to do with a father's sexual abuse of his very young daughter. I might, for instance, talk about a person's quality of fear of his or her father, or blocks to the fullest expression of the relationship. The client's denial might be quite strong. In one situation in particular, the woman saw quite clearly that when she was very young, her father consistently had sexual relations with her while her mother was away from home. The woman had completely put it out of her conscious mind for the sake of survival.

With each new regression session, I find one of the most amazing things to be the variety of descriptions of the birth process. In these sessions, it is clear that I cannot influence what the person sees for himself, for I might suggest that such and such was the case but the individual often corrects and states quite clearly the specifics of his own experience. People seem able to describe even the room where the event took place, whether that was at a hospital or at home. They see whether it was an easy experience or a difficult one and exactly who was in attendance. More than that, it is clear to them exactly what the attitude of their mother was, whether she was asleep or drugged, excited, scared or exultant. They easily attune themselves to the attitude of the doctors or nurses, other relatives in the room or midwives in attendance, but more than that, they know *exactly* what their own attitude was about the event. No two descriptions are exactly alike.

In each case, however, there has been a similar thread running through—no one has seen himself as *wanting* to come into the earth plane. Resistance to the birth process itself has been described in varying degrees. One very good reason for this phenomenon is that a Saturn cast to the horoscope specifically indicates that a regression session is needed and would be helpful because of a resistance to being born. I have recommended a regression session only when that factor was in evidence. But as I began looking more deeply into the endless possibilities that Saturn might be casting a shadow over the astrological chart, I could find hardly a single individual without such an aspect, either directly or by reflection to another planet. It may be that only people with certain aspects were attracted to me to do their astrological reading in the first place. Perhaps they came to me for consultation of the chart only when they were ready to participate in a regression session to reveal past life patterns. Unfortunately, there has never been time to do a wide-range statistical study of the incidence of Saturn casting that shadow over the chart in a specific way. My observation is that hardly a person exists who doesn't come into life kicking and screaming about having to go back to school again. Most people seem to want to tackle the Saturn lesson as soon as possible to get it over with.

With Saturn ruling the ascendant, or placed in the first house, that resistance is clearly described in the regression session. The reluctance to being born stems from many causes. A very successful businessman in a European country described his birth this way:

I'm in the womb. I pretty well fill it up because I weigh about five kilos (about eleven pounds). It feels pretty tight. It makes me want to get out of there. It is nearly time to be born, but my mother is told she must eat for two, so she eats for two. She can't sleep in a bed, she has to sleep in a rocking chair. She is force-feeding herself and me. It's very uncomfortable because she puts a plate on top of my feet and my head. Once she puts the plate on my feet and I knock it off, on purpose, but she doesn't hear me. It may be the beginning of people not hearing me.

I feel the tightness around my shoulders and head and the umbilical cord is around my neck, I think. I start pushing with my feet to get out. The water has burst, and I'm born shortly thereafter. I was pushing in the car, on the way to the hospital, and I caused the water to break. She's apprehensive and so am I. I've got to get out of there. She has lost two children before, and I'm determined. It takes a long time because it is a long way out and I'm a big baby. She's in pain, so I want to get out of there faster. I feel something pulling, like forceps. I'm angry at the doctors for doing that because it is pulling my head. My godfather hits and I start yelling. (He is a doctor.) He is all bloody. There are two nurses waiting. He's happy and smiling in spite of the difficulty. My mother is crying because she's happy, but in pain. Her tears are mainly from relief.

I'm a little ambivalent about my mother. I don't know her well. I haven't the foggiest idea of what is happening, it's all very strange. I don't know why I'm here, but I know I'll be well taken care of. I don't like being in a big body, but I hear around me the words that mean, "How beautiful," in the Rembrandt sense. I feel good then because I'm bigger than the other babies. The bigness gets me what I need, even though I don't like it very much. I still wish I weren't so big. I don't like to feel so fenced in, but my bigness gives me an advantage. It still does. I have a suspicion that the bigness is a form of self-punishment, though. In the hospital, they gave me an extra bottle after my mother's milk, saying I was so big I needed more than she could give me. People still feed me. They say, "Oh, Michael, have some more." So I make everyone happy by eating. My size means steadfastness in business areas. I think it gives me a bit of an advantage in that way.

Michael's Saturn quality describes the feeling of claustrophobia before birth and the difficulty involved in the birth process itself. His astrological chart clearly indicates his dislike for the vehicle he's chosen in this life.

Tina, an American woman who was born at home, remembers her birth in this way.

It's a cool, dark day. I'm just sort of left there. It's in the bedroom because I'm born at home. The doctor is there with my mother. People are in the other room, but he's the only one here. My mother is lying over there in pain. She isn't paying any attention to me. I am eight pounds, but there were some problems after I was delivered. She said there might have been a twin that didn't develop. I think it had to do with the afterbirth. She was just tensing up and not really wanting this to happen to her body. She made it harder for herself by resisting the birth process. It's her fear that makes her tense. I think she finds the whole birth process pretty demeaning. I think the whole sex act is disgusting to her and now the doctor has to look at the private part of her. There's no way around that, so she's very humiliated. A woman doctor might have been better. Even being pregnant shows that you've done this disgusting thing. I think she was pretty angry about being pregnant at all. I don't think my father knew how to relate to her sexually, or that he was very tuned in to her. He probably made her do her wifely duty.

There's something going on inside me. It seems like the esophagus is blocked. Other things are interfering with my getting fed, even from the moment of birth. I'm really hungry, but the doctor is tending to my mother, working on the afterbirth. She's still hanging onto the afterbirth, because the whole process is so disgusting to her, she can't let go. It doesn't seem that I have been wrapped up or even cleaned up yet. I'm just lying on a table. It is bitter cold, being December. There's a storm and the wind is blowing. I don't get sick, simply because of my willpower. It seems almost like I'm determined from the very beginning to take care of myself. I listen to my intuition and try to proceed on that. I will myself not to get sick, because no one will take care of me if I do. I feel very indifferent to her. I say to myself, "If you don't want me, then I don't want you. I'm not even going to let you know when I need you." Of course it's not true that I won't need her, but I won't let her know I do.

My father doesn't seem to know I exist until I'm about eleven months old. He seems to be in another room at the time of my birth and needs taking care of himself. I feel like I'm the strongest of all of them, so I develop a stoic attitude. I just want to get recognized as *being here*, but I don't know how. That's funny... one of my favorite expressions is, I don't know how, I don't know how. I'm not important enough to get any attention. There's something else that takes priority, so I have to take second place. Even now I get so far and then it doesn't seem to make any difference what I do. I'm just waiting for someone to come to me. I think the doctor finally wraps me up and gives me to my mother. The circumstances of my birth seem to describe my whole life!

Another young woman named Valerie also saw her mother's horror at pregnancy because it announced to the world that she had had intercourse. But her description of her birth is very different. She said,

My mother had an absolutely horrendous, awful time having me. She was in labor fifty-six hours, and she was forty-two years old just a month after I was born. I was supposed to be born on her birthday, September 8, but I was born a month early. I'm seeing my dad sitting in the waiting room with his head in his hands. He is so scared because he thinks my mother is going to die. I can see him as if he were sitting in this room, but I couldn't possibly see him because I wasn't in the waiting room. [I suggested that perhaps she was wandering around.] It makes me feel very bad. I'm not worried about my mother, but I feel the emotion and his hurt, so I'm very sad. I can also see the doctors. Everyone seems worried. Oh, it's a woman doctor. My mother is all covered with sheets, and I can't see her face. I almost want to say she's not there. What they're working on is not her. She may not be in her body. From what I've been told, she almost died.

I haven't entered my body yet. I don't think I've ever been in the body. It certainly wouldn't be a very good place to be. It would hurt because they're using forceps . . . she just can't seem to have me. It's like she's too weak to do what is necessary. I think I don't want to enter my body at all. In fact, I think I'm trying not to. I just don't want to be born! But I think my mother has had about all she can handle and if I don't get on with it, she's going to die. I've got to get this over with.

I'm just looking at somebody when I see my mother. I don't seem to have any identification with her at all, but I do with my father. My poor dad. He's blaming himself for getting her pregnant. She's too old to have a baby. He's sitting on a green couch and is just miserable. It is almost like I just walked into the waiting room and see my dad, and see all the pain and agony. . . . So I decide I'll do it and be born, after a lot of deliberation. I see the doctor and this body lying there. I see the forceps and I'm appalled by that. Oooh, I don't like that at all. He wants a child very much, but he doesn't want to lose his wife to get one. It is like a pain in the rear end to have to do this. It's like going to the dentist. I don't like it but if I don't my teeth will fall out, so I'll do it.

There's no one there to claim that baby's body. Someone wasn't ready yet. She (my mother) is scared. She's a nurse and has seen babies, helped with them and wants her own, but it's not supposed to be like this. I don't think she really wants the responsibility of a child. I feel that she knows she's in danger, but she's going to hang on as long as she can without ruining herself. It's like she's going through the motions of having a baby without really having it after all. My feeling is "It's not my fault, it's not my fault." She's blaming me! She has a sex hang-up. It's dirty and if you're pregnant, you're admitting to the entire world that you've had sexual intercourse. If she just could have gotten pregnant some other way, it would have been all right. It's like public shame. My God, I'm my mother's public shame. No wonder I was so shy all my life.

She was always pushing me to beauty contests.... My daughter got all As, my daughter this, my daughter that, but yet.... I don't want to be her public shame. That's what I'm saying as I'm floating around. It's not my fault but I'm stuck with this. My mother and I bang heads all the time. I rescued the situation and got punished for it. My dad could get me to do anything by just talking to me. It wasn't that she didn't love me, but I was the kid she really didn't want. The doctors had already told her she couldn't have a child. She had uremic poisoning with another pregnancy, had a miscarriage and was told not to get pregnant again. Everything is so clear now. We just knock heads all the time. I like things to be clear and when I would want a yes or no answer, she'd say, "We'll see." You can't believe what that woman did to me during my lifetime.

BIRTH DEFECTS REMEMBERED

Perhaps the most moving experience I've had with birth awareness came when I was working with a young man named Bob. Bob is exceptionally handsome, climbing to the top of his chosen profession because of an obvious elegance, sense of self and charm. He is also exceptionally talented in his field. When I first met him, he was wearing a dark suit that set off his handsome good looks quite nicely. As we talked, I noticed a depth and sensitivity that seemed to set him apart from other handsome young men. Bob was obviously unaware of his good looks, and his lack of self-consciousness impressed me a great deal. We seemed to have many common interests and I found myself telling him about my work with regression and past-life recall. He decided to come for a session the next day. When he arrived for our appointment, he was wearing a short-sleeved safari shirt that revealed his arms. It was now noticeable that his left arm was slightly different from his right arm. I admired more than ever the poise and unselfconsciousness I had noticed earlier.

We began the regression session by looking at an accident he'd had when he was about six years old. He'd fallen off the tricycle he'd been given for his birthday and had gashed his forehead. He was especially surprised that he had remembered the incident so vividly all his life. Now he saw how the whole family sprang to attention to get him to the hospital to have the cut stitched up. Bob was particularly aware of all the wonderful attention he had received, yet he was also very angry that he was forced to have the pain of the stitches inflicted on him after he had already been hurt by the fall. After examination of that early trauma, he realized it had been a test he set up, entirely subconsciously, to see how much attention he would receive. The setup backfired somewhat when more pain outweighed the comforting attention.

He then went quickly to the time of his birth. His memory was of tremendous claustrophobia. "I feel like I'm about seven months old inside. The frustration comes with knowing I'll get out, but not knowing *when*. I feel that I could breathe better and develop much faster outside. I've had it with this restriction. I don't think I can bend my neck, and I want to stretch. It's like my head is really pushed down on my chest and I'd do anything in the world to be able to bend my head all the way back. It's so uncomfortable." I asked him if he was prepared for what was awaiting him in the outside world. His description was related to his need for freedom. "I know what the outside world is like already. There's going to be a lot of openness, and a lot of air to breathe, and there will be a lot of colors. Inside it appears to be sort of orange, but everything will be clear and bright and white outside. I need to get to the very lightness of that."

He continued with some information he had been told about his birth. "My mother is very anxious to get it over with, because she's thirty-six and she's not having an easy time of it. My father gave her an entire bottle of castor oil the night before I was born and she woke up with terrible cramps about an hour before I was born. She described the next couple of hours as just a god-awful mess. She was barely admitted to the hospital when I was born." I asked him to look at the birth process from his point of view, and he described it vividly.

I feel everything's about to happen and suddenly, everything's very rushed. Finally, the moment has arrived and it's not happening at the right pace. I want out. I *really* do want out. I can't help it if it's hurting or not. I'm about nine pounds and my head is right down, ready to push out. I think my mother is hurting a great deal, and on top of everything else, she's having terrible stomach cramps. She's just in agony. If I can just get out, the sooner she'll get some relief. So I've got to get out fast so she won't be in so much pain.

Bob was aware of his protective feelings toward his mother even before he was born.

It feels like coming out from down underneath the ocean and the sand. It's like swimming to the top, but I can't get to the water's edge so I can breathe. I just want to breathe at the top of the water.

Finally, Bob had the feeling he was born.

It's sort of noisy. I feel myself being picked up with one hand by a doctor. I feel like my mother's cord is being severed very close to her skin. Now I feel like I'm on display. There are about five other people in the room and I'm being cleaned up and placed in a plastic bed. I feel like crying . . . I'm so tired now, because it was a real effort . . . It's like the first time I've had a chance to use my muscles . . . the nurse is cleaning me with cotton . . . My mother's just lying there, exhausted. She hasn't seen me yet. She must be seeing me now, because I'm being held up in the air.

At this point in the regression session, Bob's attitude changed. He became very serious and intense. He saw a plastic hood over him and realized he must be in an incubator. Then he saw that something was wrong with his left arm. The trouble seemed to be connected with the shoulder, at the socket. He saw himself as four hours old and feeling very helpless. He knew that helplessness came from worry about his mother rather than about himself. He told me his mother had lost two children already and he was very aware that she was really horrified because she knew something was wrong with Bob.

He continued,

I don't want her to blame herself, and I can't communicate that to her. The frustration is a feeling of "here we go again." I've come into another life and this one is not going to be perfect either. I just want to grow up one time, all the way through, without any inhibitions. I feel like I have a whole lifetime ahead of me to fight this thing.

The expression on his face reflected the deep concern and frustration, as if it were just now happening to him. Then he said,

I also feel that I'm going to try to make her feel guilty for making me feel this way. It's a calculated determination to give a little twist every now and then, when I want my way. Actually I don't really do that. I'm really more concerned, as I grow older, about how it's affecting me. Right now, at four hours old, I feel protective toward her. It's a feeling of "I wish we could work this thing out together."

It seems there are three doctors standing above me, talking about me and putting together some ideas about how they can correct this by surgery. When they tell my mother, I can see her face get very pale. She's stunned, but all her attention goes to me and all of her concern is for my welfare. My father is comforting her, with his arm around her shoulder. That makes me feel good, because I can't recall a moment of ever seeing them hug or express warmth or touching. I feel a sort of strength from their affection for each other. I only wish I could have seen them draw on that at other times.

The doctors tell her they will have to wait about six months before they will break my arm in several places and reset it. They will strap my arm to my body, and I'll have to wear a body cast for a long time. The bones will reshape because I'm so young. That gives them a lot of hope.

Bob had not remembered any trauma connected with that operation or with the wearing of a body cast earlier in his regression session. Evidently he was so determined to correct his disability in the best way possible, he developed a stoic but hopeful attitude. But he once again felt the restriction that had been so distasteful to him before birth.

The information that had already come forth into Bob's conscious mind was enough to give him a new perspective on his life programming. But that knowledge still didn't answer the question, "Why me?" We went further when I asked him to allow himself to go to a time that would give him an explanation of this experience. Bob saw himself standing on a street corner late at night, with dense fog swirling around him. He could see how he was dressed but he couldn't understand just why he was standing on that particular corner. He described himself as being about thirty or thirty-five, wearing a tall hat and frock coat. He sensed that the location was England, and from the fog, he sensed it might be London. Gradually the fog lifted a bit so that he could see more detail. To his horror, he saw a smoking gun in his hand, but became very frightened to look any further. He said, "I'm afraid of what I might see." A bit of time elapsed before he became aware of two women standing across the street from him, huddled together in fright. At their feet was the body of a man who had fallen when Bob had fired the gun. Bob knew he had shot the man in order to protect the women from attack, but he was not sure whether the man had intended to rob them or rape them. Bob was visibly upset over what he saw. He realized his shot, aimed at the *left* arm, had penetrated the body of the man and gone straight into the man's heart. He had had no intention of killing the man, only wanting to scare him away with a surface wound.

As he was able to look more closely, he felt that the two women were his mother and sister in that lifetime and that the mother strongly resembled his mother in this lifetime. He concluded they were one and the same. He said, "No wonder I still have this protective feeling toward my mother." I sked Bob to look at the face of the man lying on the ground. He was lying on his side, face down, but obviously dead. Bob said, "I can't see his face because he is lying on his side with his head turned downward and his hat is covering his face." He said he was tried for the crime and exonerated, but nevertheless spent the rest of his life feeling shame and guilt over the incident. Once again, I suggested that Bob take a look at the face of the man. I felt rather sure I knew what Bob would see. It took a long time to mentally turn the man's face around so he could see his features. Finally he gasped and said, "Oh my God, it's my father." Bob had already told me that his father had committed suicide when he was about twelve years old, leaving Bob with a mental sense of responsibility to care for his mother and sister. When Bob could find his voice again, he said, "Do you think I had to come into this life with a defective arm to pay myself back for having shot my father then? It was even the same arm." The air was heavy with the emotion of the moment. Bob finally said, "This experience was so real, it must have happened. It explains so much of my life."

Forgiveness seems to be the key to sorting out these puzzles. With awareness of the reason for his damaged arm, Bob might not be able to correct the disability, but he might find it easier to live with. Self-punishment never resolves the issue, and Bob's forgiveness of himself was long overdue. Bob might also need to forgive his father for the attack in the English life as well as the abandonment in this life. And finally, Bob's father might have carried over his own guilt into the present situation and found himself unable to live with the subconscious memory of the attack on the women over a century ago. In other regression sessions, when the person undergoing the session was able to totally forgive himself and others, a healing took place between that individual and other people in the past-life drama that was demonstrable. In Bob's case, he might not know if his forgiveness affected his father, but it might assure him of not having to relive such a difficult drama again.

In another incidence of a birth defect having roots in a past life, the situation was quite similar. A twelve-year-old girl was particularly fearful of going out in city streets alone. Her very real fear made it difficult not only for herself but also affected her mother very strongly. Jane had a difficult childhood, as she was born with a heart defect. She was very protected as a young child, and her mother worked constantly to rid herself of the guilt she felt about the situation. It was not easy for her to be a disciplinarian and ignore Jane's reluctance to do certain things for herself. An operation had closed the four holes in Jane's heart many years earlier, yet a sense of overprotection quite naturally prevailed in her mother's attitude toward her.

Jane was most eager to have a regression session, and I discovered that it was almost unnecessary for me to direct her at all. The information poured forth without any prompting from me. Jane saw herself in England, staring out of a window on the second floor of her home and seeing a red car parked in front of the house. She was quite frightened at the sight because she knew that she possessed some information that put her life in danger. She saw her mother in this life as her grandmother then. She felt unable to share her secret with anyone in the family, however, as she didn't want to jeopardize their lives too. Finally it seemed necessary to go about her daily tasks, and she saw herself on the street being chased by that car. She then knew that she was shot in the heart four times, making four holes. The information, once again, came forth with deep feelings of amazement and awe.

It would have been most unusual for Jane not to have wondered, "Why me?" during those times of enforced inactivity, pain and fear connected with her operation when she was a very young child. Yet she had always shown a most heroic style as far as her health was concerned. In Jane's case, there was no past life guilt involved, as an act was perpetrated against her. However, forgiveness was once again very appropriate to release her from the karmic necessity of having to deal with that circumstance again. Perhaps equally important, Jane's mother could forgive herself and absolve herself of any guilt she might have had in connection with Jane's birth defect. Jane's mother had suffered quite a lot in connection with the resolution of her guilt because she had taken drugs early on in her pregnancy. If she could accept that she was the instrument to bring Jane into the world and to love her enough to find the best solution for the repairing of the damage to her heart, their relationship could be upgraded to a higher level of understanding, for indeed that is just what she did in finding the best heart specialist to perform the operation. Jane's mother also admitted that to calm her own fears before the operation, she had released the situation into God's hands. That process of letting go was a courageous act in the face of the forthcoming trial both she and Jane would undergo. In the final analysis, Jane's mother felt only the greatest admiration for Jane, who said, "Let's get this over with. I want to do the operation now."

In all the instances in which there was a memory of reluctance to being born or of especially heavy difficulties that became obvious at the moment of birth, Saturn was making a hard aspect to the position of the chart that described prenatal conditions and/or the birth process itself, as well as the conditions of childhood. Frequently I would say to one of these clients, "If I could just remove Saturn from your chart, the conditions of the beginning of your life would have been quite different." I would then describe what that difference might have been and explain that for some reason or other, it was as if a shadow had fallen over his or her life from the very beginning. It might be that the soul made a choice to resolve karma incurred from the past as soon as possible, as if to say, "Let's get this over with so that the later part of my life will be easier."

In many instances, this aspect describes the need to create artificial barriers in the form of external conditions that would prevent the individual from racing into his "destiny" too soon. The older years might be the years of greatest productivity. When it is obvious that the individual is evolved, in tune with his ability to make a contribution and aware of what is needed in the world, he might be tempted to set things in motion too soon, out of sync with universal timing, unless he was held back in some way. In most situations when this heavy aspect from Saturn existed, an accompanying feeling is that of having some special destiny in life and of having to wait to know what that might be.

CHAPTER FOUR

Saturn, the Life Script
and Survival Issues

*I*n the light of reincarnation, Saturn represents the heaviest karmic burden we bring into this life to resolve. It describes areas of guilt, fear and restriction, sometimes self-imposed. But when an individual begins to work on a level of ultimate responsibility, he sees difficult conditions as opportunities for growth. The practicality of this approach may become clear as he develops new spiritual or psychological awareness that enables him to work past those blocks. He begins to realize that from a soul perspective, he did indeed create some restrictive conditions for himself. Why would he deliberately create a condition that is not productive or pleasant? The final answer becomes crystal clear with a view of past life conditions.

One manifestation of Saturn is suffering. This suffering occurs in areas where we have brought forward the greatest guilt from the past. For instance, suppose that in a past life, you organized a skiing party. The weather conditions are uncertain, and one member of the party decides it is too dangerous to go. You convince this person that everything will be fine and you'll watch for his welfare. But in spite of your vigilance, an accident occurs. This person falls and breaks a leg. He is hospitalized, suffers a great deal of pain and cannot return home from the vacation until a few weeks later. He loses money and time from work, and suffers pain from the broken limb. You, as the responsible party, feel just terrible. You wish that you could simply turn back the clock. You wish that you had never organized the group in the first place and especially wish you hadn't convinced the injured person to ski on that particular day. However, he has a different perspective. He is alive and thankful to have good doctors and hospitalization. He absolves you of all responsibility, but subconsciously you cannot forgive yourself.

With the dawn of another day, you feel better, but on some level, you've made very important decisions. First, you decide, "I'll never organize anything again." Then you say, "I'll certainly never go skiing again." And finally, "I hate cold weather, I don't like snow and I don't like groups of people." All those decisions are born from overreaction and guilt, and they are carried with you into another lifetime. But since you're in a new body and have new conditions around you, the likelihood of remembering those nonproductive decisions is very slim.

You may come back into this life with preconceived notions that have very little to do with the external programming from your mother and father. On some level, however, you may choose a particular mother or father to justify the decisions you've made in the past. You may even pick as your mother or father the very person who was hurt in the skiing accident. Then you feel overly responsible for the welfare of that parent, while at the same time you resent very much being made to feel responsible. You cannot acknowledge that the responsibility is of your own choosing because you don't remember the past life facts. You may leave home as soon as you can because you don't like the feeling of being burdened with your parents' welfare. But then you have even more guilt because you're not there to take care of things when your parents are needy.

At some point in your life, you decide to investigate all those feelings. You attempt to break the vicious cycle. You change your way of looking at life and accept that somehow you picked your particular parents for a reason. You can find out why and break the vicious cycle you've created by reviewing your past lives. And Saturn's placement in your chart can point your search in the right direction.

Often we pick other people to act as a mirror. We may attract someone negative, critical or judgmental. As a result, we feel hurt, betrayed or neglected by that person. But an evaluation of the underlying situation shows that we have drawn to us the very person who mirrors the quality of our personality that needs balance. This is especially true when we have not acknowledged that trait within.

We also pick conditions and situations to mirror our imbalances. If we are upset over outer circumstances, instead of blaming other people or life, we need to ask ourselves, "Why would I pick such a problem to resolve?" The answer is that through certain conditions of limitation, we grow and become more whole. The pain forces us to look at ourselves in a new light. If we could grow without that pain, we could dispense with negativity in our lives. Perhaps we could learn to find balance and harmony through pleasure instead.

THE MEANING OF SATURN

I use three analogies to help people understand the energy described by Saturn. The first is the analogy of the playpen. Saturn is the playpen that Mother Nature puts her children in, for safety's sake. Just as we put our small children in a playpen to keep them safe, life—our higher selves—our superconscious—chooses restrictions that will keep us from harm. Those circumstances may not appear to be safety measures when we are hampered by them, but eventually the pressure becomes so dreadful, we need to find a more productive solution. A baby is safe in his playpen, but when it is time to go to school, he must learn to cross streets. When we know the child will take responsibility for himself, we allow him more freedom. Likewise, when we are tired of pain and suffering in our lives, we begin to operate on a new level of action that will ensure better conditions. We may be squeezed or forced out of our playpen onto higher levels of effectiveness because we have outgrown certain conditions. But ultimately we must make a conscious decision to grow by becoming clear about the right level on which to operate. Limitations melt away like ice in the warm sun when we learn to take care of ourselves. We knock down the walls of the playpen and make it into a trampoline by understanding that we won't allow ourselves to jump so high that we can't land on our own two feet.

The second analogy has to do with the ego stages described by Transactional Analysis. One of those ego states is the parent. If we view Saturn as the parent within ourselves, as well as the parent in our external life, we see a different picture. A good parent exhibits all the positive Saturn qualities. He is responsible, a good disciplinarian, someone who gives a sense of security and teaches us how to structure life. But parents also say no. Sometimes the nos seem unfair to us. They are restrictive, limiting and harsh. "You can't watch television for a week because you must study for your exam." "You can't go to discothéques because the atmosphere is no good for your health." "You can't have chocolate cake or sugar because you'll have pimples." And sometimes, "I said no and that's all there is to it. Don't ask me why." As we grow up, we continue to give ourselves similar messages. "Watching television is not good for your brain." "It's really stupid to go to discothéques. You run into really bad characters and you might stir up sexual feelings." "I'm not very pretty, because sometimes I have a pimple. I'd better develop an allergy to sugar so I won't be tempted to indulge myself in chocolate candy or cake." On a karmic level, those overly judgmental messages take on incredible new dimensions and proportions.

The third analogy concerns the six of swords in the Tarot deck of cards. That card depicts a red boat going downstream, carrying a mother, child and father. The father is standing, rowing the boat with a long pole. He pushes away from obstacles in the path of the boat. He is standing so that he can steer properly, seeing beyond the swords and crosses that block the view of the mother and child, who are sitting in the front of the boat. This is the card representing journey. The father represents the higher consciousness. The mother represents the conscious mind, and the child is like the unconscious. In the journey through life, the higher self, or superconsciousness, or God self, knows where we're headed. He sees beyond the rocks in the path. If we were always on remote control, allowing the higher self to guide us, that part of us would simply push away from negative karmic situations, acknowledging their existence but knowing that it is no longer necessary to go through the pain of the association or condition one more time. The higher self knows that the healing of karma is quite simple. All we have to do is have compassion for the rocks in the path and for ourselves, for once getting stuck on those rocks. Then we simply choose to glide gently past, wishing the rock well on our way downstream.

But the snare comes when the mother and child, conscious and subconscious mind, recognize something familiar and comforting about the rocks and buy into their message of "Don't go downstream, it's not safe down there. Stay here with me in this nice safe harbor I've found. I'm your security." The "familiar" rocks hook onto our insecurities, pulling us into a vast whirlpool. It is exceedingly hard to get away from those familiar messages and conditions, even though they are negative and restrictive. But if we can comprehend that those conditions are there so we can overcome them and continue on our own life path, we can pat the rocks on the head and keep going. If we become angry or fearful about those conditions, our judgment about the past experience becomes another hook in the chain of karmic deeds. "I never want to go back there again. I never want to see that rock." And lo and behold, the same situation turns up again and again because we did not acknowledge the mutual need that caused the attraction and tie-up in the first place. Worst of all, we had no knowledge of the lesson learned. Sometimes we hook up to a rocklike person or situation because we choose to take a rest, but as we've just seen, the price of that rest may be high.

ESOTERIC VIEW OF SATURN

Saturn occupies a special place in the natural lineup of the planets. Imagine three triangles, one above the other. There are nine points in all. Considering the Sun and Moon as planets for the moment, we can place Sun, Moon and Mercury at each point of the bottom triangle, and Venus, Mars and Jupiter at each point of the middle triangle. The third triangle represents the beginning of the higher octave planets. Saturn occupies the strategic first point of that third triangle. Then come Uranus and Neptune. Pluto, representing cosmic consciousness in this case, stands alone above the other groups of triangles. The quality of energy embodied by each planet represents one step along the way to that cosmic consciousness.

Saturn, at the beginning of the triangle representing higher consciousness, acts like a breaking point. It can be a barrier to further development or the platform from which to leap into the exciting but unknown areas represented by Uranus, the planet of enlightenment. It describes the point in the development of consciousness at which we each choose to go higher or cautiously to dig in where we feel safe. We cannot ignore Saturn. It stands at the gateway like a rock that demands a secret word to roll it aside. The secret word, in my opinion, is *compassion*, or *forgiveness*. But on the face of that rock are inscribed many of our past words and deeds. It may be possible to roll back the rock without understanding all those words and deeds from our past, but it may not be possible to reconcile the karmic situation fully without greater awareness of just what happened before. We need to know what we must forgive within ourselves.

In terms of the metaphysical, every word and deed is recorded in the Akashic Records. All the kind and good things we've done are there, as well as all the negative things. Before our spiritual voyage is complete, *all* those negative acts must be balanced, even if it takes thousands of lives and experiences to do so. Saturn points the way toward those past karmic issues to be resolved, and we can see those negative deeds and acts and hear the words we need to hear in a regression session.

Saturn's Placement in the Astrological Chart

The astrological chart is divided into twelve sections, or "houses," each describing a separate department of life.

In interpreting the astrological chart for purposes of reviewing past lives, it is essential to consider the aspects to Saturn (an *aspect* is the mathematical relationship of one planet to another) as well as its placement in the chart. By *placement*, I mean the house that Saturn is *placed in* as well as the house that Saturn *rules*. (Each house is ruled by one of the twelve signs. Because Saturn rules the *sign* of Capricorn, it also rules the *house* in the chart that has Capricorn on the cusp (or dividing line) of a particular house.

	SIGN	RULING PLANET	
♈	Aries	Mars	♂
♉	Taurus	Venus	♀
♊	Gemini	Mercury	☿
♋	Cancer	Moon	☽
♌	Leo	Sun	☉
♍	Virgo	Mercury	☿
♎	Libra	Venus	♀
♏	Scorpio	Pluto	♇
♐	Sagittarius	Jupiter	♃
♑	Capricorn	Saturn	♄
♒	Aquarius	Uranus	♅
♓	Pisces	Neptune	♆

If you do not already have a copy of your astrological chart, you can order one from

Jupiter Pluto Communications
204 E. 77 Street
New York, NY 10021

A natal chart costs approximately five dollars, but it may be advisable to write in advance to find the exact cost. You will receive a computer printout that shows the wheel of your astrological chart, the placement of the planets within that wheel and the placement of the signs. From this, you will be able to determine what house Saturn is placed in, what house it rules (the house that Capricorn rules) and what aspects it makes to other planets. Later in this chapter, we will discuss Saturn's aspects in more detail. For now, let's take a look at the meaning of the individual houses in the chart.

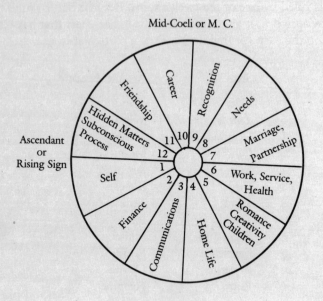

Mid-Coeli or M. C.

The placement of Saturn indicates the specific area of life in which the most severe lessons are to be learned, the areas of responsibility are the most pronounced and restrictions are most likely to occur. If we let the negative pressures of Saturn condition us to remain in our stuck position, or the position of safety, we are choosing not to roll back the rocklike door. When we take on the responsibility of tackling our lessons and resolving our karmic judgments and relationships, Saturn becomes a true platform of security. It becomes the good parent who watches us cross the street, knowing that he has given us the information and security to enable us to make good choices and decisions in life. Saturn becomes the trampoline that enables us to leap to the heights, knowing our commitment to responsibility will bring us back to earth. Saturn becomes our life-supporting gravity.

When I first began doing regression sessions, I started with people who had Saturn placed in or ruling the twelfth house or the first house in the horoscope. Those placements describe heavy karmic guilts that are obvious from the moment of birth. For instance, if Saturn rules or is placed in the first house, the infant is born with a feeling of not being wanted, which results in a decision to put up barriers to protect himself from the pain of rejection. He says, in essence, "I won't eat too much, I won't take up too much room (or space), and then I'll be wanted."

With that first-house placement of Saturn, the individual feels a deep insecurity and at the same time a deep responsibility. He becomes parentlike and is judgmental about his own behavior and life as well as toward everyone around him. His idea of safety is to stay in control. But he also needs to be needed. He may be masochistic and take on burdens that prevent him from enjoying life. He will allow himself to be "dumped on," and it may take a long time before he will be a good parent to himself. He tends to store resentments until they turn into walls, preventing anyone from reaching him again. After a regression session, he understands why he chose to come into life with all those preconditions and judgments.

Indicating an even deeper need to review the past is the placement of Saturn in the twelfth house of the subconscious. With this position in the astrological chart, an individual comes into life with a feeling of karmic, racial guilt. I am never sure what that will mean in the present life, for it may have nothing to do with the present-life race or sect. It describes a guilty feeling of responsibility toward a group or community from the past. This placement indicates either a guilt of commission (having done something that caused suffering for a group of people) or a guilt of omission (having neglected to do something that might have saved a group from disaster). In either case, the individual cannot allow himself joy or true success in this life, simply because of his nagging subconscious memories. He watches opportunities pass him by, knowing that he could have those things in his life if he could only reach out to grasp them. He may feel a subconscious paralysis and have deep-seated fears. He may have nightmares. He may be afraid to open the doors of his subconscious mind for fear he would find a monster lurking there. If he is courageous enough to bring that monster into the daylight, he will see that it is very tiny and easily vanquished.

SATURN RULING OR PLACED IN THE FIRST HOUSE

The first house represents the personality and describes the basic survival issues that we adopt at the moment of birth. It demonstrates our behavior patterns and indicates the specific viewpoints that follow us throughout life. A first-house Saturn describes the conditions of the birth process itself and indicates that the birth was a prolonged, slow and perhaps painful event. The child takes on a stoic quality that may even mean stiffness in the body, as if he or she were steeling himself against life and more pain. The personality is serious, for birth has already demonstrated that life is not just fun and games. Tension can develop in the shoulder areas, for this placement describes the "Atlas complex" of taking the weight of the world on the shoulders. The child instantly becomes the parent, not only to himself but to everyone else around him. He may not trust that his parents or the people around him are capable of caring for him. He can feel a deep sense of rejection and may even feel very unwanted. He is cautious by nature, able to take only one step at a time. He cannot be pushed, for he must ensure that he is on safe ground before he can advance further. On a karmic level, the individual has chosen to take on very heavy responsibilities in this life. But he may not be ready to assume the major task he came here to perform until he is older in years. Therefore he chooses restrictive situations in childhood that will teach him basic structure and responsibility, just in case he may be tempted to be frivolous and ignore his karmic duty. He chooses to build a strong character very early in life. Early feelings of rejection ensure that he will do just that. For the truth is, he may have come into the world very reluctantly. He says, "Please don't make me do it again. I don't like the restriction of the earth plane. I don't want to be born to those people. I can see already how difficult it will be and I'm not sure I can handle it all another time. Suppose I fail again?"

These self-imposed judgments come from a past life in which he was in a very strong position of responsibility and experienced great guilt, either by omission or commission. He tends to beat himself up and become very masochistic in the present life. Self-forgiveness can be extremely difficult, because he carries the shadow of a past event for which he blames himself bitterly. The more pain he can endure, the more cleansed he may feel. But self-punishment is not the way to reconcile this deep subconscious guilt.

Saturn pressures early in life act like a squeeze play for him. When he grows beyond the four walls of his self-imposed play-pen, he simply cannot ignore the sense of destiny any longer. His higher self says with a sigh, "You've had a chance to play your game of self-denial long enough. Now it's time for you to find your destiny." Usually the first-house placement of Saturn describes a prebirth decision to take on the real-life purpose or task later in life. He may erect walls that will keep him on earth, tied by gravity long enough for the timing to be in line with his age and development. He is an old soul, but if he were born with full consciousness, he might very well have decided to postpone his coming into the earth plane until conditions were better. As it is, he purposely chooses to wear a crown of thorns until the time is ripe for his real contribution to be revealed. As a result, he may get stuck, like the rock, and refuse to grow into his own shoes of destiny. In that case, life becomes almost an imprisonment. He knows clearly what he is capable of but sees himself developing a shy or insecure personality that automatically prevents his breaking through the barriers of self. This behavior can cause intense pain.

As he grows older, he gets bored with the game. He becomes tired of the self-punishment and finally says, "Let's get on with it. What am I to do?" When he is truly ready to assume his ultimate responsibility, he can accomplish more than anyone else, for his very persona has been melded and shaped by the forces of the cosmos, making him rugged, capable and solid as a rock that has withstood the test of time. His fortitude is formidable. He can take on a load of pressure and even thrive on it. He represents the ultimate in the serious, prestigious, reliable person we can look up to and respect. He sets long-range goals and steadfastly climbs to the top of the mountain of his own ambition, born from that inner sense of destiny.

This quality of Saturn in the chart applies if Saturn is in difficult or hard aspect to any planet in the first house as well, for it acts like a shadow over the quality of energy described by that other planet. (It also applies if Saturn is in difficult aspect to the ruler of the ascendant.)

SATURN RULING OR PLACED IN THE SECOND HOUSE

When Saturn is placed in or rules the second house of finance (or if Saturn is in hard aspect to the ruling planet of that house or to any planet in the second house), responsibility with finance is the key word. This aspect indicates a "poor" complex. The individual may be born to a wealthy family or to an impecunious one, but his attention must go toward building security with money. The environment may foster his sense of deprivation. He may have had judgmental parental messages such as "Get a good steady job. A penny saved is a penny earned," but whatever the circumstances of his life, he is not a spendthrift. He may worry about money and feel a sense of defeat about ever having more than just what he needs. He can be judgmental about people who are extravagant or carefree about financial matters.

In any case, it is necessary for him to focus attention on matters connected to security. Since Saturn means responsibility, he can fulfill his sense of duty by making sure to build a solid base of financial security. He may be an accountant or a business manager, or he may simply need to develop practicality in connection with money. Usually the individual spends too much time worrying about funds. He avoids financial responsibility by denying that money is important at all. He wishes someone else would simply take care of it. A sense of defeat about funds may prevent him from taking on or expressing his true capability within the financial arena. He may tend to limit himself because of some karmic guilt about money matters.

The deeper karmic issues involved may have to do with memories of starvation or deprivation from a past life. He may develop a dependency on someone else to provide funds, or just the opposite may occur. He doesn't trust anyone else to provide for him and denies potential sources of income, just to be on safe ground. If, for instance, a person starved in another life, he would be very security-conscious in this life, and rightly so. That kind of memory would be hard to erase. Another situation that could have occurred, especially in the time of the French Revolution, for instance, was the expectation that if someone arrived with funds *in time*, a life would be saved. If that someone did not make it, it is easy to see how fear of dependency on another person has become a life-or-death issue for that individual. Those overshadowing memories overwhelm and paralyze a real ability to make money in the present time. Guilt is another major factor. If one had been incredibly wealthy, not knowing or ignoring the fact that other people were starving, the shock of such a realization could cause denial in present-life situations.

When true awareness of the cause of the worry, fear or guilt about money dawns, the individual develops a different attitude. He may have a talent he hesitates to explore professionally for fear he won't make enough money. He chooses to get that steady but boring or limiting job just to make sure he knows where the next meal is coming from. Yet with acknowledgment of the cause of the problem, he can begin assuming another kind of responsibility for financial well-being. He can feel more secure about doing that when he learns to restructure his present needs and develop new concepts about money.

SATURN RULING OR PLACED IN THE THIRD HOUSE

Since the third house in an astrological chart describes communications of all sorts, including the learning process and the *later* interaction with people, when Saturn rules or is placed in this house, the individual may be overly cautious about all such activities. In early school years, the person may be a perfectionist about the learning process and actually try too hard. He may think that he must be perfect and will never live up to his own expectations. The result is a tendency to say, "Why bother?"

This house also describes relatives, siblings in particular. The person may have a past-life association with a sister or brother, or relatives in general, that gives him a sense of responsibility for their welfare. The reverse may be true in that the siblings take on a parental role toward the individual and can be judgmental of him or her. Generally speaking, there can be a coolness in these relationships until the people involved are older and wiser. Strong ties and a deep sense of security become stabilizing forces once the walls of judgment are broken down.

The individual's manner of speech may be slow and methodical. He seems to fear being wrong or incorrect in his vocabulary, or perhaps a fear of ridicule makes him very cautious about saying what he thinks. He hesitates to commit himself to an idea or agreement. He may dislike talking on the telephone.

In the positive sense, Saturn in this placement allows the individual to deal with the communications world in some way or another. He may adopt a field related to discussions or communications that represent security. He may block a real desire to communicate as a writer, an idea person, an actor, a speaker or a negotiator. Only he can know where he levels off for the sake of security. One gentleman who had come to me for a regression confessed to being a frustrated singer and actor. His messenger service business represented tremendous security, but later in life, some of his latent talent in the area of communications emerged in a new way. He began to study voice and became an expert in comprehension of voice production.

Why are some people willing to take risks in areas of communications, while others have a real fear or hesitancy to express themselves? If in a past life, a person was a public speaker, a singer, an actor or a politician and was ridiculed, punished or ostracized for it, he can come into this life with a real fear about exposing himself again. One man saw himself being killed in a past life when he stood on a platform to advocate moderation to the rebelling colonies of America. The shot that went into his body set in motion patterns of limitation with words that were deeply ingrained. One of the most obvious ways to avoid speaking, writing or communicating on a profound level is to think oneself ignorant. It is an easy out simply to think oneself incapable of self-expression, and if a person *thinks* he can't do something, he can't.

In connection with siblings, karmic ties can be so strong that rejection in this life comes not from a mother or father but from an older brother or sister who really did not want a new baby to steal the show. As so often happens, that very same older brother or sister may be given some responsibility for the care of the younger child. "Watch your sister. She's not as old as you are." "Take your little brother with you to the picnic. He wants to go with you." Even without past life ties, those injunctions are enough to turn one against the little brother or sister, as it puts the older child in a parent position much too soon in his or her life. He continues telling the younger one what to do, thereby restricting a relationship that might otherwise be a happy one. Perhaps in a former life, one of the siblings was indeed a parent, the other a child. Those memories are still active and alive.

There may be great guilt in connection with a younger brother or sister from a past life. In that case, the older child may want nothing to do with that person in the present. Saturn can also indicate loneliness due to the absence of a sibling. Medical science now presumes that multiple pregnancies can occur in which one fetus simply doesn't develop. The doctor and the mother may never know she was slated to have twins. But the other fetus inside the womb knows! There have been instances in which the surviving infant feels tremendous guilt, emerging in a regression session, that he or she may have taken all the food, all the space and inadvertently (or deliberately) forced the other fetus out of the way. In another instance, a girl whose twin was epileptic felt that it was her fault. She punished herself by denying her ability to talk, think and communicate brilliantly because her twin was defective in those areas. With a review of the real situation, she became aware that it was not her fault—it was simply her twin's karma. Her reason for joining him in this life was to help him bear his burden by showing patience and love, not guilt. Knowing this, she could allow her true compassion to emerge.

SATURN RULING OR PLACED IN THE FOURTH HOUSE

The fourth house describes home, land, property, life-style and programming from the parent of the opposite sex. When Saturn is ruling or is posited in this sector of the chart, a sense of rejection usually comes from that parent. The parent may have a stoic nature and exhibit conservatism and a judgmental quality that prevents close association with the soul entering the family. He or she may feel burdened, giving the child a sense of responsibility to relieve some of that pressure. The helpless feelings that come forth when a baby is newborn and sees the extra burden he places on that parent can be paralyzing in the extreme. He feels that he must honor and obey that parent at cost to himself and his happiness. He may not be able to go beyond the limiting messages inherent in the life of that parent, and he may even deny himself the kind of life-style he desires in order to keep company with the limitations in the life of that parent. How could he live a grand life if he sees his father or mother suffering?

In a former life, that parent may have been judgmental, an authority figure, one who punished the soul entering the earth plane, or someone the newborn feels a sense of responsibility for from the past. The infant usually thinks, "Oh no! Not him (or her) again." The sense of never being able to escape from that parent comes from the guilt of the past association. This parent expresses the rocklike messages, "Don't go downstream, it's not safe. I know best. I've lived longer than you and so my experience is more valuable than your ideas." The truth is that the parent is fearful that if the entering soul accomplishes great things in his life, it will show him up or he will somehow lose the parent-child association. He can give permission to the child only in direct proportion to the permission he was given as a child. He tends to pass on the conservative, cautious attitude that was part of his upbringing. If the child only knew that the parent was insecure— and he does on some inner level— he might take time to reassure that parent that he will be safe and that he loves the parent for his desire to provide a safe harbor.

In another instance, a young man examined his relationship with his mother. He felt a sense of responsibility for her welfare, yet he also felt a distance between them. He knew he didn't want to be too close to her for fear he'd never have any freedom in his life. He wasn't able to feel a sense of detachment about her. He knew her early childhood had been difficult, because she was shy and had a tempermental mother. He knew she had been neglected by his father but had taken this abuse without complaint. He had a hard time analyzing his feelings for her because he felt that he must almost be her parent rather than the other way around. In a regression session, he saw himself married to his mother in another life. The relationship was one of great love and joy. Upon her death in that incarnation, his sadness was so tremendous that he felt he never wanted to establish closeness in a marital relationship again. After he became aware of the deep love between them, he was able to express his feelings for her more openly, without the paralyzing fear of loss or the opposite one of never getting away from her in his life. He assumed the right kind of compassionate responsibility and very much enjoyed the times they shared. The walls dropped away to release a caring, loving mother-son relationship.

SATURN RULING OR PLACED IN THE FIFTH HOUSE

With Saturn in this position, creative self-expression may be blocked. The fifth house rules the gambles in life. It is a gamble to fall in love, have a child, give a party, invest in the stock market or express a talent. When Saturn is placed in this sector of the chart or shadows a planet ruling or placed therein, an individual may block or deny his creativity, his need to have children or his romantic nature. Procrastination, fear or an overly judgmental sense of perfectionism can mitigate the pleasure that could come with such activities or associations. An individual with this placement of Saturn naturally looks for someone who represents security in a romantic situation. She will opt for the person she can depend on rather than the fiery exhilaration of being swept off her feet. In their relationship to children, many women find that their off-spring represent areas of responsibility that can prevent them from expression of their own talent. One gifted dancer was supportive of her daughter's career onstage rather than developing her own. In her later years, she broke through the insecurities that had prevented earlier self-expression. Using children as an excuse can cause a person to adopt the attitude of "I can't, because I must take care of my children." That may be an excuse for the fear of failure that goes hand in hand with the denial of self-expression.

In many instances, these individuals may express their talents in a technical rather than a freely creative manner. An artist with such an aspect may produce fine technical pieces of art rather than something flamboyant or original. Many talented musicians become audio engineers rather than performers. The denial of any talent at all can be a wonderful way to avoid one's destiny in connection with such areas of life. With such a placement of Saturn, one may call in or attract children who adopt a parental, judgmental attitude toward their parents. Deep insecurities on the part of the offspring may lead to a role reversal in which the child is more conservative and judgmental than the parent.

On the karmic level, there may be a valid reason for this fear of expressing latent talent. If great pain in another life accompanied creativity or situations with children, one would hesitate to go through that pain again.

I once worked with a talented singer who was tremendously frustrated over the lack of apparent success with her career. She knew she stopped herself, but she could never understand why she deliberately sabotaged the very result she thought she wanted most—recognition of her talent so that she could have freedom of choice with the roles she performed. She also felt that if she allowed herself to have love or romance in her life, she would forfeit her career altogether. She observed other people finding supportive partners to share in their creativity, but she was always attracted to someone who seemed judgmental and rejected her if she exhibited her vocal abilities.

A look at her past made this restricting subconscious viewpoint understandable. She saw herself as a famous opera singer in a past life. She was involved with her voice teacher to such an extent that he controlled her life. She was allowed no friends, no social life or pleasures as a result of her fame. He was tyrannical, brutal and had her completely terrorized. Therefore the memory of having paid such a price for a career that should have brought joy and great benefits had psychologically conditioned her to avoid such pain again. Her talent is still abundant in this life, but an inner judgment said, "Not again." So she went about sabotaging herself quite brilliantly by picking men in her life who did not enjoy her voice or who would not be supportive if she had a full-blown career. She was able to release all those mental blocks and began to make decisions about how much time she was willing to devote to her career and how much to her personal life. She made it her goal to find someone who shared her pleasure in music and who loved her for herself.

Saturn Ruling or Placed in the Sixth House

A sixth-house Saturn describes someone who is a workaholic. But those working habits may be the security issue that prevents the person from rising to the true level of his or her ability. If he overloads himself with work, he has no time to investigate his real need for *service*. Regimentation, discipline or taking on too much of a workload can be a masochistic way of staying safe. Health becomes an issue when the person is unable to say no. He may become sick from overwork so that he can free himself from momentary pressures. This person may have deep-seated guilt about not working in another lifetime. Guilt over misuse of a chance to be of service in another lifetime may prevent him from working at a normal pace or with a moderate routine.

Usually the person with this placement of Saturn finds boring, routine jobs that prevent growth. He may have karmic health problems that act as a block to finding a fulfilling choice of work. He can take on tremendous responsibility with his job in order to provide himself with a sense of accomplishment and fill up time.

As long as he can work, he feels he's needed and is contributing something to life. But the contribution he makes may not be what he is ultimately capable of expressing. Health problems may be his way of forcing himself out of his own playpen. One brilliant man developed a fusion of the spine, a true Saturnian malady, that forced him to stay in bed and think. He had been avoiding his destiny by busying himself with golf and visits to the racetrack. But as a result of his forced inactivity, he devised a new technique that was incredibly valuable in his specific field. He said, "I would have wasted my life if I hadn't created such a brilliant ploy to remain still. Because I had to stay in bed, I was forced to think."

A karmic necessity to develop a sense of service to humanity may be accompanied by great fear and reluctance to assume such a task. One woman remembered several lives in which she was caught in the glamour of political power and intrigue that cost her dearly. In two different lives, she saw herself beheaded as a result of her associations. She also saw a lifetime in which she was married to a wealthy oriental man and therefore had the luxurious kind of life-style that enabled her to assume the task of teaching the local villagers. The joy of this memory was in great conflict with the fear of wasting her life in associations that were exciting but extremely dangerous. She created a situation in this lifetime in which she had no choice but to work. Financial necessity forced her to find jobs that were eventually boring, burdensome and nonproductive, until she found her niche with a specialty that provided her with a true sense of service. Eventually she developed health problems that forced her into a more productive field of endeavor. But more important, she finally had to face the fact that she could assume only so much responsibility for others before she had to take care of herself as well. She achieved a balance by finding yet another level of work that allowed her more freedom from regimentation.

SATURN RULING OR PLACED IN THE SEVENTH HOUSE

The seventh house is the part of the chart describing partnership activities. These can range from joint endeavors to business associations to actual marriages. In present times, it describes a live-in relationship, whether it is an actual marriage or not. With a Saturnian cast to this house, fear of relationships with present-day partners that could become restrictive, heavy and burdensome after a while may prevent the individual from having any relationships at all. Early in life, the individual may avoid marriage altogether or marry for safety's sake and become trapped on some level, forcing an eventual redecision about the marriage. He or she may pick a "rock" as a mate, someone who is ultracautious, conservative or rejecting. If security issues are involved, such as finding a father figure or finding someone to take on the major problems and burdens in life, any attempts to find full self-expression may be very difficult. Naturally, if Saturn is well aspected in the chart, potential exists to find that perfect person who does indeed represent the supportive, secure, stable force one needs in life. But most often, what appeared to be a form of stability becomes instead a tender trap as the partner may have deep insecurities that do not appear on the surface.

The issue of *who* we attract as partners and *why* can easily fill a whole book in itself. The person picking the Saturnian individual needs to work on his own security issues before he chooses a mate. If he picks someone who is judgmental, aloof, cool and parental, it may be his way of staying safe. That way someone else can establish the limits he needs for a sense of security. He may choose a mate with a very prestigious background or from a country whose cultural traits lead to a reserved personality. Because of his childhood programming, he may not be able to allow warmth, comfort or joy in the relationship.

Usually in this instance, there is a strong karmic tie to be resolved. The rejecting partner may have been rejected in another life or may have done something that causes guilt to rise like a wall between the two people. A strong sense of responsibility on the part of the Saturnian person may also bring with it some resentment that he is placed in that role. He may have deep insecurities that masquerade as coldness or an inability to be demonstrative. In that case, when he or she is most judgmental, he may be begging for love and understanding. He may not know how to express affection or ask for affection in return.

The karmic law works in strange ways. From lifetime to life-time, it is literally an eye for an eye and a tooth for a tooth. One young woman found herself trapped in a cold, loveless marriage. In her regression session, she saw a Japanese lifetime that was very similar to the plot of the opera *Madame Butterfly*. She saw herself as a famous actress, in love with an Englishman. At this point, her story took a departure from the Butterfly saga. Her family looked down on this foreigner and refused to allow a marriage. Like But-terfly, she was pregnant, but she went into hiding to have the child. She did not kill herself, but her rejection of the Englishman was very painful for both of them. She had her family and career, but he felt he had lost everything.

In this life, they met again and a similar drama unfolded. This time his family rejected her. She was once again pregnant before the marriage. In that time, such a condition was terribly damag-ing to her reputation, and she suffered a great deal of humiliation. They were married, exonerating the situation with his family to some degree. In the other life, she gave her child away to a family who were not of the same social position but were kind, good, loving people. She watched the development of her baby from a distance and provided very well for that child. In this life, the same couple who took her baby in Japan were distant cousins. Since they were unable to have a child of their own, they hoped they could adopt the child she had conceived before marriage. She learned of her cousin's unspoken desire to adopt her child once again, but it had never entered her mind that she might have to give up her baby in the present time. She felt she had chosen her husband and an early marriage only to enable her to bear the child she had so wanted. In fact, her husband had been unresponsive, distant and cold. But because of the awareness of the past life conditions she was able to forgive both him and herself and thereby resolve their karmic tie.

She might have been horrified at the secret hopes of her cousin to take her baby if she hadn't discovered that a similar situation existed in the past. Instead, she could feel great compassion for her cousin, childless and longing to be a mother, grasping for what might have been a perfect solution.

SATURN RULING OR PLACED IN THE EIGHTH HOUSE

An eighth-house Saturn is indicative of a real fear of being obligated to anyone. The thought of owing money or being beholden can turn into a terrifying need to store worldly goods against a possible time of want. The perfect slogan for someone with this aspect in his chart is Neither a borrower nor a lender be. The rub is that with such a sense of what is fitting and proper, the other side of the eighth-house coin may be neglected. The eighth house is the natural Scorpio house; transformation occurs with the realization that one also has a contribution to make to humanity. Since Saturn puts up walls of security, the way this particular individual meets his needs is to deny himself any help, comfort or financial aid coming from outside his own abilities; he also does not acknowledge any deep-seated need to contribute to mankind. Isolationism is often his philosophy.

If the time comes when the person needs something, whether that be a mortgage for a home or an increase in salary, he can only request such aid by feeling justified. This blocking of the flow between himself and humanity may be hiding anger, sorrow, pain or memories of hard times in a previous life. The illustration of the French lifetime comes into play again with this position of Saturn. If one were waiting to be beheaded, hoping someone would show up with enough funds to buy freedom, and those funds were not forthcoming, the person comes into this life with a deadly fear of any expectation of aid from another human being. Yet his very reason for entry into this earth plane is to take on some level of responsibility for his fellow man, and a financial flow might be necessary to fulfill that task.

A good example of that fear of obligation involves the story of a woman visiting in the West who met another woman from an entirely different part of the country. They were both busily doing their needlepoint. The second woman quite spontaneously said,

"We must have perfected our needlepoint sitting in the French jail waiting to be guillotined." They began a spontaneous regression session that eventually included other people having lived at that time. Since I was friendly with all these people and was on that same vacation trip, I was privy to the drama that unfolded without the aid of a formal regression session. (I will describe in more detail the events that took place in another chapter.) The first woman felt that during that lifetime, when she finally became aware of the horrible starvation prevalent in all of France, she had tried to feed people but it was like trying to stop the dam after it had already broken. She died with a tremendous sense of helplessness. In this life, she confessed to having nightmares if she owed anything to anyone and great pain if she thought anyone was hungry. Those attitudes, born from fear, had to give way to more compassion about present world conditions. She felt that she must somehow help feed the starving peoples of the world.

SATURN RULING OR PLACED IN THE NINTH HOUSE

The ninth sector of the astrological chart describes matters connected to travel, higher education, promotional efforts, the publishing world, distribution and the higher mind, or philosophical considerations. It can indicate the reputation, in that it describes the ability to be promoted or advertised. When Saturn rules this house in any kind of association, there can be an actual fear of being well known or publicized that may come from a past life. If, for instance, a person had been well known or involved with publishing or promotion of ideas in the past and had been ridiculed or killed for his stand, he would certainly want to avoid being placed in the spotlight in the present time.

One woman remembered a past life as a man, when she was involved in a publication advocating the abolition of slavery. The more angry his neighbors and family became, the more inflammatory his articles became. He went so far as to help slaves escape. Because of his opinions and actions, he was subjected to a great deal of ridicule. In this life, the individual was born into a black family and in a female body, changing both sex and race. She now understood how it felt to be in a black body and to be discriminated against. However, she did not take it upon herself to espouse the black cause. She merely tried to live her life as best she could. Eventually she became the target of some unfair hiring practices. Once again she had an opportunity to speak her mind about important issues. This time she took on a major corporation and instituted a lawsuit, which took courage in view of her past life memories. She was very frightened about it until she realized that it was precisely for this reason that she was born into this life. This time she decided to be more moderate and win her point through diplomacy and in a legal way.

Since the ninth house also describes flying or international travel, when Saturn is in difficult aspect to a planet therein, a fear of flying may be pronounced. New techniques have been developed to enable people to get over their fears, but perhaps an even better way to resolve the problem would be to conduct regression sessions that would enable these people to see where their fears began. If, for instance, a person had died in a plane crash, he would quite naturally be apprehensive when he boarded an airplane.

Many times a ninth-house Saturn can indicate an instant aversion for another country. For some time now, India has provided a strong lure for people interested in gaining enlightenment. One young woman, whose many friends were constantly inviting her along on their spirited pilgrimages, still had a strong aversion to the idea of going to India. During her regression session, she found out why—she discovered that she had starved in India, in a former life, when she was only two years old. That painful memory prevented her from investigating for herself what the Indian culture and environment might have to offer.

SATURN RULING OR PLACED IN THE TENTH HOUSE

When Saturn rules or is placed in the tenth house, it describes the quality of the relationship with the parent of the same sex. The association of that parent with a future choice of career becomes clear when we consider that generally we emulate the parent of the same sex, in his or her public life, more closely than we emulate the parent of the opposite sex. Most often, for instance, a woman follows in her mother's footsteps, even to the point of her social behavior. She rarely follows her father's public life. In other times, a woman simply got married and had children, just like her mother. The idea of following in mother's footsteps has taken on a different twist in modern times, however. Many times the daughter remembers her mother's frustration over her domestic position; so the daughter tries to fulfill the unfulfilled potential of her mother. If the daughter knew that her mother had a frustrated desire to sing or to be an artist, she might consciously choose that avenue for expression in her own career.

One young woman recalled her astonishment over the letters her mother had written to her when she was away at school. She was amazed that her mother had never tried to write professionally. Quite naturally, this daughter became a writer. She had never realized quite why she had chosen this profession until the patterns became clear in her regression session.

When Saturn rules this house and is not well aspected, the judgments that the parent of the same sex placed on the offspring are also reflected in the offspring's choice of career. But these blocks go even deeper, as we can more fully understand by taking a look at past lives. Public life that represented a great burden or restriction can prevent an individual from wanting to assume a mantle of burden again. However, since he is subconsciously programmed toward responsibility, he is likely to take on unreasonable burdens instead of assuming ultimate responsibility.

During her regression, one young lady clearly saw the reason for her unreasonable sense of responsibility toward her mother. As she was describing her birth, she realized that she did not want to come into life; but more important, she realized she didn't want to be born to this particular woman. She said, "I don't understand it. I love my mother, but I feel tied to her. Even at the time of my birth, I knew I would never be able to get away from her. At least I have my own apartment now, but I speak to my mother two or three times a day. If I didn't call her or talk to her when she calls me, she wouldn't be able to understand it. The problem is that I allow this to happen."

As she went into past life situations, she described seeing a man on a white horse with a beautiful harness and trappings. He was standing in the center of a town while many people brought him flowers and objects of tribute. He seemed to be a prince of some minor principality. She felt it must be fifteenth-century Italy. Another scene flashed into her consciousness in which he was once again surrounded by people singing and expressing joy at the pleasure of the occasion. There seemed to be jousting and games of all sorts. In general, life seemed to be especially pleasurable for this prince—except for one thing. He was married to a woman who was very religious and who disapproved of any frivolity in his life. His patience at an end, he simply had her put to death. He was then able to continue his enjoyment of life without the constant judgments of this woman. It was then time to identify the people in the Italian life. She knew herself to be the prince, but it came as a great shock when she associated the wife in that lifetime with her mother in the present. She could only comment, "No wonder."

This young woman and I both felt that the revelation was important enough to share with other people. She was willing to talk about her new awareness on a radio program in conjunction with a therapist and with me. Thus her mother heard the story for the first time. The young woman prefaced her story by saying, "Mother, I love you." She felt a great release in connection with her mother and was able to put their relationship in better perspective. She said she now felt free to devote more of her time and attention to building the career she really wanted. She had her mother's full support.

SATURN RULING OR PLACED IN THE ELEVENTH HOUSE

An eleventh-house Saturn describes the ability and the desire to interact with people, especially in groups. That sector of the chart describes friendships as well as organizations and projects involving many people. With Saturn overshadowing all these situations, there may be difficulty in being involved with many people. If the person is connected with an organization, he finds it difficult not to feel lost in the crowd. He may have a tendency to pick people who are Saturnine, overly conservative or merely judgmental. Long-time friendships may be especially important no matter what the basis for the association might be. The individual may choose friends who will act as a rock, or playpen, to give him restrictive parental messages that represent safety. He may then find it impossible to break away from these friends who have remained in a rut as they grew older, thereby giving him a built-in excuse for not fulfilling his potential. This behavior is demonstrated by the person who stays with the same group for twenty-five years, going to the same social events or taking the same vacations together. Familiarity breeds security. However, individual accomplishment is likely to be stymied.

Group solidarity is not always restrictive, however. The eleventh house can represent great comfort in connection with group activity. One woman undergoing a regression session recalled living in a group situation at the time of Christ. The Essenes were a Jewish sect who devoted themselves to the cause of selecting the young family who were to bring the man called Jesus, later to become the Christ, into earth plane existence. As she was describing her daily life then, her face took on a beatific glow. She saw clearly how joyous was her existence in that life. In present times, she became associated once again with a group of people who were involved in spiritual practices. They met once a week to devote themselves to high motivations in daily living.

With this aspect in the chart, group karma comes into play in past life situations. There may have been a feeling of responsibility for a particular group of people that implies a need for that association once again. This can be very positive, yet if the individual cannot find productive associations from the past, he may either cling to groups for some kind of security or resist the idea of group involvement altogether. He may have past life memories of associations in which his sense of responsibility was tested. Situations such as having survived the massacre of Masada in biblical times or having been in a concentration camp leave vast scars in the area of closeness to a particular group or cult of people. Yet memories of having been an Essene or a Tibetan monk, where joy and peace reigned, give a very positive kind of programming.

One young woman with Saturn ruling her eleventh house of friends found great comfort in her associations. She was willing to endure a great deal of negativity, torment or jealousy before she would consider detaching herself from their company. She had the same unreasonable attachment to her mother and father as well, and as she grew older, the friendships she formed or the casual acquaintances she had in her life became of paramount importance. She was even terrified to be alone.

In her regression session, she saw a little boy of five or six, very dark, with big, black eyes, wandering through streets that seemed to be in Italy. He was quite alone. She deduced that it was during World War II and saw terrible devastation in the streets. The little boy didn't seem to notice that many people were dead or wounded. She knew then that the little child was in a catatonic state and was terribly alone in his inner world. Realizing that the little boy was herself gave her reassuring confirmation that even today, she was still looking for someone, anyone...even the wrong people...to give her some kind of comfort. In the present life, the very beautiful young girl, dark with very large eyes, had just cut her hair only a short time before her regression session. It was in the style of a boyish haircut and was very short. From the neck up, she looked like a little Italian boy. After her session, she felt that she had cleared up her terrible fears and was able to be more independent. She cut away from some of her former, negative associations and became manager of a restaurant where she was in contact with people every day. She put herself in a position of caretaking with the right kind of responsibility. She did not form close ties with anyone except people who would return the friendship in kind. Her acquaintances were innumerable because of her job, yet she was quite selective about true friendship.

SATURN RULING OR PLACED IN THE TWELFTH HOUSE

When Saturn is posited, or ruling the twelfth house in the horoscope, or shadows any planet that may be ruling or placed in that sector, the indication of the need for a regression session is very pronounced. Twelfth-house and first-house placement of Saturn are the most important in relation to the need for a regression. With twelfth-house placement, there is a vast need to clean out the karmic garbage pail, because it describes a subconscious karmic racial guilt. I am never able to describe what may lie behind that placement, for the racial guilt may have nothing to do with a present race or nationality. It appears that a grave sense of responsibility that was not honored makes for intense self-punishment on a deep, subconscious level in the present day.

This aspect manifests as a paralyzing inner fear preventing the person from allowing himself true success. He tends to sabotage himself without understanding why or how. He may have a profound desire for a particular opportunity that comes this way only once. He plans for such a chance, longs for it, and when it arrives, he finds that all he has to do is reach out his hand to pick the plum. Yet he cannot move to receive what is waiting for him, for he feels paralyzed to the point of inaction. It is as if his arm is stuck to his side, and by the time he releases that arm to reach out, the opportunity has vanished. His timing is off, but more than that, he just can't seem to allow himself the prize he so desperately wants.

Usually there are memories of imprisonment from a past life. In one case, a brilliant therapist saw herself literally chained to a wall in a prison. She saw one shaft of sunlight that entered the small room and used that as a frame of reference to retain her sanity. She could have prevented such a situation if she had betrayed her family, but she didn't, and with that refusal, she herself was betrayed. She knew she had used that life as a time for great spiritual growth. She saw that she had transcended the limits of her physical body in that previous life and was now gifted with insight far beyond that which she gained through her career training.

Another man, a gifted psychiatrist, had let go of many opportunities, such as scholarships, awards and the like, simply by not reaching out to take them when they were presented to him. His self-punishment was evident to me but not to him. In his regression, he saw himself as a ruler of a sector in Germany. He had also been betrayed and saw that he was drowned. He felt that it was his own fault for being naive and trusting. He also knew that he had let down the very people who depended on him for gentle and wise leadership. He was able to identify himself through historical reference, but he already knew a great deal about this well-known German ruler. In his youth, he had a fascination with the architecture that had been erected by this particular man and had even visited most of the sites of the buildings designed by the king. The mystery of this ruler's death had never been resolved. He was thought to have drowned, but there was the suspicion of suicide. The shame of such a suspicion was still harbored in the subconscious of the young man until the present time. He had been unable to tell his subjects what really happened, and even to this day wanted his reputation to be cleared of any taint of weakness. His frustration came from not being able to let anyone know that he had been murdered. He had tried to balance the scales by healing people, yet he felt so overburdened and tired that his work was becoming detrimental to his own health. He was much in need of a new life-style. Finally, with subconscious blocks removed, he began to explore the many choices and life-styles that were available to him. In his case, especially, forgiving himself and others for the mistakes of the past was essential for his own future growth. Without that clearing, he was only hurting himself by punishing himself unmercifully in the present.

When Saturn shadows this sector of the chart, not only is racial guilt stressed, but also the individual hesitates to open his doors of intuition and inspiration for fear of finding his own particular monster lurking inside. With the cleaning out of past life memories and the bringing to light of the tiny dragon within, he effects his own transformation very effectively.

ASPECTS TO SATURN

As I began doing more and more regression sessions, I discovered that the need for a regression session was equally important when Saturn is in difficult aspect to another planet that rules or is posited in the twelfth or first house of a chart, as it is when Saturn is placed in one of those houses itself. When that aspect occurs, it is as if Saturn casts a shadow over the quality of energy that would usually be expressed by that planet. For instance, if the Moon rules the first house or is placed therein and is in hard aspect to Saturn, instead of easily showing the mothering, nurturing qualities of the Moon, the individual puts up walls around his feelings, tending to deny those emotional needs. He might have children, a manifestation of the mothering facet of the Moon, but revert to being more of a disciplinarian than a nurturing parent. In other words, more of a Saturn quality is expressed than a Moon quality. I refer to this hard aspect of Saturn as Saturn *overshadowing* another planet.

An aspect is the mathematical relationship of one planet to another. I have described aspects thoroughly in *Astrological Aspects, Your Inner Dialogues*. However, for the purpose of reviewing past lives, it is important to know how to find Saturn aspects in your own chart. Along with the diagram showing the wheel and the placement of the planets in that wheel, you should have a table that indicates the aspects of each planet to another. Find the column relating to the Saturn aspects and compare the symbols I will give you to the symbols that are listed on that chart. You can then determine which are soft aspects and which are hard aspects. Then find the section in this book that describes the different aspects you may have in your chart. You can read about situations in the lives of others that will give you a clue as to what may be locked in your own consciousness.

The Two Kinds of Aspects

There are two kinds of aspects—beneficial, or *soft* aspects, and difficult, or *hard* aspects. Soft aspects describe areas of ease in life. Hard aspects describe difficult conditions or inner conflicts that represent opportunities for growth. For the purpose of regression into past lives, we need deal only with hard aspects; as they represent a block to the natural expression of energy. For the purpose of reviewing past life blocks we are only concerned when Saturn is in hard aspect to a planet.

Hard Aspects

Semisquare	∠	45 degrees
Square	□	90 degrees
Sesquiquadrate	⊡	135 degrees
Opposition	☍	180 degrees

Soft Aspects

Semisextile	⌄	30 degrees
Sextile	✳	60 degrees
Trine	△	120 degrees

Neutral Aspects

Conjunction	☌	0 degrees
Inconjunct	⊼	150 degrees

Although the conjunction and the inconjunct are normally considered neutral aspects, they become hard aspects when Saturn is one of the planets. When Saturn is involved in a conjunction, it is as if the heavy Saturn judgment is squelching the energy of the other planet. When that conjunction is resolved through life's experiences, the individual has a serious determination to exhibit the quality described by the other planet. In other words, the Saturnian sense of responsibility supports the quality of energy from the other planet rather than restricting it.

In the case of the inconjunct, great growth is indicated when the two qualities of energy are resolved. But the growth comes through reaching out, like stretching a rubber band to its limits. However, for the purpose of locking into past-life conditions, we will consider the inconjunct a hard aspect.

All hard aspects describe growth conditions that arise from conflicting inner messages and the resulting confused outer conditions. When viewed from a present-life point of view, aspects indicate psychological patterns that can help us understand what is going on externally. So aspects clarify the *what* of the conditions of our lives and, to some degree, can tell us *why* we react the way we do. But when we look at aspects in our own charts from a past-life perspective, we can begin to understand *why* we came into this life with such conditions in the first place. The in-depth look answers the question, "Why me?"

Sun	☉	ego, sense of self-worth
Moon	☽	emotions, vulnerability, compassion
Mercury	☿	intellect, analysis, rational thought
Venus	♀	love, beauty, harmony
Mars	♂	action, ambition, sexuality
Jupiter	♃	enthusiasm, joy, expansion
Saturn	♄	responsibility, dedication, structure
Uranus	♅	enlightenment, freedom, spontaneity
Neptune	♆	inspiration, idealism, vision
Pluto	♇	power

Saturn/Sun

For instance, when Saturn is in hard aspect to the Sun in a natal chart, the present-life interpretation could be that the individual was born with a lack of self-worth and may not have received the ego strokes as a child that would reinforce his ability to be a leader. From a past-life point of view, however, the interpretation is a bit different. A lack of sense of self-worth may be due to the fact that in a past life, something happened when the person was in a kingly, leadership role that caused him to come into this life with no conscious sense of such a position. Guilt about the former misuse of authority or the memory of dreadful consequences as a result of his leadership make the person want to forget he was ever in that position. If he blocks his awareness of the "royalty" within himself, he doesn't have to accept any responsibility for its expression in the present. He may not allow his strength to show. But an inner or subconscious knowledge of who he *really* is causes him to hope that someone else will give him recognition and acclaim for what he does and make him feel better about himself. If not, his lack of self-worth is reemphasized and the vicious cycle continues. Eventually he must take the responsibility of acknowledging who he is and give himself permission to release his blocked self-esteem. That implies taking on a higher level of responsibility in life and becoming the leader again.

Saturn/Moon

When Saturn is in hard aspect to the Moon, the present-life interpretation is that a person tends to cut himself off from his emotions and become very depressed. He may feel rejected by his mother, or he may have attracted a mother not comfortable with expressing her nurturing qualities. She may have had great difficulties in her own life that prevented her from exhibiting compassion and caring for her offspring. The person, therefore, represses his natural emotional nature and may not allow emotional security into his life for fear that it will be taken away when he least expects it. He tends to protect his own emotions rather than be vulnerable and show compassion for others.

With a past-life perspective, the interpretation is that because of a painful situation in which an involvement, with children for instance, may have caused a great deal of guilt, the individual denies that he possesses deep feelings for children, his own or those of the world. He may not be able to bear anything that represents pain for helpless, little beings. Therefore it is safer not to be involved. He denies his ability to be compassionate and caring for fear he won't be able to solve the problems shared by mankind, such as a need for food. He can deprive himself of food or comfort to try to make up for his past-life guilt instead of taking on the responsibility to do whatever he can, whenever he can, to rectify an imbalance. He may feel he has to rescue people instead of simply showing them how to help themselves. Eventually he must work through his painful emotional reactions to take on a new level of compassion for people who need his aid, and perhaps for his mother in particular.

Saturn/Mercury

When Saturn is in hard aspect to Mercury, an inferiority about intellect is strongly indicated. The person may have been told as a child that he was to be seen and not heard, or that he was not very intelligent. He feels he has to be on very sure ground before he expresses an opinion; he can repress originality of thought. He can be comfortable quoting a person he considers to be an expert rather than sticking his neck out to express what *he* thinks. He may be overly cautious about making a decision or researching a project. He can be critical or a doubting Thomas. He can worry about being right.

From a reincarnation point of view, he may have been a person in a position to make important decisions, for many people or simply within his own life sphere. If he made what turned out to be a wrong choice or if he caused pain for himself or others by not taking a strong stance, he comes back with deep-seated fears of making the same mistake all over again. If he thinks he is not smart or knowledgeable enough to be a decision maker, he doesn't have to assume the responsibility for the consequences of such a choice in present times. He may create outer conditions that force him to take a look at what he really knows. For instance, if he leaves decisions up to someone else and suffers because of it in the present life, he may have to work past his own fears and feelings of inadequacy to express himself more positively. He must resist a tendency to negativity. With technical knowledge, described by Saturn, he can feel safe about what he knows. Therefore, rather than overwhelm himself with details, he may have to develop the security of expertise in a particular field.

Saturn/Venus

If Saturn is in hard aspect to Venus, the love nature comes under scrutiny. In present-life interpretation, the individual will find that the demonstration of affection makes him want to run away from involvement. He can therefore feel much safer with a person who is aloof or cool rather than with someone who does a lot of touching or hugging and demands it in return. He may feel a lack of total fulfillment in love because of that distant quality. He may inadvertently select a more Spartan life-style or deny his own artistic ability rather than allow himself an easy and creatively expressive life.

From a past-life point of view, deprivation of love may have brought forth dreadful memories. He may have lost someone important to him and felt loneliness in the past, or have taken himself away from a loving situation or have deep guilt about past associations. This aspect can indicate the possibility of suicide in the past. Therefore, in the present, he feels he must repay that debt by not having fulfillment with love or life-style. He may not allow himself to be indulgent in any way, for fear his guard will be dropped and he will suffer a loss of love or life-style again. He can punish himself unmercifully by deprivation to try to resolve his own karmic debt. With awareness, he can repay his karmic debt by learning to show love, developing trust in connection with love or through the development of an artistic ability that can bring beauty to the lives of others. His greatest gift may be to learn the meaning of universal love.

Saturn/Mars

When Mars is badly aspected by Saturn in the chart, the person may block drive and ambition in the present time. He can have a fear of violence, or simply deny his sexuality and aggressive urges. He may have been told as a child that sex is dirty, or that it is not ladylike to be aggressive or ambitious. He may block initiative that could help him be more resourceful, for fear of what he might do if he let himself go. He can attract a great deal of frustration into his life. He may deny the anger he feels and not be aware of a sadistic quality apparent in some area of his life. Sadism might come from another person or an outside source, or exist in the denial of himself to other people: "Now you can have me, now you can't."

In reviewing a past-life situation, there may be a terrible memory of guilt over a violent act that was perpetrated by him, or lingering fear over what was done to him. Memories of the misuse of sexuality, such as incest or rape, can prevent him from natural enjoyment and a feeling of freedom in connection with his own sexuality. Sometimes memories of the violence of war make him fearful of any action that might imply danger. He can't even tolerate an argument. He may repress his primal qualities of energy to the point that he manifests physical symptoms or drinks to excess, because only then can he release his rage. He may have to acknowledge hidden anger or rage and learn how to transmit that energy into productive behavior such as exhibiting courage, daring and ambition. To rectify the karmic balance, he may have to become a fighter for reformation of the very conditions that caused him guilt or repression in the first place.

Saturn/Jupiter

Jupiter is the planet of expectation, enthusiasm and joy. If Saturn is in difficult aspect to this planet in the natal chart, the individual may not want to set goals for fear of being disappointed. He may repress his natural enthusiasm, neglect his ability to encourage others (or to teach) and generally refrain from allowing the greatest luck in his life as a result of his own expansive nature. He sits on his contagious enthusiasm.

From the perspective of reincarnation, he may have been punished in a past life for expression of his religious feelings, or he may have had pain connected to religious groups or organizations. In this life, he may not want to acknowledge his own deep religious feelings or express them to others, for fear he will be ridiculed or punished again. He may have set goals that were unattainable or that hurt others, and he may feel that he must punish himself in some way for his lack of judgment at another time. Self-interest or selfishness from the past can cause the person to deny himself good fortune in the present. He may feel he has to earn everything good that comes his way and not depend on "luck" in life. He may have memories of extravagance that caused pain for others and that make him deny opulence in his present existence. The karmic reconciliation cannot come through denial but through exhibiting his humor, philosophy and knowledge in a way that will encourage others to expand in those areas of their own lives. He learns to be a permission giver or a teacher by showing the right manifestation of good fortune or philosophy in his own life.

Saturn/Uranus

Since Uranus is the first of the higher octave of planets, it describes a new level of awareness. With Saturn blocking this energy by difficult aspect in the natal chart, the person may not be comfortable with insights or anything that sets him apart from others, or with any situation that puts him in the spotlight. He can fear his genius potential or deny it altogether. He may resist any expression of special inspiration or enlightenment in his life, preferring to stay safe and pretending to be just like everyone else. He may repress any rebellious tendencies, putting himself under dreadful pressures to be sure that he conforms to what appears to be the conservative view or the norm among his contemporaries.

With a review of a past-life situation, the person may reveal a level of prestige, awareness, genius or enlightenment that set him apart from his fellow man or that represented great danger. Running away from responsibility or showing a rebellious quality may have brought about pain, death or hardship to others. Many times this indicates a lifetime in a highly developed civilization, such as Atlantis, where a person developed a level of inspiration that he is unable to use in his present time. He may have come in as a beacon for mankind, but at a time premature for his knowledge to be revealed. Therefore the limiting circumstances in the present life may give him a sense of boredom that is hard to deal with or a suicidal complex. Repressed nervous energy may give him health problems that slow him down or that cause him to take on a new level of discipline. In effect, that may prevent him from impulsive action that would ordinarily deter him from his destiny. Timing is an essential ingredient in his overall success. He may have to learn how to tap his own inspiration instead of looking to others for information, for his view of the world is from a higher perspective and somehow sets him apart. He needs to learn to be of this world but inspired by another. He is a truly free soul underneath any layers of what appears to be a conservative outer demeanor. He can use that combination to great advantage in his work with others who might not respond to someone too avant garde.

Saturn/Neptune

When Neptune appears in the horoscope in adverse aspect to Saturn, a description of a cynical approach or outlook is accurate. The person may have a caustic way of speaking or an underlying attitude of "what's the use." Rather than trusting his powers of intuition, the person needs to not trust or hope, for fear he might lead himself down the garden path of unrealized fantasies through a naive approach to life. The circumstances of his childhood can be such that he develops a lack of faith. If he sees conditions of hardship for those he loves and knows they had dreams of something better in life, he takes on a cautious approach that will keep him safe from disillusionment. He may have been told not to be a dreamer and not to indulge in fantasies.

But when this aspect is seen from a perspective of reincarnation, he understands why he cannot trust his intuitive powers and why he selects the very conditions in his present life that will prevent an unrealistic or impractical outlook. He may pick the very people he trusted in the past in order to reconcile any karma in the relationship. He may have had powers of vision that he ignored, or a special sense of perspective that caused him pain in another sphere of existence. He may have been too trusting, too naive or too idealistic, thereby ignoring danger signals that caused harm to himself or others in the past. He has poetry in his soul and is a potential prophet. But he may have to repress that part of himself momentarily to develop the other part of his intelligence, that is, the factual, practical part, to give balance to his conceptual abilities. Rather than deny his visionary abilities, he needs to take responsibility for expressing the vision he utilized in a past life, but this time in a practical manner. When he develops a realistic approach and combines it with his vision of how he wants things to be, he can inspire others to lift their sights to the ideal conditions that are possible in life.

Saturn/Pluto

Saturn in difficult aspect to Pluto describes unwillingness or fear of showing power or achieving a powerful position in life. It can describe a basic abhorrence of the politics of life, whether that be governmental politics or merely the personal politics of group situations. The person may fear being caught in a situation in which he cannot hold his own, or even being trapped in a mob or crowd. Repression of the positive expression of his magnetism and potency may result in manipulation of some sort. This manipulation is really a release of energy when he feels totally blocked or squelched. Not being aware of his force for good, he feels he must go underground simply to get his own needs met. He learns eventually that anything he attains by ulterior methods carries penalty and lack of ultimate gain. He finds that his own feelings of revenge only backfire to cause more trouble in his own life. When he realizes he hurts no one but himself, he can finally transmute his own rebellion and childlike game playing into activity motivated by the desire for the good of everyone concerned.

When this aspect is viewed from a deeper level, that of a past-life condition, it becomes clear why a person fears involvement in a political situation. Usually he sees himself having lived on a level of opulence that implied some sort of compromise of his own principles. He can see himself as having swung from the priestess (priest) in one life to the courtesan (playboy) in another. He may not be able to forgive himself for having resorted to the lower, manipulative level of his power, especially as it has carried some penalty in the past. He may have been executed, betrayed or compromised in some way that makes him very cautious in the present. Therefore he doesn't dare acknowledge that he possesses any power or ability to influence others for fear he would have to rise to a power level again.

If he had been punished previously or had the rug pulled out from under him, he needs to review his feelings at that time. If he was able to rise above the condition or go around the person who caused his pain, he may have developed the potential to fly like an eagle, soaring above negative conditions in the present, to find what universal plan is in store for him in the here and now. If he resorted to revenge, he comes back with a negative power and force that may frighten him. Therefore he tries to squelch or repress the darkness he sees within his soul. The transmutation of difficulties in his own life depends on his ability to change his motivation. With the motivation of the will to do good, he becomes a dynamic force for the development of that quality in others.

II

Past-Life
Memories

CHAPTER FIVE

Saturn and the Sun

ne of the more common observations that people make while reviewing their birth during a regression session is that as tiny infants, they are not acknowledged as *persons*. The individual may observe that the doctors and nurses did their job very well but in a perfunctory manner. There seemed to be a lack of real celebration or of a banners-waving, flag-flying kind of welcome. There was no sense of "Hey, well done. It was a rough trip but you're here and that's all that matters!" The person may have observed great happiness on the part of the parents or hospital staff but not in a personal way. The individual feels alone in his journey and as if he has landed in strange territory.

This is particularly pronounced when Saturn is shadowing the Sun in the natal chart, for the Sun describes the ego and sense of self-worth. In the final analysis, the individual feels a lack of acknowledgment for who he really is and usually goes through life feeling unrecognized no matter how much acclaim comes his way. The sadness that sets in is like putting a shade over a bright light. The Sun describes not only the ego and sense of self-worth but the real essence of the soul quality. If a person is denied by others often enough, he quite naturally begins to deny himself and his existence. He feels unimportant, and may be motivated to get the acknowledgment he craves and feels he deserves in a variety of ways, sometimes by being lured on by the reward or ego stroking he hopes to receive for a job well done. His diligence is rarely acknowledged fully, however, as he was programmed for *lack* of acknowledgment at that all-important time of birth.

Why would a soul pick such conditions and a set of parents who might not know who he is? It seems masochistic to come into this world needing recognition, feeling that one deserves it and then finding the very circumstances and people who may not be able to give it. On some level, it may be to his benefit to remain in hiding in this life. He is not consciously aware of this, however, and seeks constant reassurance instead. In many cases, when the person becomes aware that his parents or associates are not able to acknowledge *themselves*, he is better able to throw off the feeling of rejection. He learns not to relate external conditions to himself or to value himself by the amount of attention coming his way. He learns to give *himself* permission rather than to wait for that green light from others.

When the Saturn/Sun aspect is evident, it seems that past-life karma is particularly heavy in connection with rulership, royalty, dominance or leadership. If, for instance, an individual had a lack of privacy or was badly punished, killed or imprisoned because of his strength or position of leadership, he would not be so happy, in this life, to exhibit those qualities again. One criticism of reincarnation is that everyone claims to remember being a king or queen. That is certainly not the case, but when the Sun is overshadowed by Saturn, it is quite likely that a past-life memory of having attained leadership status will surface. During the session itself, I must wait patiently for the person to let go of his own judgment about seeing himself in a rulership position. I may have to almost pry it out of him, because his reluctance to think highly of himself is so ingrained.

One gentleman undergoing a regression session described being born into a country where the underlying message is, Don't think much of yourself. In the United States, for instance, many children are brought up with the admonishment, Don't get a swelled head. These children are being condemned to live an ordinary life even before they have a chance to spread their wings. But on a soul level, the individual seems to need that restrictive conditioning to work past in order to purify his feelings about a special quality, leadership ability or kingship he once had. He may not have been able to carry out this function of rulership or he may have performed his duties at such a sacrifice that the desire to once again put himself under pressure is naturally stymied. In either case, however, the secret knowledge of who he really is produces frustrations that must be reconciled in the here and now. He must learn finally to give himself the acknowledgment he deserves.

FATHER AND SON REUNITED

There were two such cases in which this was clearly demonstrated. Each situation involved two people, a man and a woman, who saw themselves closely connected in another life. In the first instance, the man and woman scheduled their individual appointments one right after the other on the same afternoon. This back-to-back arrangement was necessary because they had to drive a great distance together to reach me. They arrived at my door hand in hand, having decided who would have the first session and determined that the woman would wait at a nearby restaurant or do some shopping while her partner began. As he finished and was leaving by my front door, she was walking down the hall toward us to begin her appointment. She was bubbly and enthusiastic, saying such things as, "How was it? Did you remember anything? Is it scary?" He was in a state of profound awe over what had emerged from his subconscious and could hardly respond to her at all, certainly not in the same lighthearted vein. Clearly they had had no chance to compare notes or to go into collusion about what they saw, but both of them remembered being together in the same previous lifetime and saw exactly the same scene.

In the second situation, the couple had plenty of time between appointments to decide on a common story, but the dramatic in-

cident emerging from the woman's mind was so moving and inde-
scribable that she would not have shared her experience with her
partner. She really wanted to know if he would reveal the same
lifetime in his session. In both situations, the couples saw exactly
the same scenario, but each from his or her special perspective.
The second was verifiable by a little research into history and
started a group drama quite extraordinary in its scope. All four of
these people had Saturn casting its shadow over the natal Sun in
the horoscope.

In the first regression session, the young man, whom we will
call Jack, saw himself standing on a large terrace or projection
from a building that was high enough for him to review many
troops passing in front of him. He described large columns that
decorated this platform and also described the people in his family
standing beside him. He saw himself as king, married to a difficult
woman. They had sons, one of whom he described as the young
woman who had accompanied him to the regression session. He
saw himself as having good character and being a good king.
Then he said, "It's nighttime in a desert. The Moon must be very
strong because it is all lit up. I'm a little in back of the men,
talking with the generals. An awesome army appears on the horizon. The very moment that I see them, I accept the reality that we
will all die. Before I saw them, we were trying to devise a strategy
for when the battle would take place. Even though I see that
army, I continue to discuss the strategy, knowing the generals and
the men will enter a battle that they will quickly die in. I know
that none of us will be alive within twenty minutes. I encourage
everyone, saying 'You must get on this hillside to combat the
enemy,' but I do it only for the generals and the men, engaging
them in order to distract them. I'm killed by a Greek soldier with
a sword through my stomach. There's a great sadness. I know that
I have reigned well, and now I will die."

Jack became aware that the woman he was married to in that
lifetime was his mother in the present time. It was clear to him
that the wife in that time was violently opposed to his going into
the battle in the first place. His comments were, "In that life,

there was a battle, pain and death and my mother (wife) saying don't do it. In this life, Mother says don't do it. My subconscious memory of opposing her is pain and death. So, having learned my lesson then and feeling so guilty for the death of all my men, I've chosen to live this life complying with all her wishes. If I was in my other life, I would be embarrassed to have me in the kingdom. I'm a coward now."

Jack discussed the relationship of his birth memories to the memory of the past life. He observed, "When they brought me to my mother in this life, she disgusted me by her inability to acknowledge my power, even if I was only a newborn baby. If I had proceeded to *be* powerful, she would have experienced my disgust and my wrath in the most vicious fashion. I would have destroyed her. I certainly would have exiled her immediately." I commented, "So, you've chosen not to exile your mother at the cost of your own power." Jack's expletive was born out of a moment of shocked awareness. He then added, "I really feel like I can begin to live like a king now. That is very powerful. It's almost that I have to find a kingdom. Whew. I don't feel frightened anymore. The things that seemed to overwhelm me in my areas of work and responsibility seem, after this, like ordering eggs for breakfast instead of cereal. I can do things now with a yawn. This is so incredible. All those feelings I got into earlier in the session make sense now. I was so disappointed by my father and my mother. Neither of them knew who I was! I didn't belong to them. What it feels like now is that I never have to apologize to anyone. I don't mean I'd step on people, but I'd show my natural strength in a way that is different from what I've done before. The reading of the astrological chart was like an academic exercise, hints about what was to come for me. That was just incredible."

During the earlier part of Jack's regression session, he saw this conflict between his present-life desire to be anonymous and his past-life determination to make that powerful king known. Jack was born with Aquarius on the ascendant, with Saturn ruling the twelfth house of subconscious memories. He said many times, "I feel so different. I just feel so different from everyone else."

A great turning point in his life came with the death of his father. At the time of the funeral, he was sent to stay with a neighbor. He felt hopeless, since he knew his mother didn't have a lot of warmth to give him. Even though his father had been rather perfunctory with Jack, there might have been a chance for comradeship—but that chance was taken away forever. He was left to be dominated by his mother. Soon after his father's death, he started school for the first time. He was very scared and tried to remain invisible, but the *real* Jack wouldn't let that happen. For a former king, notoriety was better than no notice at all.

He said, "All the children were told to go to the bathroom. They lined us up, five at a time, but I couldn't go to the bathroom before all the other children and there was no privacy, so I didn't go. Just before lunchtime, I had to go so badly, I wet my pants. I saw the puddle literally running out on the floor, and so I blew the anonymity right there and then. In a way, I had control over my mother by that action. She was very embarrassed and I was able to get my own back a little bit." This clarified the reasons for the obvious manipulation that went back and forth between him and his mother as he was growing up. As a result of deeper understanding, Jack felt he had reached a turning point in his relationship and awareness of new insights for others, which he could infuse into his therapy practice. He also felt able to let go of all the nonproductive games in the relationship with his mother and therefore to women in general.

He expressed new feelings for Kate, the woman who had arrived with him for the session. All his concerns about their relationship seemed to fall into place because of his own new perspective.

In her regression session, Kate became aware of a near-miscarriage when her mother was carrying her. She described her mother having a bad fall and worrying about losing her child. Kate said, "I don't particularly care what happens. I really feel that. The doctor gives her a shot of something that stops the miscarriage and the bleeding and then everything is okay. I think I do a little bit to try to help the miscarriage along. I feel like I'm pushing and swimming out. I'm not doing a lot, but since she had miscarriages before, I didn't figure it would be that hard. It didn't work, however."

I asked Kate to go to a past life that would give her an explanation about this life and that would help her understand *now*. She said: "I see a person, a man about twenty-five, clean-shaven, nice-looking, slender, on a horse. It's also a nice-looking horse, not with reins, but with cloth. I'm holding something like reins but with gold edging. I'm not wearing armor or anything. It's much looser, softer, like chain mail underneath with a tunic over it. I have something on my head, but not full steel things. It's some kind of protection like a metal cap. I'm holding the horse like this and with my head over my shoulders I'm saying, 'Come on into the fray.'" In her description, Kate went back and forth between "I" and "he." She continued:

He's not like the superior or highest leader, but he's like a prince, who has a king for a father. He's leading a battalion or an entourage. He thinks it's going to be fun; he's excited about it. The people behind him don't want to go because they're afraid. It's his first battle and he's very happy about this fight. I don't know why he's not wearing full armor. All the people behind him are galloping by now, and he has the flags waving and is extremely happy about this adventure.

In front of him it is very dark, almost like night, like a woods. The horse shies away from the woods, but he urges the horse against what he wants to do. He says, "We have to go forward." It's so dark in this forest... very dark... Oh, it's like an ambush. People are in trees, very dark people. They're Visigoths... very mean people. They don't have many bows and arrows at all. They have short swords and knives. As soon as he's into the forest, he turns around and is off the horse. He screams "retreat," but the horses rear up and a lot of horses have fallen by now, at least twenty-five. Others are prepared to fight, but you can't fight them because they jump down from trees and are standing in a circle. The young man can't see anyone, but meanwhile a lot of people are being mutilated. That's what they do is mutilate, cutting off parts of the body and leaving you there to die and suffer. His

[123]

friend is on the ground and he's crying from pain because his leg has been chopped off.

The young man is in a panic. He has failed his people; he is not hurt at all... not a scratch on him. It wasn't supposed to be a big deal, like going on an intelligence or scouting trip, but he's lost everything. The enemy don't touch him, like they know he is the son of the king. Hours later, or days later, he is crawling among men who are dead. There are some horses grazing, but he's the only one left alive. He goes back to his father, crawling on his hands and knees, and says, "Kill me, for I have failed you and our country." His father says no.

I asked Kate if she recognized anyone around her. She replied, "Is it possible that I'm the young man? It feels like it. I think I am. The court is old, a very large place with lots of torches and light marble. I'm French, maybe not in France, but it's the fourteenth century. There are more women than men. Only a couple of old men are left. I ask where my mother is. My father says, 'She's taken to her bed, because she's very ill.' My mother doesn't like me very much anyway, but my father is very kind to me. He says it isn't my fault. My mother is very beautiful, the most beautiful woman in the land, and she's very proud. She rules my father and she doesn't like me, because she thinks I'm weak... too small, too slender, and I don't like to kill things. My father understands that. After this my mother won't grant me an audience to see her. I'm the one who is to rule, but my mother talks against me and ridicules me for being foolish enough to get ambushed. I have a younger brother who will take over."

At this point in the regression, Kate became very sad. She continued, "I'm in disgrace, especially with my mother. I live but I'm treated as if I'm retarded or a fool. I don't have any power, because you don't get a second chance. They took away all my swords and all my ceremonial clothes. I was really alone. I looked like a servant boy, yet I was a prince. This ambush was a terrible warning to the kingdom not to expand but to stay within the walls of our city." In response to my question, she described her father in more detail. She said, "My father is heavy and full-faced and tall... for those days a very big man. This is going to sound stupid, but his eyes and his mouth are similar, but bigger, but he reminds me of Jack. . . . It's Jack." (In the beginning of her past-life review, Kate had described herself as being in a male body, standing on a large terrace with columns, along with her mother and father, reviewing the troops marching in front of them. The description was the same as the one Jack had given in the beginning of his past-life memory.)

If we were to create a bit more of the scenario between Jack and Kate, we could well imagine why the wife and mother didn't want another battle to take place. Kate's description of the wife and mother as having great influence over her father fit Jack's description of his wife (current mother) as being difficult. Jack, Kate and I did not have another session in which we might have filled in some details, but Kate did see two other lives in which Jack was present and important to her.

She saw herself living in the Swiss mountains as a young girl, with Jack as her friend. She said, "We're sitting and talking on the grass and we're both very young. We're talking about what we're going to do. I think there's a famine. There's some trouble of some kind. Someone moves me away from him and tells me I can't see him or be with him. There are tears and fights and they lock me in a room. He doesn't know where I am. He goes around looking for me and all I can do is cry. Finally I'm let out, but I'm to marry someone else. Jack can't do anything about it, because he can't get to me at all."

I asked Kate if she was ever married to Jack in another life. She said, "My first inclination is to say yes. I see him, I see me and I see a baby. He's wearing a Quaker hat, so it seems to be in a Quaker lifetime." She concluded her regression session by talking once more about the vision of her life as a young prince. She said very simply, "I can see that incident as having something to do with being afraid of doing anything wrong and not trusting *anybody*. I have no desire to be in a leadership position again."

LOVERS FROM ANOTHER CENTURY

When the time is ripe for the exploration of the subconscious mind, information seems to come forth in amazing ways. The individual may not know that the time has come, but when the student is ready, the teacher appears. When a person is ready to tap deeper matters, an opportunity arises. So it was when I met Connie. Neither of us was prepared for the momentous turn of events in our lives. I read Connie's astrological chart, and after that she had an immediate desire to do a regression session. She didn't ask what it entailed, or how much time it would take, or how she would benefit; she just knew she wanted the experience. So it was with the follow-up session for the man in her life, Jim.

I met Connie while having lunch with friends in a small northern California town. Her restaurant was very charming and the menu exceptional. I was pleasantly surprised to find such lovely and tasteful surroundings in a very small town. When I met Connie, I complimented her excellent choices. As soon as she walked into the room, I noticed a distinctive elegance about her. She had an aura of strength and command, coupled with a gracious kind of dignity. When she discovered that I was an astrologer and that I did regression sessions, she asked for an appointment.

Connie has Saturn in a semisquare aspect to her ascendant, and that usually points to a real need for a regression session. More than that, she has Saturn conjunct her Gemini sun, opposing her Moon but ruling her tenth house of career. These aspects describe a resistance to being born and a special reluctance to exhibit the dominant, dramatic leadership qualities that are naturally hers. She might have felt a rejection from her mother due to financial worry and restrictions. At some point in her life, Connie might have to come to terms with the need to earn her own money or to take on the responsibility for expressing latent talent. Children could provide a sense of stability but may also provide a built-in excuse for not expressing that creative potential. A breakthrough may be necessary in order for her to feel worthy of commanding a good salary. Since the Saturn-Sun conjunction rules the tenth house of public life as well as the second and fifth house in her chart, she might first avoid a public life or career. Later on, those same areas become her focus of attention and also provide a sense of security. The fifth house describes her relationship with her children but also the tendency to attract a romantic situation with strong karmic overtones.

Since Saturn describes her mother and her father (with Saturn overshadowing the planets ruling and posited in the fourth house of home), Connie may have felt rejection and a karmic identification with her parents. There may have been an undercover role reversal. Her mother may have been the strong, dominant one, while her father may have repressed his potential for being the nurturing parent. Each parent would have tried to be the good, but judgmental, disciplinarian. Connie probably would not have received the nurturing she needed from either parent (especially from her father) or the example of real strength and support she needed from her mother. Her mother's subtle message may have been, "Don't get a swelled head."

With Jupiter conjunct Pluto conjunct Venus in the fourth house (describing the relationship with her father and the desire for a grandiose kind of life-style), all overshadowed by Saturn, the karmic memory of an opulent life-style is connected to some feelings of guilt that may prevent her having such luxury again. The desire is there, but the subconscious strings attached make an individual think twice before taking on such a responsibility again. However, it's very possible that she will reclaim an expansive way of life as she grows older. Once old karmic patterns are broken, shared artistic work with a partner or mate can provide a lavish income.

The present-life conditions indicate her father's inability or unwillingness to have the abundant life he also may have been accustomed to in another time. He may have guilts and fears about the power he seems to possess. With Pluto conjunct Venus, he may worry about his desire for total self-indulgence, so he simply denies himself the temptation. Connie would inherit those feelings by osmosis as well as through her father's overt or subtle judgmental messages in the subject of lavishness, self-indulgence and power. When Pluto is placed in or rules the fourth house of home or life-style, memories of power and grandeur incline the individual to the desire to recapture his personal kingdom. With the Saturn blocks in this life, the individual finally allows himself the present-day correlation of that kind of existence only if he feels it is for the benefit of all, not just himself.

This sort of astrological analysis always leaves me feeling short of fulfillment, because I can't describe more fully the *why* of the matter. Why do such opulent memories exist? Why is such frustration connected to those issues in present times? Obviously there are karmic lessons connected to those issues that must be recognized and reconciled in the here and now. When I read a chart to an individual, I try to express these salient points in such a way that his own thoughts about the issues will be stimulated. That seems to be the first step toward present-day resolutions. The Saturn-sun aspect is particularly important, because the sense of self-worth is the issue. Insecurities may be prevalent, but there is a *reason* such insecurities or denials of self-worth are necessary and even productive in this life. That aspect can also indicate a serious quality that demands much of the self. The person may want grave responsibility in order to feel needed. Connie's regression session confirmed all this in a more profound way than I could ever have expressed it.

In the beginning of her session, the most important thing to emerge was the sense of isolation that had haunted her all her life. She was born on a farm to a family that struggled for survival. She wrestled with a sense of being different from the moment of birth. She said,

Not only do I feel different, but everyone in my family treats me as if I'm different. My brothers are a little bit afraid to talk to me. They keep their distance. It's really funny. My mother is always asking me for advice. My entire life has been that way. In school, everyone was my friend, but I didn't really have a close friend. I remember walking down the hall and everyone moving out of the way. It really bothered me. I tried to be nice and then everyone would say, "Thank you for being my friend," like I was doing them a favor. I would think, "Thank me for being your friend... but I like you!" I felt totally connected to my grandfather. He never treated me differently. He treated me like I was special to him.

I was always embarrassed about my clothes, so I learned to sew at the age of six. Then I could make my own clothes. We couldn't really afford the kind of thing I liked and I had to be careful not to appear ungrateful because I wanted something nicer. I felt guilty about that. I even wanted nicer furniture. Then I wondered why I couldn't be content with what we had. My family were such sweet people. What difference did it make? But it did make a difference to me. When you live on a farm, you don't always set the table properly, but at a very young age, I wanted to have the plates and napkins arranged in a pretty way. I would always set the table and ask everyone to sit down and put their napkins in their laps. Everything had to be just right.

I was always getting things I didn't go after. The last time I was home, I was going through an old photograph album. All through school I was queen of something—Football Queen, Queen of the Fall Festival—and I even saw a picture of a little boy crowning me queen in the first grade. People were always voting me into things I didn't want. I didn't want to be different, I just wanted to be like everyone else.

After reviewing some particularly painful situations in this life, Connie immediately went to the age of two weeks and described what she saw. "I feel like I can't get my breath. I'm coughing and coughing and it really hurts. I hear the doctors saying that I could die at any moment. I'm turning blue and I'm really in pain. Someone is holding me. I realize it's my grandfather. I think he's the first person I'm aware of holding me and comforting me." The tears that began trickling down her cheeks were real indeed; the sadness was quite obvious. She continued, "I want to tell him I don't want to stay here. He is convincing me it's going to be all right. He says, 'You're here for a very special purpose and you can't leave us.' I hear my parents talking about not having any money and that times are rough. I just want to turn around and go back. I know I'll have to be really careful and not eat too much. I will have to be good and not cause any trouble. I become a very quiet, shy child." She described her birth and commented, "I don't feel my parents are really ready for me. It's mainly financial and I am not really ready for this life either."

I asked her to go to a time that would give an explanation of the circumstances of her present life, and the first thing she said was, "I see myself coming down a long flight of steps. I have on a beautiful gown, really elaborate, with a real high collar and big sleeves. There are a lot of flounces on the skirt. I have lots of jewelry around my neck and there are jewels on the dress too." I asked Connie where she was going and she replied quite spontaneously, "I'm going to some sort of very special occasion, like a coronation." Suddenly she said, "Oh, it's my coronation. I'm going to be queen!" This revelation came as a complete surprise to her. Even with her eyes closed her attitude was wide-eyed. "There is a huge hall, like a banquet hall, with a huge table. There are tapestries and chandeliers. Everything is heavy and wood carved...massive...the chairs at the table look so big, they're almost too big." I asked her if her parents were there and she said, "No, they're dead. My little brother has just died. He wasn't a baby, but he wasn't grown up either." At that point, I asked what country this might be and she said, "England." I asked her name and she said, "Anne." The thoughts that ran through my mind were very distinct. I said to myself, "She's Elizabeth, not Anne." I felt chills run down the back of my neck. As a student of that period of English history, I knew that Elizabeth was crowned queen upon the death of her sister Mary, but Mary's coronation took place after the death of the young King Edward. I was fairly sure Connie was unaware of who she was talking about, and she didn't mention Mary's reign at all. Elizabeth had been very close to her younger brother but was ill at ease with her sister because she was a rival for the English throne.

I asked Connie to look around the scene to see if anyone was there whom she knows in this life. She described her adviser then, as her father in this life. She said, "He is always telling me what I can't do. In this life, my father did the same thing. I always felt rebellious toward him. I would do what he said to do, but I was really mad. I was very resentful toward him until a few years ago. But I did what he said to do in that life and in this one too." Her description of her father fit clearly the description I saw of him in her chart.

I asked her how people reacted to her. She said, "Everyone

loves me. They think I am wonderful because everything I do is for the people. I don't seem to be doing anything for myself. Every decision I make is what's best for the people. I try to do things for people who are poor, because my father seemed to be more concerned about himself than the people. I am more concerned about the country. He was more egotistical and wanted fine things for himself. I have to sacrifice myself because all the people are depending on me. It seems I feel he didn't really do what was right and I am going to do what is right, come hell or high water. [Queen Elizabeth's father was Henry VIII.] I have a strong sense of moral obligation. I am in a constant battle with myself because I'm not able to do anything as far as my personal life is concerned. Everything has to be hidden." She began to cry softly at that realization. I then asked her to describe other people she might know in this life. "I have a very, very distinct picture of the kitchen. I see my mother, in this life, down on the floor, scrubbing like a servant. It is a monstrous kitchen with a monstrous stove. A pipe is going up to the ceiling, and a fireplace has a pot hanging in it. There is a big wooden table in the center that is worn off in places. It is like a working table where round places have been smoothed out of the wood. It's a table where they make bread and it has little dents all over the top."

Suddenly she began crying quite hard, and I asked her what she was seeing. She said, "I'm looking in the corner where there is a doorway." I again asked her what she was seeing, but her tears prevented her from answering me for quite a while. It was obvious that she was feeling great emotion over the scene before her. At long last she said, "It's Jim." Jim is the young man Connie is in love with in this life. She met him while she was traveling and convinced him to move to her home town to help her with her restaurant. She was having difficulty reconciling her feelings toward him because he was younger than she, single, attractive and not the person her family might approve of as a future mate. When I felt she was ready to go on, I asked, "Why are you crying?" She replied, "Because I can't have him." I asked her to explain that, and she continued, "For one thing, he's married, but the real reason is they won't let me. It's not right for the country. It wouldn't be good for the kingdom or the people. He's not the right person." I asked if she was ever able to marry him, and she said, "No, I have to be very careful not to let my adviser know how I feel about him. Everything I do in the relationship has to be sneaky. We can't just say anything to each other and we can't go anywhere together. He has to appear to be just a friend." The tears began to flow again, and eventually I asked why she was crying. She said, "It's just the same thing all over again. Everything has to be whitewashed." After more specific questions about the situation then, she continued, "My adviser won't let me marry him or even see him. He keeps telling me it will cause trouble. He (Jim) is around me all the time at the court. It's like I just have to have him with me. He is supposed to have a function at the court, but I actually create a job for him and give him a title as well, I think. I have to have a good reason for him to be there. There are always men around trying to persuade me to marry them. There are so many people bringing me gifts, trying to do things for me, and he is one of my suitors. I think his family are a bit dishonest, which makes it even more difficult. He's not royalty either. But the first time I see him, it's like the feeling of meeting a long-lost friend. It is a complete and total communication and feeling of comfort. I don't have to pretend anything with him; I can just be myself. He uplifts my spirit and makes me feel good about everything, making sure that all is smooth for me. He is around me for a few years and then he is married. He is really impatient because I won't do anything about our love. I am supposed to be a virgin, but we are having a relationship that no one knows about. I have a maid who helps us go away together. We go for rides in the country and really have fun. She covers for us."

I asked how she found out about the marriage and she replied, "Someone tells me. He is afraid to tell me himself, but a man who is watching everything he does is really eager to tell me the news. He says in effect, 'Now you can just forget about him.' I am so upset I get really mad and banish him from the country. I say, 'Now you've done it. Now you'll have to pay for it.' Everyone is trying to get me married. They keep telling me to get serious about someone. They keep picking people they think will be good for the country. I pretend to enjoy the whirlwind that starts, but I am really thinking about my love. I had given him a ring, but I take that ring away from him when he gets married. He didn't know that I'd react so violently or that I'd banish him from my sight. It's just too painful to have him right there in front of me when I can't have him. I can never let anyone know how I feel. I have to be really hypocritical, because if I don't do everything just right, there is someone else to take my place."

I asked Connie to tell me about the other person. It had become increasingly obvious to me that Connie was unaware of the details of her description from a historical point of view. She was recounting everything from a deeply personal and emotional perspective, yet her observations were historically accurate. I deliberately avoided leading her to what I knew to be correct. Connie said, "It is another woman. She isn't well. She isn't as much in control as I am and does not have a strong constitution. She is really emotional. She is always putting pressure on me because she has children and I'm not even married. I think I make her physically sick through my mental power." I asked her the name of the other person and she replied, "Mary." [Mary, Queen of Scots].

She continued telling me what came to her. "I think I had him put in prison. He wasn't married very long. He didn't want to be married to her, so he got her out of the way so he could come back to me. I wanted to lock him up so he couldn't be with her, but I really didn't have a good reason. After he kills his wife, I have to lock him up, even though I'm glad he has done it. It doesn't look good if I don't punish him for the crime. Even though it is painful to put him in prison, I know he understands that it's what I have to do. Later I pardon him. He gets sick and pleads with me to let him out of prison. Other people say I can't do that. I am skirting dangerous ground with that one. They're ready to pounce on me anyway because I'm not married." Emotion overcame Connie once more. She described his death. She told me that she was dying inside but did not dare show any grief at all. She concluded her story by skimming over the rest of her life as a lonely woman with a tremendous sense of responsibility and pressure from the outside world.

After the regression session, Connie told me how tired she was. She was looking down at the table in front of her and suddenly lifted her head and said, "I know who my mother was in that life." The emotion of that realization showed clearly on her face. "When you asked me my name, there were two names that popped into my head. I said Anne, but I think I was Elizabeth and my mother was Anne." I told her what I knew about that period of history and confirmed much of what she had recounted. The hour was quite late and we were both overly tired. We decided to meet the next day to confirm the details by checking an encyclopedia. We also made an agreement not to tell Jim any of the details of her regression. We hoped he would be willing to do his own regression session and we didn't want to prejudice him in any way. If he also recounted the events of that time, we'd have an interesting corroboration of her memory.

The next day we met like conspirators to pore over the encyclopedia. As she read, her expression was one of profound amazement. "Look at this," she said, and pointed to a paragraph about the Earl of Leicester, the love of Queen Elizabeth's life. It stated that his real name was Robert Dudley. Since I knew that already, I didn't see the significance of her astonishment. She finally said, "Don't you know Jim's last name? It's Dudley!"

Subsequently I did a regression with Jim. As we had agreed, Connie had deliberately kept the details of her session a secret. I was not at all sure that Jim would recall anything that remotely resembled her story. I was not really interested in proving reincarnation or that the information buried in a person's subconscious is in fact real. I am more interested in the effects such a session will have on present problems. So I was not really prepared for what poured forth from Jim. He was a willing subject, even though Connie had rather insisted he do a regression session as well.

Jim also had a Saturn-Sun aspect, but in his case it was a sesquisquare, perhaps more difficult to resolve than other hard

aspects in a chart. Most interesting to me was the conjunction of
Saturn-Pluto in the tenth house of career, ruling the financial second house and the fourth house of home. The tenth and fourth
houses also describe parents and, with an additional Saturn-Venus
square, it was clear that Jim did not feel as though he belonged to
his family either. Jim had Libra rising, with Jupiter conjunct
Venus in the second house of income. If Jim could reconcile any
negative programming about money that may have come from
parents, he could be especially successful in financial areas. To me,
Saturn squaring that lovely conjunction of the two benefic planets
describes a "poor" complex. It may also indicate a resistance to
allowing love in his life as a result of early feelings of rejection.

Jim reviewed painful times in his childhood when he indeed felt
like a stranger among strangers and finally saw an incident that
took place when he was only a year old. He said, "The seats are
pretty scratchy. I'm just wearing diapers and a shirt, no booties or
socks. There is a train wreck and I'm thrown across the aisle. I am
asleep, lying on the seat, when it happens. I hit a wall across from
me and hit my head on the right side. I'm more scared than hurt.
I wonder why I'm not crying. I think I'm too scared. I just clam
up." I asked Jim if that is his reaction in the present. Lots of tears
began welling in his eyes. I asked him what he was thinking. He
replied, "I just don't understand why they would let me fall. It
doesn't really hurt and I think I'm just mad. My fright and anger
are all mixed up." Then he said, "I think I'm unconscious for a
while after the wreck. That's why I'm not crying. I think I decide
I'd better keep my eyes open and look after myself." Finally he
said, "I think that's when I decide not to trust anyone ever again."

With no further questions on my part, Jim began to shiver. I
asked him to tell me what he was feeling. He didn't answer, and
once again, I asked him to talk to me and share what he was
thinking. Finally he said, "I'm so cold." I asked if that was a past
life or the present and he replied, "Another life. I'm just so cold."
He said he was wearing a bathing suit. I asked what country he
was in and he replied, "Denmark comes to mind. It's cold, really
cold." I asked if he was in a swimming pool and he replied, "A

lake." Jim continued, "I'm swimming by myself. There's a dock somewhere. I have a mustache and I'm heavier than I am now, but about the same height." I asked him if this is where he lived. He shook his head no. Jim was shivering quite hard by now and was clutching his stomach. I stopped to ask if he wanted a coat around his shoulders and he said yes, but later commented that it didn't help because the cold was from inside.

He was in such obvious discomfort, I knew he was experiencing a deep emotional reaction. He asked if we could stop the session, but I assured him it was necessary to go on; I couldn't leave him in the middle of a bad memory. Finally I asked him to describe the scenery before him. He continued, "I'm looking up through the water. I can see through it, but it is as if I'm under the surface. I'm alive, but I can't straighten out, and I can't get to the surface. My stomach really hurts. I've been trying to figure out why my stomach hurts so much. There are three people standing above me. There's a lady in a big, big dress. It's big at the bottom, straight at the top with a big collar. There's a man with her. Someone is standing and someone is sitting down." After a slight pause, he said, "I'm not sure I'm in water at all. It's like I'm seeing them through glass. They're just looking at me. It's like they're standing there waiting for me to die."

With that awareness, a fresh batch of tears poured down Jim's face. He was clearly hurting on more than a physical level. I asked him to describe his station in life. He replied, "I'm rich, very rich. I'm noble. I'm part of them. We don't have to do anything, we're so rich." Then he came back to the emotion he was feeling so strongly. "I'm shocked that they're my friends and they're not helping me." I asked if he recognized any of the people from this lifetime and Jim replied, "I feel like I know them. I don't like the man standing there, but she's someone I love." I asked if he recognized her from this life and he began sobbing. He said, "It can't be, it can't be..." As a last question, I asked, "What country are you from?" He didn't hesitate before he said, "England."

It seemed appropriate to stop the session at that point. As he came back to the present, he said, "I want to see Connie." In anticipation of what Jim might experience about that moment of seeming abandonment, Connie was waiting for him outside. As they clung together, there was no need for Connie to ask him what he had recalled. I quietly slipped out of the room.

One of the facts that emerged from the foray into the encyclopedia was that the Earl of Leicester had died of cancer of the stomach. Although Jim did not describe the scene at the English court in the same way that Connie had, I felt rather sure that he was recalling the same moment in history. I subsequently did my own research into the stormy and passionate romance of Elizabeth and Leicester. I found corroboration of much of what they both had said that might be unknown to a casual student of Elizabethan history. It was clear to me that neither Connie nor Jim had done any research into that period. It was more interesting to me that some of the facts that emerged were less important to the regression sessions than the very real emotional reaction on both their parts. However, the facts were astounding.

In *The First Elizabeth* by Carolly Erickson, she describes the relationship between Elizabeth and Leicester toward the end of his life. "Three days after word reached the capital that the [Spanish] Armada was within striking distance of the English coast, the Queen appointed Leicester to be commander of the Camp Royal at Tilbury. The appointment warmed the heart of the sick old earl, who ever since his return from the Netherlands campaign, had suffered nearly as much from Elizabeth's coldness and angry neglect as he did from the illness that was slowly killing him." More information about that time was gleaned from *Sir Francis Bacon* by Jean Overton Fuller. In the chapter entitled "The Armada and the Death of Leicester," she says:

When the Armada was sighted sailing up the Channel, Elizabeth wanted to go down to the coast. Leicester, as chief of the land forces, wrote her a very sensible letter, saying that to see her exposed to real danger would distress rather than hearten her troops, and that his love would not permit her to hazard her person further than Tilbury. [Elizabeth did review the troops at Tilbury.] Shortly after Drake's great victory at sea, Leicester and the Queen dined together, and Leicester mentioned his health. She suggested he should take the baths at Buxton, and on August 27 he wrote to tell her he was setting out. On his way to the spa on September 7, 1588, her birthday, he died.

Elizabeth's reaction to the shock was violent. She shut herself up in her room for the whole of the day, night, and following day, admitting no one, even to bring food. In the end Burghley ordered the door to be broken down. After her own death, Leicester's letter of August 27 was found, marked on the outside in her hand: His last letter. It was in the casket inset with jewels which she kept beside her bed.

Many of the events that Connie described were confirmed in *The First Elizabeth*. It was noted that Elizabeth had a mania for jewels. Connie's description of the coronation dress with "jewels on the dress, too" was quite accurate. Her perspective about her relationship with Dudley, later Earl of Leicester, was interesting. In the regression session, Connie presumed they had fooled everyone into thinking they were just friends. In the literary description, it seemed everyone knew they were having an affair. In fact, the rumor of the time was that Sir Francis Bacon was actually a child of Elizabeth and Leicester. The historical account of the death of Leicester's wife, Amy, was somewhat different from the harsher account revealed by Connie in her session. The sequence of events was also somewhat out of order in Connie's account, for Leicester was suspected of killing his first wife, Amy Robsart, but it was his later marriage to Lettice Knollys, after he had given up any hope of a marriage to Elizabeth, that so infuriated her.

In *The First Elizabeth*, Carolly Erickson says:

Yet Leicester had a potent weapon of his own, calculated to wound Elizabeth cruelly. He began a flirtation with Lettice Knollys, the dazzling, auburn-haired daughter of Francis and Catherine Knollys, universally praised as "one of the best-looking ladies of the court." Lettice was a stunning beauty, more vivid in her coloring than her second cousin Elizabeth and with none of the queen's aloof intellectuality to blunt her allure. Lettice was everything Elizabeth had once been and was no longer: young, ripe, nubile. And she was Leicester's sweetheart.

The disloyalty cut deep; so too did the loss of the Earl's constant, affectionate presence. Elizabeth was humiliated, her vanity punctured. They quarreled openly, in front of the whole court. She had the last word... but suffered nonetheless. They wept and made up—after a fashion.... They [Leicester and Lettice] were secretly married sometime after Lettice's husband died in 1576. Simier [Jean de Simier, master of the wardrobe to Francois, Duke of Alencon, who hoped to marry Elizabeth] found out about the marriage, and told Elizabeth.... The discovery of Leicester's treachery shocked, then enraged her. It was like Leicester to act behind her back; his pusillanimity was as contemptible as his deceit. As for Lettice, that traitorous "she-wolf," no words were harsh enough to describe her. Leicester, though, would have reason to fear for his life. She ordered him seized and shut up in an isolated tower in Greenwich park, to await stricter imprisonment in the Tower of London.... She had thought better of her initial reaction to the discovery of his marriage, when in cold anger she had ordered him imprisoned. He had spent the week in involuntary isolation, but it was given out that he had merely been shut away to take medicine, and after the week was over he left court to stay at one of his own houses.... Clearly he had forfeited a measure of that sentimental concern Elizabeth had always felt for him, and he feared to lose his power and perhaps his wealth besides.... He felt like a faithful dog being whipped by an ungrateful master.

Perhaps the most astounding fact that emerged was Connie's casual account of Leicester's killing of his first wife, Amy Robsart. The court was in such an uproar over the scandal that a demand was made for a formal investigation into the charges. According to Carolly Erickson, "Dudley, presumed villain and absolute master of Elizabeth, was before long sent away from court, to his house at Kew. There he stayed, frustrated, anxious, more than a little bewildered, while she coped with the tumult. Dudley lamented elegantly [to Cecil]. He 'sued to be at liberty, out of so great bondage' and found himself 'too far, too far from the place he was bound to be'—at court, by the side of his beleagured lady the queen."

In *Francis Bacon*, the account is more vivid.

The constant companionship between Leicester (still known as Lord Robert) did not escape the eyes of the court. Count de Feria, the Spanish ambassador, wrote to his king on April 18, 1559,

"During the last few days, Lord Robert has come so much into favour that he does whatever he likes with affairs and it is even said that her Majesty visits him in his chamber day and night. People talk of this so freely that they go so far as to say that his wife has a malady in one of her breasts and the Queen is only waiting for her to die to marry Lord Robert." Leicester's wife, Amy Robsart, was ill with what modern medicine might have diagnosed as terminal cancer. On April 29, De Feria wrote again of the affair and said, "She speaks like a woman who will only marry a great prince and then they say she is in love with Lord Robert and will never let him leave her." He reported again in November 1559 that the duke of Norfolk had threatened that if Lord Robert would not abandon his pretension to the Queen's hand, he would not die in his bed.

By the following September, Bishop de Quadra, who had succeeded De Feria, wrote to the king of Spain: "She had promised me an answer about her marriage, but now she coolly tells me she cannot make up her mind and will not marry. After making many pledges of secrecy, Cecil said the Queen was conducting herself in such a way that he thought of retiring. He clearly foresaw the ruin of the realm by Robert's intimacy with the Queen, who surrendered all affairs to him and meant to marry him. He begged me to point out to the Queen, the effect of her misconduct and persuade her not to abandon business entirely, but to look to her realm.... He ended by saying that Robert was thinking of killing his wife, who was publicly announced to be ill, although she was quite well, and would take good care they did not poison her.... The next day the Queen told me, as she returned from hunting, that Robert's wife was dead or nearly so, and asked me not to say anything about it. Certainly this business is most shameful and scandalous and withal I am not sure whether she will marry the man at once, or even if she will marry at all, as I do not think she has her mind sufficiently fixed. Since writing the above I hear the Queen has published the death of Robert's wife, and said in Italian, 'Que si ha rollo il cuello.'" (She broke her neck.)

Amy had been found at the foot of a staircase, after sending the servants out for the day. Leicester desired there should be an inquest. It was shown he had not been at Cumnor, where she died, and a verdict of accidental death was recorded. It seems she was suffering from a cancer of the breast with extension into the neck, causing spontaneous fracture of the spine. This would be likeliest to occur while descending stairs, and would be consistent with the absence of damage done to her bonnet, such as should have been obvious, had she been pushed from the top of the staircase. The author goes on to say,

> Cecil, therefore, did Leicester wrong, and he was not the only one. Mary Queen of Scots was reported to have said, "The Queen of England is going to marry her horse-keeper, who has killed his wife to make room for her." For Elizabeth to have married Leicester in these circumstances would have further fed scandal. From being everywhere with him, now she was hardly seen at all, but withdrew into herself, in Whitehall Palace, for the winter.

The intrigues and the continuing ups and downs of the relationship between Elizabeth and Leicester lasted throughout their lives. The rumor was that Elizabeth was pregnant with Leicester's child and that during the time she was isolated after the death of Leicester's wife, she could have been carrying the child, later to be adopted and named Francis Bacon. It is recorded that Elizabeth made her confession to Bishop de Quadra on January 15, 1561. He dutifully reported to his king, "She wishes to confess to me and tell her secret in confession, which was she was no angel." De Quadra interpreted this to mean that she was not a virgin.

The passion between these two people was the subject of many letters and comments from Bishop de Quadra to the king of Spain. It seemed Elizabeth wanted confirmation from the king of Spain that he would approve of her marriage to one of her servitors. She went so far as to ask for a letter from the king advising her to marry Lord Robert. Robert also asked the bishop to intercede and ask the king to advise Elizabeth to marry him. It seemed she needed proof that such a marriage was upon advice and not to satisfy her own desires.

There were many rumors of a secret marriage, but evidently such a ceremony never took place. A report in Stowe's *Historical Memoranda* gives an account of a proposed quiet wedding set for

April 12, 1566. "She was late and he gave up waiting. In fact, she had set out with two of her ladies-in-waiting, but he met her on the way, and they simply rode back to Greenwich Palace. The Queen had not gone through with it again. With such frustrations, it is said that there was further withdrawal on Leicester's part after this."

Elizabeth and Robert Dudley actually met as children, when they were both eight years old and were confined together in the Tower of London. There was a special empathy between them even then. According to Erickson, "Though Elizabeth was not a confiding child, she confided in him. She told him very seriously, he recalled many years later, that she had made up her mind never to marry." It is no wonder that Connie described her relationship by saying, "The first time I see him it's like the feeling of a long-lost friend." She also said, "I think his family are a bit dishonest. They're not quite on the up and up, which makes it even more difficult." Erickson uses these words to describe Robert's father: "John Dudley, a crafty soldier ambitious for influences..." and later, "the disaffected English did not forget to rail against the merchants... and above all to denounce the councillors, especially Dudley, for their corruption and misgovernment." During the reign of Edward VI, Elizabeth's brother, who ascended to the throne when Henry VIII died, religious shifts were intertwined with political ascendancy. Dudley emerged as the actual, though untitled, ruler of the council and the king. By December, 1549, he was firmly in command of the council. The elder Dudley now ruled England through the twelve-year-old king. He could not have achieved that position without a great deal of shrewd, perhaps underhanded political maneuvering. He was ultimately tried for treason, convicted and killed.

Elizabeth maintained a surface friendly relationship with Mary Queen of Scots but was constantly on the alert for any signs of treachery from her rival. For Mary was considered the logical person to succeed Elizabeth to the throne. There were plots and subplots to put Mary on the throne. Elizabeth finally had her put to death in 1588, during the time of threat from the Spanish Armada. Elizabeth maintained the upper hand during their entire relationship and refused to allow Mary to see her in person, even though Mary put forth many protestations of her devotion to Elizabeth. Connie described the emotional relationship quite accurately in her regression session.

Robert Dudley was already married to Amy Robsart, an heiress, when Elizabeth actually came to court, just days before her brother Edward's death. Connie was clearly talking about Leicester's second marriage to Lettice Knollys when she described her anger and his imprisonment. In Jim's regression, the hurt over the coldness exhibited by Elizabeth (Connie) at the time of his death was expressed with real emotion. Historically the passionate and stormy relationship between Elizabeth and Leicester had cooled as she grew older and there was even more pressure on her to marry. However, her appointment of Leicester as chief of the land forces during the time of invasion from Spain clearly shows that he was never totally out of her mind and heart. Her grief over his death was genuinely devastating. It signaled a turning point in her life.

I saw Connie about six months after her regression session and asked her to describe the changes or benefits that may have come as a result of the sessions. Connie replied, "The first thing I noticed, immediately after the regression, was that I no longer felt like I had to live my life according to what someone else expected of me. That in itself has been tremendously important. I have also had a lot of déjà vu, especially between Jim and me. We would be laughing and just having fun and I would get flashbacks." Jim volunteered, "One thing I have never understood about our relationship is my attachment to Connie. I understand the emotional part, but I would rather do something for Connie than take care of my own business. For instance, I can't stand the restaurant business, yet I'm there working very hard. After a few months, I was ready to leave. I hate the hours, the pettiness, but I just can't leave her. I know what she's going through and what she has to deal with. I try to persuade her to sell the restaurant and leave this town, as we have no social freedom here. Yet I continue to stay somewhere I don't like just to be with her. It's such a contrast from my past. Nobody could ever tie me down before."

Connie then told me she had had spontaneous recall of other lives where they were together. She said, "We were living in this country two different times. I saw myself in a print housedress and an apron. He had on pants with suspenders. It was somewhere close to the beach, probably the East Coast. He left me then...on horseback. He left me for someone else then, too. I saw myself very upset. I had children and I felt really abandoned. The other life was really beautiful. It was a tropical, gorgeous, lush environment. We were artists together, living in some heavenly paradise. We were very successful then." Jim is an exceptionally talented artist in this life as well.

About a year after our first meeting, Connie called me on the telephone. She said, "Something has happened that is so personal, I can't tell anyone but you and Jim." She was reluctant to reveal any more on the telephone but promised to go into more detail when we saw each other next. When we were together, she said,

One morning I woke up and remembered a dream I had had. I was sitting at this enormous desk, just huge, and I was writing with a feather pen in a script that was different. I was very dressed up in a big dress with a high collar and big sleeves, and I was writing a poem. When I woke up, I tried really hard to remember that poem. I could see some of the words but I couldn't remember it. I had to get up, as I had pressing appointments, but a few days later, I decided I would meditate and try to remember that poem.

I lay down and went into a real deep state of meditation. I visualized the desk and the chair, and I started to "read it" off the page. I'd see some part of it, then jump up and write it down. Then I'd forget, go back and lie down to see some more lines. I could see some lines very clearly, but then it would skip and go on to the next verse. Three or four lines would be very clear in one verse, but only a couple in another. It was an extremely personal experience.

The only thing I could think of that day was to find out if that poem exists. I went to the library and found a reference book that is an index for poetry. The poems are listed three ways: by title, first line and author's name. I had seen the title as "On Monsieur's

Departure," so I looked first under the titles in the reference book. I was a bit disappointed when it wasn't there. Then I decided to look under the first line. I wasn't sure that I had remembered the first line, but I thought I had been able to see the top of the page in my meditation. I decided I wasn't going to go to the author first, just on principle. I wanted to find that first line and then see who wrote it. It might have been by someone else.

As I was turning the pages, my hands were just shaking. I was going down the list and...my God...there it was...the first line of the poem. The author was Queen Elizabeth. I was shaking so hard, I had to sit down. I was just stunned. When Jim arrived, we tried to find a book in the library that contained the whole poem. We discovered there was only one book that contained that poem. The book was so rare, it was in the rare book section of a university library in a nearby city. I was so shaken, I couldn't go there, so Jim went to find the book. When he arrived at the university, he discovered that he needed permission even to see the book. It took a few days to get that permission, but when he did, he went back and was able to copy the poem word for word.

I asked if I could see the poem as well as the lines that she had written. Connie was just a bit reluctant to show me the two pieces of paper. She considered that a very personal experience, but she knew I would be sensitive to her feelings. First Connie showed me a piece of paper written in her own handwriting with several lines unevenly spaced. The spaces between certain lines indicated that the lines were not consecutive. Connie explained the reason she felt the poem had not been titled in the rare book. "Evidently I didn't give the poem a title because that would have given away my feelings. I wrote the poem after the Earl of Leicester had died. Since I couldn't show my grief at the news of his death, I spent a day by myself and poured out my feelings on paper."

There seemed to be no way that Connie could have stumbled on the poem by accident in her schooldays. There is always a possibility of an individual's ability to tap into a universal stream of consciousness, or the Akashic Records, as they are known, yet that is quite a feat in itself. These lines seemed to be etched into Connie's subconscious mind. The lines Connie remembered were:

I grieve, and dare not show my discontent;
I love, and yet am forced to seem to hate;
This too familiar care does make me rue it;
Oh be more cruel, Love, and so be kind;
Let me float or sink, be high or low;

The poem in its entirety is as follows:

I grieve, and dare not show my discontent;
I love, and yet am forced to seem to hate;
I do, yet dare not say I ever meant;
I seem stark mute, but inwardly do prate;
I am, and not; I freeze, and yet am burned,
Since from my self, my other self I turned.

My care is like my shadow in the sun,
Follows my flying, flies when I pursue it;
Stands and lies by me, does what I have done;
This too familiar care does make me rue it;
No means I find to rid him from my breast,
Till by the end of things it be supprest.

Some gentler passions slide into my mind,
For I am soft, and made of melting snow;
Oh be more cruel, Love, and so be kind;
Let me float or sink, be high or low;
Or let me live with some more sweet content.
Or die, and so forget what love e'er meant.
                              —Queen Elizabeth I

Connie and Jim have a deep and abiding love for each other. They have had many lives together to resolve the relationship that was established centuries ago. If Connie were to focus on the very beginning of their association, she might find the roots of the attraction and be able to go past the blocks that prevent her from trusting and commiting herself to Jim. Connie has confessed that her greatest fear about him is his attraction to other women. Evidently she was very jealous and possessive of him in Elizabethan times, even though he proved his devotion to her countless times. She has another memory of a lifetime in which Jim abandoned her and their children. Those scars can be very deep. She is sure his attraction to others is only an ego gratification for him and has nothing to do with a lack of love for her, but she hesitates to trust him completely. She is always afraid of him leaving her again.

On the other hand, she allowed public opinion and fear of judgment from her family to inhibit the full expression of their relationship, then and now. Jim described the frustration he feels because, once again, Connie can't seem to make up her mind. He is aware of a tendency to want to run away from the situation, but he has decided to stick it out. He wants to convince Connie of the sincerity of his love by patience and continuing supportive demonstration of that love.

After the discovery of the poem written by Queen Elizabeth to Leicester, both Connie and Jim have an entirely different perspective on the situation. For one thing, Connie no longer feels her life revolves around her restaurant. She has decided to continue its operation as long as it is productive, but she has rediscovered an executive ability that can be channeled in many directions. After the memory of the lifetime spent together as artists, where they were very successful, new ideas have come to mind about work they can do together. They have decided to focus on promotion of artistic, creative products.

In Connie's astrological chart, with Jupiter conjunct Pluto and Venus, it is clear that she can derive tremendous income from the sales and production of creative works. Jim's chart reveals a Jupiter conjunct Venus aspect in the house describing money, and ruling the eighth house of income on a residual, commission, bonus basis. He also has an ability to express his power through a stronger commitment to career and financial potency from home base. The comparison of their astrological charts indicates a connection that is long lasting and continuing. Jim's ascendant is exactly trine Saturn in Connie's chart, indicating great stability in the association. Her Moon is exactly trine Pluto in his chart, describing dynamic and powerful emotional ties. In fact, there are twelve matching aspects within a one-degree orb that clearly shows the continuing growth of the relationship. Their decision to have the courage to put away the negative memories and focus on the successful ones has enabled them to build a deeper, more committed relationship.

Jim and Connie are not the only people who have such attractions that need to be resolved. For with anyone, when an attraction is strong or a dislike is intense, some kind of past association has paved the way for that reaction. It is not important for Jim and Connie to live in the memory of the Elizabethan era. It is important to focus on the here and now.

What emerged from the regression sessions can give Connie and Jim tremendous insight about their present-day relationship. In Elizabethan England, there were many problems that prevented them from being together. However, it was really Connie's fears that prevented her from marrying her lifelong love. History might have been quite different if Queen Elizabeth had followed her heart and married the Earl of Leicester. In Connie's memory, she had indeed married Jim in a later life and was abandoned by him. Jim has taken giant steps to express his love for Connie in the present and to reassure her constantly by demonstrating his continuing support of her life choices. The high drama and public awareness of their private lives is fortunately missing in present time, so any obstacles to their relationship may be simply fragments of memory filtering through to present-day circumstances. At least Connie and Jim have a chance to talk about their fears and resolve them on a deeper subconscious level, no matter what the outcome in their present life. Perhaps most important of all is the revelation of leadership and strength they both possess that can be used in the present for enrichment of their own and others' lives.

CHAPTER SIX

Saturn and the Moon

raditionally the Moon has been associated with the female sex. It relates to the *anima* part of the personality. That term was used by Carl Jung to describe all the characteristics ascribed to women, such as receptivity, vulnerability, sensitivity and nurturing. In this age of psychological awareness, Jung knew that those characteristics are not confined to women, and, indeed, the Moon is found in the charts of everyone. Certainly a man with the Moon strong in his chart can easily take on the role of the nurturer in a household. But the Moon describes another important quality in the chart. It indicates the areas where a person will identify with the common man and sense what that person needs almost intuitively. His greatest satisfaction may arise from areas in which he can express that intuitive, sensitive concern and in which his response will be in connection with feelings and desires we all share in common, such as the desire to feed the hungry. When an individual, male or female, allows himself to be open and aware of the feelings and problems we all share in common, greater compassion emerges.

Everyone shares, to some extent, the same basic concerns about loved ones, survival, home and family. When someone begins to feel compassion for a person experiencing pain connected with those issues, he opens the channels for greater communication and rapport in all his relationships. One very beautiful Tibetan meditation suggests that we look at the suffering of our mother and father. When we acknowledge the degree of trauma in the lives of our parents, our hearts must open at least a small amount, allowing us to have greater comprehension of the problems we all have to face on the earth plane. We learn that no one is exempt from suffering. The Moon has been found to be strong in the charts of writers, for instance. Perhaps writing about one's own suffering, pain or emotional needs enables another human being, reading the material, to identify with and feel better about his own lot in life.

The Moon has been described as a cold planet. But, in the interpretation of an astrological chart, it is clear that the Moon indicates areas of tremendous sensitivity and may therefore only *appear* cold. If the Moon has many difficult aspects, the person can seem to be very self-protective, simply because his feelings are so close to the surface of his life they are too much to bear. In many cases, the Moon indicates areas in life in which the person may hide his vulnerability, appearing unconcerned rather than allowing feelings to show, especially if he felt abandoned early in life. He feels he has no one to depend on and can be deeply hurt over the situation. He can hardly take care of his own emotions, much less those of others. So he appears above it all. (The strength and placement of the Moon in a chart describe the degree of that sensitivity and vulnerability.) Moreover, in certain emotional situations, he is likely to go into symbiosis with the person who is suffering. The identification with the feelings of another person is particularly difficult in cases of close relationships. Therefore the overly sensitive person may feel he has to close himself off emotionally to avoid taking on an extra burden of pain. All this may be done subconsciously, for the Moon describes reactions on the emotional level, where a person has no natural, conscious protection.

Intellectual awareness of the patterns in life can help the individual reconcile some of his emotional reactions, for Mercury, the planet of observation and analysis, is the natural antidote for the overreaction of the Moon. If we analyze the problem and develop a more objective outlook rather than just reacting emotionally, we are ahead of the game in finding a solution and leading a more emotionally rewarding life.

The Moon also describes oral needs and the process of feeding oneself and others. An individual with the Moon strong in his chart may have a strong emotional need to nurture or feed other people, either literally or figuratively. In former times, women traditionally took care of the preparation of food and provided sustenance for their husbands and children. The roles are naturally changing with the times, but in reality, only a woman can give birth and breast-feed her child. So ultimately the Moon describes motherhood and the strong symbiosis that occurs when that feeding process takes place.

In the light of reincarnation, however, we have all been mother and father, man and woman. Perhaps the only way to understand complex emotional difficulties in relationships is to examine those changes of roles from the past. This is particularly important when Saturn overshadows the Moon with a difficult aspect. The confusion and misunderstandings that exist when people do not react emotionally the way we expect them to must have their roots somewhere, especially if coldness exists when warmth is expected. Those roots may lie buried deep in a past-life relationship.

Perhaps the most mysterious relationship of all is that between mother and daughter. Volumes have been written and many films made to depict the tangled feelings that can exist between two women who may still be tied by a long-since-severed umbilical cord. This is a relationship that should be the happiest of all, due to the deep connection made during the prenatal period and the following early stages of life. But it is often the most troubled. For many daughters, their mother presents insurmountable problems. The same may be true for mothers whose daughters seem uncaring or unresponsive to their overtures. Feelings between mother and daughter can range from seeming indifference to outright hatred. We may pick the very woman to be born to, who represents the greatest karmic tie to be resolved.

When Saturn is in difficult aspect to the Moon there is an indication of rejection from the mother. There can be a barrier, either psychologically or physically, that prevents the natural flow of feelings from mother to child. This is not only true in mother-daughter relationships but also in mother-son situations. The child may have a deep sense of rejection or loss in connection with the mother. Basically, with Saturn overshadowing the Moon, there has been a lack of mothering in life.

Sometimes this aspect describes a coldness or aloof quality coming from the mother. This may be due to burdens in her own life that prevent her from expressing her natural nurturing feelings. The Saturn/Moon aspect can represent sadness or fears which condition the mother to cut off her feelings. The child may develop a sense of obligation, and it may become the overriding quality in the relationship. In many cases role reversal is the result with the child feeling responsible for the mother's happiness and well-being. He may feel his birth was the cause of her unhappiness. Quite often, the child sees this role as having been forced upon him. He cannot see clearly that he chose to feel parental toward the mother as a result of some guilt in the past. It is as if *he* is the burden that forces the mother into a restricted position and he must pay for being born. But after viewing a past life situation, the reason for the guilt can become crystal clear. In some cases, the newfound compassion can effect healing on a very deep level. For developing compassion for the miseries of others doesn't mean taking on their burdens. It opens the doors for mutual caring.

Healing of Mother/Daughter Relationships

Kate came to me for a regression session before her chart was done. As she walked in for her appointment, she said, "I only want to accomplish one thing. I want to understand my relationship with my mother." Kate had felt tremendous anger toward her mother ever since she was old enough to realize that her mother was an alcoholic. I stated that although it was quite possible that one of the strongest emerging factors in her regression session would concern her mother, I could not guarantee it. I informed her that her subconscious mind would direct the session, not either one of us.

Kate reviewed much of the pain and humiliation she had suffered in this life, not only in connection with her mother but also with the death of her husband, and then went to a past-life situation. She saw herself as a woman in southern Germany. The period of history was around 1850, and she saw it as a time of political unrest. She saw that she was walking in the woods, unobserved, as some people were discussing plans to blow up a railroad train. Her husband in that life was to be on that train and, in spite of her pleading with him to cancel his trip, was determined to ignore her warning. Therefore the act was a personal tragedy for her as her husband was killed in the explosion. She was able to identify the leader of the group and, taking justice into her own hands, had the leader imprisoned in the cellar of her own home. It was clear that the woman who instigated the sabotage would never see the light of day again.

Kate identified that woman as her mother in this lifetime. It was clear to her why she was so upset at the prospect of being born to her in the present. It was also clear to her why she had a compulsion to be a lawyer in the present life, against all odds. Fighting for justice might balance the karmic scales. When Kate opened her eyes at the completion of the session, she expressed great concern about her mother's welfare. She knew that two wrongs would not make the situation right, and wanted very much to make that up to her mother. She said, "The first thing I will do, when I am able, is send my mother to a rehabilitation center so that she can stop drinking. I've always expressed my anger to her, but now I must begin to show my compassion and love." We talked about the disease of alcoholism and about the issue of unconditional love. It became clear to Kate that the only way to show her real love and compassion was to accept her mother's addiction. She said, "When I visit her next, I'll take her a bottle of champagne." Kate also visualized her mother standing in front of her and said things to her that she had never been able to say in person. Primarily she expressed her compassion and caring for her mother's welfare.

A few months later, I received a call from Kate. She sounded exuberant and told me she had a wonderful story to tell. When we met, I noticed a radiance about Kate that unmistakably emerged from a new kind of inner joy. She said, "I have something special to tell you. I did exactly what I said I was going to do and took my mother a bottle of champagne. Our relationship since that last visit has improved noticeably, and of course I told her about my regression session without telling her any details. Last week, I had a telephone call from her, and she expressed interest in doing a regression session herself. She volunteered to me that she had always suspected she had been imprisoned in some past life. She said, 'I can feel myself with heavy iron chains around my ankles walking down three cold stone steps.' But the best of all came just before I called you. She telephoned to tell me that after thirty-six years of heavy drinking, she has stopped—cold turkey! She had been dry for over two months before she called me to give me the good news. I feel the regression session and the awareness of what I did to her and the resulting talk healed our wounds. It was very important for me."

Kate was not the first person who reported a healing that had taken place between two people without the other person being involved directly with a regression session. When I finally erected Kate's astrological chart, I saw Saturn squaring her Moon, indicating the karmic tie that concerned motherhood.

Another young woman stumbled on a past-life tie with her mother rather dramatically through her regression session. I read her astrological chart and described her unwillingness to be born. I also indicated that she felt a deep sense of responsibility for her mother. Laura confirmed this overridding tie to her mother by saying, "I can't understand it. I feel absolutely bound to my mother. I love her, but it doesn't make sense that I am now thirty-two years old and only recently have I been able to move into an apartment of my own. I still call my mother every day. It was very hard to make the break."

As Laura described her entry into life, she said, "Oh no. Look who I am being born to. Oh this is going to be dreadful. Oh no, I'm trapped for my whole life." It was only when she went to a particular past-life that she could understand the dread she felt in being born to this woman. Laura saw herself as a man, riding a beautiful white horse. The horse wore fine trappings with beautiful ornaments on the harness, and the rider himself was dressed in regal splendor. Laura saw herself as a prince and realized it must be in Italy, perhaps in a minor principality. Nevertheless, the lifestyle was quite grand. In this particular scene, she (he) was in the center of a town where banners were flying and the townspeople were celebrating. Yet it didn't seem to be a day out of the ordinary, rather the kind of festivity that permeated their existence.

Laura then saw a different scene in which there was another celebration, this time in front of the castle where she lived. The crowds were lusty in response to the jousting and festivities of all kinds. She saw herself in a box decorated with finery fit for a prince and filled with beautiful women, cheering for the men on horseback, who raced full tilt toward each other, lances drawn. At another point, she was a participant in the jousting and received many favors thrown by these women in the form of flowers, ornaments from their clothing or handkerchiefs coyly given. The life Laura saw held only one thing to mar the constant joy and pleasure of wine, women and song. She saw herself married to a woman who was devoutly religious. The woman dressed in black and harangued constantly about the sinfulness of the festivities. After years of this nagging, the prince simply had her put to death. He was then able to enjoy all that life had to offer, unfettered by the dour presence of his wife. It came as no surprise to me to hear Laura identify this woman. She said, "Oh... it's my mother. No wonder I feel so responsible for her."

Laura was courageous enough to participate with me in a radio show during which reincarnation and regression therapy were discussed. Before we began to tell Laura's story, she said, over the air, "Mother, I love you." She had not revealed the nature of her regression session to her mother but chose to tell her publicly what had emerged. Laura felt that after the experience, she would continue with a more normal expression of concern and caring about her mother's welfare. She felt released, on a very deep level, from the burden she had carried for centuries unconsciously.

Past-Life Persecution by Present-Life Mother

Belinda, a most capable woman, is the executive director of a new-age teaching center that she founded with her husband. Belinda has a quality of serenity and assurance that has obviously come from years of steadfast determination to hold true to what she believes to be her special destiny. During the years she waited for her husband to be free to marry her, she faced all kinds of obstacles that could have dissuaded her, including the disapproval of his family and especially that of her own mother. Her mother was highly critical of Belinda's faithful attachment to this very enlightened man, which had developed when Belinda decided that she wanted to study astrology. She found a teacher who had an excellent reputation and in fact was quite well known in his country for developing unique theories. She had no idea that they would become emotionally attached and fall deeply in love with each other at first sight. Her teacher was married to a woman who was homosexual, and therefore the marriage had never been consummated. However, because of the law of the country, he was unable to divorce her in order to marry Belinda. So it was up to Belinda to live in the knowledge of their love without any expectation of a future marriage. In her generation and social stratum, this situation was quite scandalous. Her mother threatened to disinherit her if she did not break off the relationship. However, Belinda was determined to stay true to her heart. Seventeen years later, the laws changed, and her teacher was free to marry her.

They shared many happy years of productive work. Belinda developed her own practice and provided invaluable assistance to her husband in his writing and research. When her husband died, some of her sadness was mitigated by the determination to keep their work alive. They had started the new-age center together, and although Belinda was not too keen on running it by herself, she rose to the occasion with great success. Although she had forgiven her mother for the pain she had caused, now that her mother was also dead, many bitter memories refused to disappear. Belinda asked me to do a regression session with her to clarify some matters.

Belinda was born with Sagittarius on the ascendant and with Capricorn as an additional ruler. Saturn, the ruler of Capricorn, is posited in the tenth house of public life and career, but that is also the sector of the chart that describes the relationship with the parent of the same sex. With several difficult aspects to Saturn, Belinda was born with a negative karmic tie to her mother.

Belinda reviewed her present life and saw the conditions surrounding her birth. She said, "My father is excited about having a child, but he wants me to be a boy. I've always been his daughter, for many, many lives. But when I see my mother, I feel like saying, 'Uh-oh. Things are going to be very rough.' A warning voice says, 'Be careful, things aren't the same, but you'll still have to watch your step.'" Belinda wasn't quite sure she knew what was meant by that warning voice, but she did know she would have to be careful. She said, "All through my life, when I was about to have some joy, I'd hear that voice of caution." I asked Belinda to examine a lifetime that would help her understand the conditions in the present.

Without hesitation, Belinda said, "It's in Spain. The name Burgos comes to my mind. I don't know why I say that but that's the name I hear. I'm a young girl about twelve years old. We have quite a nice hacienda. It's square, but spacious and very pretty. My father then is my father now. He's very important in the town, like the mayor or governor. My mother in that life is my present mother's cousin. I have been very close to her, especially when things were difficult. In that life, she's very religious. In that day and age, a very prestigious thing to do is send a daughter to a convent. So it is decided that I will enter the convent. It's a joint decision between my mother and father. I don't have a choice. I'm a girl who is so full of joy and life, but my attitude is dutiful. The convent is nearby, so I don't feel so badly about leaving my home. It's fun at first, but the mother superior of the convent doesn't like my spirit. Everything I try to do is wrong. If I try to do something nice, she misinterprets. She criticizes me constantly. I become angry, not sad. I try to stay out of her way, but it's too hard. She spoils it all.

"I can feel that I'm going to hate her, but that comes later on.

She's quite a bit older than the other nuns. For some reason, she singles me out for punishment. If I'm reading, she's jealous about my eagerness, intelligence and joy. After many years, when I'm twenty-one, I begin to hate her. She..." Belinda paused, and I could see her face changing. I ask, "What's happening?" She replies, "I'm burned. She pushes me on a stove or...I have a feeling there is someone who teaches me. I go to see a man to be taught and someone finds out. That person tells the mother superior and then I'm not allowed to go out of the convent. I am broken-hearted. She's going to make an issue of this. Of course they want me to testify that he was molesting me, but I won't do it, because it is not true. They throw me into a dungeon, but I don't care. It's my choice not to denounce him. All I did was sit with him reading. It feels like a younger sister in the convent is jealous of me and tells her [Mother Superior] to win her favor. Oh...I'm studying astrology with him...it's my husband in this life! My father is broken-hearted. He won't believe I'm evil, but there is nothing he can do."

I asked Belinda if there was a trial. She replied, "There is some kind of public exhibition. The bishop makes an issue of this. I think the mother superior believes she was doing her duty, but the bishop takes it further than she wanted it to go. There is some sort of a room like a courthouse. I've been in the dungeon all this time. It seems that the trial is before only churchpeople, and I'm found guilty. When I'm sentenced, I'm very badly hurt. I'm condemned to being burned at the stake."

Belinda was speaking very quietly now. "I'm very scared of the stake. I think I learn how to leave my body. Just a minute ago I felt all hot, but now I don't feel a thing. It is a public execution. The townspeople are there." Belinda became very quiet for a time, then continued. "It comes to mind that I'm sorry for a little girl named Anna who is watching all this. She is only seven and she is so shocked." After another pause, she said, "Little Anna is you." I confirmed this by saying, "I know." (Belinda was one of the people who also saw the Spanish incarnation, first revealed to me on my train ride through the Pyrenees. A therapist from England also pointed up my lifetime in Burgos during her regression session.)

When Belinda opened her eyes, she was very solemn. She said, "The mother superior was my mother in this life. Once again she hated my husband in this life, just as she hated him as the teacher in that time. She almost cut me out of her will because of him, but for some reason, she changed her mind. I risked everything to be with him in the present. We fell in love at first sight and I simply couldn't walk away from him. My father, then and now, was quite a spectacle, a very dignified, important man. I think the mother superior had to live with the memory of what she had done. In this life, she actually talked to a minister about punishing me again. It's ironic that astrology is once again an issue. I said to myself so many times, 'I don't dare close my eyes or blink. I have to stay in control.'"

I asked Belinda if she thought there was another life in which this antagonism with her mother began. It seemed as though the mother superior had already taken a dislike to the young girl even before anything transpired that would cause such a reaction. Belinda said, "The first relationship was in an Atlantean temple. My mother was jealous of me then. It seems that in each life, I've had to learn to live with her. It was very hard in this life even before my husband entered the picture." We agreed that the penalty for harboring a grudge or any resentment was having to be closely associated with that very person again. It seemed extremely practical to develop compassion and tolerance in order to avoid the pain of repeating a difficult relationship again and again. The words "let it go" can take on a whole new meaning in the light of reincarnation, for they do not describe only an altruistic sentiment. They form a very practical maxim that may help to avoid unnecessary pain in a future life.

Compulsion for Motherhood from a Past Life

When Connie finished her regression session (see Saturn-Sun), she said to me, "I know who my mother was in that life." As often happens when someone has a special insight from a regression session, they suggest to a friend that he or she also share in the experience. So Connie felt sure that Jennifer (whom she had seen as her mother) would want to make an appointment with me. Once again, we agreed not to disclose what Connie had revealed through her session. Jennifer made an appointment, more to satisfy her curiosity than to get help for a specific problem, but as an actress she also felt she might open up some extra creative energy by reviewing her past experience. She was open and ready for the process. As she had had a great deal of therapy in her life, she was not resistant to the images that came into her mind.

She reviewed her childhood, and although her therapeutic work had helped reconcile the loss of her father when she was only two years old, she had new insights about that when she took another look. Jennifer had always felt that she didn't know her father because he committed suicide when she was so young. Her saddened childhood was made even more so because when she was only four, she went to live with a distant relative in a city far from her home.

Jennifer knew that when she left home at that young age, she was motivated by a need to help her mother. Although she was also excited by the prospect of adventure, she adored her mother and was only too aware of the hardships in her life due to the loss of her husband. She saw the moment when her "second mother" arrived to meet her. This woman was very magnetic, strong and intelligent, a contrast to her soft, sad, subdued mother. The new "mother" brought her a beautiful dress and promised toys as well as an exciting adventure in school if Jennifer wanted to come with her. It would be only for a few months, and then Jennifer would return to her mother's home during the summer months. It was clear that if Jennifer didn't want to go with her relative, her mother would not force it upon her. Practically speaking, it would be for the best, though, as Jennifer had a variety of people caring for her while her mother worked, none of whom she liked very much.

So Jennifer put on a facade of excitement about the visit. Her mother felt Jennifer would have experiences she couldn't provide for her in the small town where they lived. So each person, Jennifer and her mother, protected the other. The sadness of parting was covered by another side of the coin: relief on the part of the mother that Jennifer would be well cared for, and curiosity on Jennifer's part. However, Jennifer was very homesick. She never revealed this to her mother and exhibited very little to her second family. She started acting very early in life, not to appear ungrateful. Her summers were spent with her mother. But she was very much alone, as her mother worked during the day.

So deep down, Jennifer was a lonely child, covering all that by exhibiting a very strong personality. A scene popped into her mind that conveyed the actress within. She saw herself in her second mother's bedroom, dressed in scarves and furs, peering into the mirror saying to herself, "I am the princess of the world." Her second mother thought that everything Jennifer said and did was very precious, and she wrote copious letters to her mother to keep her appraised of Jennifer's progress. And Jennifer knew how much her second mother loved her. This woman said, "I couldn't love you more even if you had been born to me." So Jennifer had a deep sense of security even though she always had sadness as a counterpart.

Jennifer reviewed a scene in which her mother had fainted. She saw herself at age three absolutely panicked for fear something would happen to her precious mother. She felt this was the moment when she decided she must make her mother's life a little easier. She felt very powerful inside and sensed that she had a great deal of control over her life even at this young age. So her desire to relieve her mother of the extra burden she might impose set some esoteric plans in motion. She knew, in retrospect, that if she caused some things to happen and she wasn't totally thrilled with the results, she had no one to blame but herself. Therefore she could never complain or ask to come home again.

Next Jennifer reviewed her father's death. Jennifer first saw herself at two years old. She thought she was returning to her house from the nearby town. She was holding her mother's hand, and she could feel the pavement beneath her feet, so she knew she was not wearing shoes. As they approached the door, she saw many people standing on the porch. They seemed very sad and compassionate. As she and her mother approached the doorway, some of the people took her mother into the house and helped her into a chair. Jennifer was somewhat ignored at the moment, but then another person led her down a long hall to the kitchen, where she was placed on a counter and given a biscuit to eat. She was evidently crying for her mother, because she was taken into the room where her mother sat slumped in a chair and was placed in a small chair close by. It was then that she realized her father was dead. She also realized her mother had grabbed her up at the sound of a gunshot and had gone next door to notify a neighbor.

Jennifer reviewed this scene with the same tears pouring down her face. She said, "I know that I'm crying because the tears are wetting the biscuit as it goes into my mouth. To this day if I'm upset, I want to eat something. But what is significant about my tears is that they have nothing to do with my father. I seem to know what has happened because I'm utterly disdainful about him. I want to tell my mother, 'Who needs him? I'm here to take care of you. You don't have to worry.' My tears are due to the fact that she doesn't turn to me for comfort at all. She doesn't seem to know I'm there at that moment. It's almost as if I had thought she would want him out of the way. I don't feel responsible for his death at all, yet I do feel that perhaps if I had been a little nicer to him, I could have turned the tide and helped him over some rough spots. At that moment, I feel anguish because if I had known she cared so much or that she would be so lost without him, I might have been able to do something to prevent his despondency. I feel very abandoned and alone at that moment."

In the review of her birth, it was clear that Jennifer was not wanted at that particular time. She had known that her mother and father had an almost storybook romance. Her father had been married before to a woman who knew she was going to die. This woman was evidently remarkable, because she began to collect special things for her husband's new wife. Although he insisted he would never marry again, she insisted that he would and that he would also have the children they had never been able to bear together. She had borne two or three sons who were either still-born or had died shortly after birth. Jennifer went on to say, "There was a great deal of prophecy that surrounded my father's marriage to my mother and the advent of my sister and me. But after my sister was born, my mother had several miscarriages, some almost full term. When she was finally pregnant with me, the timing was very bad because of the depression. I see myself being born on the kitchen table! There seems to be a doctor and a midwife, or perhaps just a kind neighbor is also in attendance. I see the steam coming out of a big kettle on the stove and my mother being carried off to bed after my birth. She doesn't seem to be able to greet me. I'm not sure that she doesn't wish I were also stillborn. I think I chose this family almost rashly. It's as if at that moment I feel, I have no one to blame for this but myself! This predicament I find myself in seems to be because of my defiance. As if I had tried to be born to someone else and when she rejected me, I plunged in without checking things out properly."

Jennifer saw a prenatal scene in which her mother was telling her father about the pregnancy. He was very upset. Jennifer saw her mother crying, lying on the bed, with her father standing over her. In astonishment, Jennifer said, "I can't believe the attitude I have at that moment. It is as if I make a very defiant, rude gesture and say to him, 'Who needs you?' It appears as though I was born with that same outlook toward him and life. I suspect now that the bravado was a cover-up for a terribly sad feeling of not being wanted. I'm sure I decided to be a good girl and not give anyone any trouble. I probably decided right then that I'd leave home as soon as possible to be out of their way. Amazingly enough, I accomplished that within a few short years."

After Jennifer had a chance to assimilate all she had viewed about her present life, I asked her to go to a life that would deepen her understanding about the difficulties she had experienced.

She said, "I think there is a time when my family really got me into a mess politically. I have always been deathly afraid of politics. It seems too tricky, because you always gamble about being on the winning side." Suddenly Jennifer began to identify with a terror she said she had carried with her all throughout her life. She said, "I have had almost constant anxiety that I've had to push away from in order to exist. I remember that I was so terrified when I first began working in New York that I had to become fearless in order to cope."

I asked Jennifer to go to a time when that might have started. Her face became very pale, and she began to cry. Her crying was not gentle, however; she began to wail. She seemed to be seeing something very terrifying. She was so upset, she was not able to talk for a few moments. I encouraged her to put into words what she was experiencing. She said, "I'm in a tiny room, crouched in a corner, waiting to be executed. I'm like a small terrified animal, I'm so scared. It isn't fair, and I can't get to the person who could prevent this. I might even be pregnant, but that seems to be the issue behind my impending death. I can see out of a barred window overlooking a cobblestone road. It is like I'm on the floor above a driveway of cobblestones, but no vehicle goes on this roadway. Oh . . . it is the road where I will walk to the place of my death. It is to be a public execution and I see crowds of people gleefully awaiting my death. My guard is very sympathetic to my plight, but he can't do anything to help me or he'd lose his life. Someone is very vindictive toward me. He won't even let me get near him, because he knows I could convince him of the truth if I could see him. He wants me out of the way." Jennifer paused to consider what she saw. She said, "It's no use. There is absolutely nothing I can do to change this situation, and I fall back on my deep religious feelings. I've spent most of that time of imprisonment praying to God to turn this around if possible. I think I'm considered something of a witch, in fact, but I'm not. I see the clothes I've recently taken off and they are quite elegant. In fact, I haven't been in this small cell-like room for very long. I was living in a beautiful house, with my ladies-in-waiting to attend me. I don't think they are my real close friends, however, because there is no one near to give me comfort."

I asked Jennifer to identify the country where she is. She replied immediately, "England. In fact, I'm in the Tower of London awaiting my execution. I seem to be a very unpopular queen. I think I am..." It took much persuasion to convince Jennifer to name herself. "It seems I am Anne Boleyn. Of all the people in history I would least like to be identified with, I am sure I am she." I gave Jennifer a moment to consider all of this before I continued. "Let's review your death, so that you can dispense with it once and for all," I suggested. She was very sad but took on an air of great dignity by sitting up very straight and holding her head high. "I ask them to wait until I give them the signal to chop off my head. I compose myself and I see myself walking down that cobblestone roadway, past the jeering crowds to a slightly raised platform. There are some people seated nearby, but it seems there are crowds just a little way off in the distance. I beg for the mercy of God to help me keep my dignity, and suddenly I feel great calm and peace inside. I am innocent of the charges, so I walk to my death in innocence. I seem to be looking down on the people as if I am floating in the air. I think I leave my body, so I feel no pain at all. It looks like I take on a great air of purity and the crowds, far from continuing their taunts, are suddenly very quiet."

With this, Jennifer did a very strange thing. She began to laugh. She laughed and laughed until tears poured down her cheeks. I began laughing in response and asked her what was so funny. When she could stop laughing long enough to speak, she said, "It's all a cosmic joke! They can kill us and torture us, but we're still here!" I said I thought the session was over, but when Jennifer opened her eyes, I asked if there was anyone in that life that she knows in this one. "You bet I know some people. My business manager is Henry VIII. He's a very powerful man, and although we were very attracted to each other from the moment we met, I wouldn't have an affair with him. It was like life or death when I thought about having an affair with him in the present. I remember what happened when we were alone together. He is very persuasive, but I had a sudden unreasonable feeling of panic. It was so bizarre." Jennifer suddenly said, "My father then was my father now. I think he pushed me into the whole messy situation and was greatly benefited by my marriage to Henry. In this life, it is like we were face to face again, and I think he couldn't live with his guilt. My son was my brother then and was killed along with me. I think we were accused of having an affair. In fact the whole issue of my death is that I was supposed to be sleeping with a lot of men. That simply wasn't true. I was sacrificed for political gain, and because Henry wanted another woman as his wife."

Jennifer was suddenly very tired, but I suggested that she talk to her friend Connie to share what she had experienced. We agreed to have another meeting so that we could discuss the issues involved when she had a chance to be more objective. She did want to tell me one more thing. She said, "When I was in California about a year ago, I met a lovely doctor who was working with color healing. I was very interested in what he was doing and happy to find a medical man who was willing to try alternative methods. We had dinner and felt very comfortable with each other. I said to him, 'You must have been my physician in another life.' He looked at me and said, 'You were Anne Boleyn.' I simply laughed and dismissed it then. It was just too much for me to consider seriously at the time."

When I next saw Jennifer, some time had elapsed. She had many new insights to share with me about her regression session. She said, "I was able to identify my present-life mother in the life of Anne Boleyn. She was a lady-in-waiting and a good friend of my mother in that life, who was my second mother in this life. They knew each other very well. It was almost like my mother gave birth to me for her in this life, since she wasn't able to do it herself.

"It's funny about the birth of children in my family. There were so many stillborn babies or deaths early in life, just as in those days in England. Jennifer paused for a moment and seemed stunned by a thought. I asked what was going through her mind and she replied, "My father's name was Bolin. It is not the exact name, but it is close enough to be a bit shocking, and my sister's name is a female derivative. She must have been part of the family as well. Since my father was the same then and now, I understand how I felt I could have done something to prevent his suicide in the present. I could have forgiven him. Perhaps it is not too late. He was a handsome man in this life, but he would have been just as dogmatic now and he would have made my life a living hell, I'm sure. No wonder on one level I was relieved. But the most important thing I have to tell you is about seeing Connie and realizing that I was her mother then. I abandoned her by allowing myself to be killed. I know I was devastated about leaving her then. By chance, I had a stack of pictures with me when I saw her. Among the pictures was one of my business manager. I didn't say anything to alert her, but when she went through the photographs, she stopped when she came to his picture. She said to me, 'He was there, you know.' I said, 'Who do you think he was?' Connie said to me, 'I think he was my father!' Now how about that? Either we're all a bit loco, or we're really seeing the same situation."

But Jennifer had one very profound experience that belied her attempts to make light of the situation. She had read a book and had visited London since our session together. She continued, "I read a book by Carolly Erickson called *Mistress Anne*. In the book, she confirmed so much of what I had sensed, but the thing that amazed me was the description of her time in captivity before the execution. She was taken to the Tower and allowed to live in the house Henry had built for her but that she had never lived in before. So she did live in her former grand style. It was said that she was despondent, but would suddenly laugh uproariously, as if it were all a huge joke. Do you remember how I laughed at the end of my regression session? I can promise you that never happened to me before. I couldn't have made up that spontaneous reaction.

"When I went to London, I reluctantly decided to visit the Tower. I had such lumps in my stomach. I took the tour, and the Beefeaters described the events preceding her death and showed the spot where she was beheaded. It made my spine crawl. I also saw where she was buried. But the Beefeaters stressed that she was taken directly from her plush quarters to the execution spot. I felt very disoriented at that. Everything else felt so real and true. So afterward I walked around by myself. The house that Henry built for her had a green grass lawn, not cobblestones, and was directly in front of the execution spot. In my regression, I saw cobblestones and a walkway that kept me out of view of the crowd of people until I rounded a corner. I said to myself that memory plays tricks, but I knew I had not made up the whole scene. As I went through one of the apartments built right into the wall, I came upon a small cell-like room. I was absolutely transfixed. It was the exact cell that I had seen in my fantasy, except that everything seemed much smaller than in my mind's eye. That room was directly over a broad cobblestone walkway that led in the exact direction I had seen before. If I had gone down that walkway, I would have had to turn to go to the execution spot!

"In the book, it was said that Anne Boleyn was not pretty. She was not typical in her looks, and since there were many blond beauties around Henry, no one quite understood why he was attracted to her. She also had a sixth finger on one hand and was considered a witch. I have always been self-conscious about my hands, but more than that, my second mother always said to me, 'You're not pretty, but you're smart.' Even though she loved me a lot, she said that to me over and over again. I wanted to be pretty more than anything, but I think she was my mother then and constantly reassured me that Henry would be captivated by my intelligence and my charm even though I didn't have the same blond good looks as other women in the court."

Jennifer's chart reveals the Saturn square Moon aspect that indicates problems in connection with her mother, motherhood and the nurturing aspects in life. Her Moon is conjunct Uranus in the tenth house of career. That house describes her mother as well. So with such an aspect, it was clear that not only was Jennifer's mother frightened and vulnerable as a parent, she was suddenly removed from Jennifer's life. In connection with a career, Jennifer might be very sensitive to any possibility of recognition in her life and set up conditions, with Saturn square that aspect from the sixth house of work, in which she would overwork, develop health problems or take on an overload of responsibility. All that might be an attempt to avoid the spotlight again, for it indicates a fear and nervousness that Jennifer described very well. Jennifer seemed to finish what had been left undone before by making sure she would have children in this life. Although she might have chosen once again to abandon them, it became a motivating force in her life always to keep them with her. She knew why she had such a compulsion in this life to have children and why they represented her greatest security. She also confessed to an unreasonable fear about allowing deep emotional attachments in her life. In her case, to allow herself to be vulnerable was like a death sentence.

In each of the cases I described, mothering urges came into conflict. Kate had a son whom she cared for and loved as a single parent. Laura had no children because of her ties to her mother and because she had no man in her life. Belinda chose not to have children simply by falling in love with a man who couldn't father a child until they were both in later years. Her vision of the suffering of little Anna showed her concern for children, however. Jennifer had three children in this life but was a single parent after all as a result of her husband's early death. Therefore, she wasn't able to devote herself as totally to their upbringing as she would have liked. In each case, some kind of limitation was connected to the relationship with the mother and in turn to children. For each woman, developing nurturing feelings on a broader scale (e.g., working compassionately for the children of the world) may be the antidote to the karmic block.

CHAPTER SEVEN

Saturn and Mercury

ercury is the planet of the mind. It is indicative of all the activities associated with the left brain, such as dealing with details, facts and plans. It is related to the ability to organize, discriminate and collect data. It is primarily the part of the mind that observes, researches facts and makes choices. It describes clarity of thought, the learning process, communications and discussions. When Saturn is making difficult aspect to Mercury, all those abilities seem unavailable, repressed and difficult. A person tends to be judgmental about his ability to collect facts, speak and think, and that results in worry, negativity, doubt or overattention to detail. The individual with such a difficult aspect may become nitpicky and self-critical rather than observant and intellectually aware.

Since Mercury describes intellect, when Saturn overshadows that planet, one may doubt his intellectual ability or his learning potential. He may think he has to study longer than is really necessary. He may hesitate to speak his mind or express himself unless he has lots of data to back him up. A person with this aspect can be a doubting Thomas. His viewpoint is, "Prove it to me." On the other hand, he may believe anything that he reads in print, quoting someone else he considers to be an expert rather than speaking his own mind or expressing original opinions. He may ask many, many questions of others because he doesn't trust his logical mind to give him answers. But he may not really listen to the answers to his questions, as he has another ready to ask right away. He can hide behind his mind. If he can convince someone else to commit himself to a plan of action, he is relieved of the responsibility in case such a plan is not productive. He is free to make inward judgments about what has happened without risking exposure of his own ideas. He protects himself from criticism all the while he is being inwardly critical.

Sometimes this aspect can describe a slow, methodical way of thinking and speaking. It describes some difficulty in being objective or in trusting one's own sense of reason. The negative judgments the individual expresses are only reflections of the negative messages he has received in this life. He can do a lot to change his way of thinking by realizing he is merely repeating his parents' messages. He may have been told early in life that he mustn't think he is too smart or else... "people won't like you," "you won't be popular with the opposite sex," or "children should be seen and not heard." He may have simply copied those judgmental patterns by watching the behavior of his mother or father or other family members. Nevertheless, those negative thoughts protect him in some way and keep him safe. He may decide that if he shows his real intellect, he would reveal himself to be smarter than other members of the family and lose them as a result. Or he may fear the responsibility involved if he really acknowledges his ability to be a decision maker.

Edgar Cayce said, "The mind is the builder." In fact, the decisions we make about dealing with life and viewing the people around us set the patterns that are manifest in everyday life. Therefore our ability to make choices and to be clear and objective determines the circumstances of our lives. If we block that ability, deny or doubt it, the outer circumstances reflect that block by producing limited opportunities and difficult conditions. Objectivity may be the very asset that is lacking when this aspect is in evidence. It is probable that denial of the ability to think and reason may, on some level, be profitable for the person. If he thinks he can't, he can't. He is absolved of the responsibility and commitment to make good choices for his own well-being or that of others.

An overly cautious attitude about the thought processes may come from a past life. With Saturn in hard aspect to Mercury, no doubt serious blocks to expression, thinking or learning come from past-life conditioning. For instance, if a person had been killed, ridiculed or imprisoned for speaking out, he would naturally come into this life resisting expression of that kind again. Usually this aspect is related to a memory of having had to make an important decision, not only for oneself but for others. If that decision proved detrimental to himself or to many people, it is clear why he would carry guilt and blocks to the expression of that energy into the present.

Since the conditions in one's present life are so directly related to thought processes, it is essential that one clear away any mental blocks. In fact, with Saturn in hard aspect to Mercury, there is even more reason to heal past wounds, resolve self-doubt and develop constant vigilance over the mental processes. If poor choices existed in the past, one must be especially diligent to observe any tendency to negativity in the present. Otherwise the same conditions are perpetuated ad infinitum. To take that a step further, present-day thought sets in motion not only the conditions that will exist for the balance of this life but also for a future life.

There are two examples of individuals having made bad choices in the past that caused difficulties in the present. In one situation, the decision affected many people. In the other, the decision was confined to a family situation but nevertheless produced tremendous guilt feelings and restrictions in the present.

LACK OF TRUST IN FORESIGHT

In Andrea's regression session, a wealth of information simply poured forth. Many facts seemed very close to the surface of her consciousness. She began by describing a time when she was very

sick. She described her mother's bedroom in great detail, for that
room played a significant part in a painful experience for her. It
was Thanksgiving time and she had turkeys on her mind, so she
decided to draw a really beautiful one on the walls of her mother's
bedroom. She said, "I don't like to share a room with my sister, so
I go into my mother's room. It has such nice wallpaper and it is
brand new! There is a chair at the window, so I take out my
broken crayons to draw a great big turkey. It's fun to draw with
broken crayons instead of new ones. I can be hard with this one
and if I break it, I don't care. Oh, I love those tall tail feathers! I
make the turkey as big as I can make it. I use a lot of purple, but it
doesn't look like a turkey too much. I thought I could do better. I
am clearly disappointed that it doesn't look so much like I know I
can draw it. I'm really enjoying drawing that turkey."

Andrea went on to describe the frustration she felt when the
turkey didn't come out the way she thought it would. Her voice
was that of a disappointed child, and tears were running from her
eyes. "I'm so surprised the turkey doesn't look like those pictures
in the book because I know I can do that. It doesn't look like a
turkey and I worked and worked on those tail feathers. I'm so
upset because my muscles don't work like they're supposed to. I
know I can draw, but I don't know why my muscles don't work
right. I don't like being a child very much." She went on, "I was
going to give the turkey drawing as a gift. I've been sick about a
week and I need to get some attention."

Then the underlying motivation to draw on her mother's walls
began to dawn on her. She continued, "I know I will get punished. My mother's doing the washing and can't hear what I'm
doing. My sister is in her crib. She's not too old. In fact, she just
got here. I don't like Ann. I get sick and almost die." Now the
tears really began pouring from her eyes. "I'm sitting on my dad's
lap. He's holding me and he's telling me everything's going to be
all right." But then the punishment came. "I'm starting to put my
things away when she comes in. I had finished my drawing. She
comes in from the bathroom and there's nothing nice about it.
She's so angry she doesn't say anything. Oh, she's so angry. She

takes my crayons and puts them away. I thought she was going to hit me but she doesn't. They have just papered the bedroom and I've drawn all over it. Oh, she's so angry. I have to sit on the toilet with the seat down while she finishes the laundry. She's so mad, she just yanks me around. I would rather be spanked than confined...all the hot water and that awful washing machine. I love mechanical things, but all those clothes are so dirty and the room is so steamy. It's just awful sitting there."

As Andrea talked about her reaction to the punishment, another realization dawned on her. She began to be almost hysterical in her expression of her feelings. "My dad has to work where he gets his clothes all dirty. He hates it and I blame my mother. Daddy is a scholar. He should study spaceships and space travel. I don't know whether she makes him work like that or if he does it himself. She likes the things that money buys, even though she pretends not to. But I know better! Daddy chooses. He could have done something else...it would have been hard, but he could have done it." After a pause she said quietly, "I'm not sure she's happy."

Andrea went to a past life without any prompting, bypassing the circumstances of her birth. She said, "My head hurts. I'm trying to see something. I'm a man and I'm a leader of some kind. I seem to be on a ship and I'm a lookout....Ah, I'm a Viking." I asked her to describe what she saw about that ship and the situation around her. She continued, "It's day, but it's slightly overcast. I'm looking hard out to sea, but I don't know what I'm looking for. I suspect I'm on the lookout for trouble, but I don't know whether it's another ship or something from the land. I'm on the part of the water that is now the North Sea. There are over a hundred men, but no women, on the ship. I think we're using oars. It seems to be a warship, but if it really is a warship, I don't understand why we seem to be looking for a settlement. We're quite near Ireland." Andrea paused to sort out her confusion about the ship, the men and their purpose for being out at sea. She said after a moment, "We didn't have to leave where we were, but I have convinced them to leave. I think I'm a kind of magician or . . . I think I have dreams . . . I seem to have the sight . . . yes, I had a vision. I know that we'll be happier, but I'm also afraid because I know we'll lose some people. We'll have to fight, but eventually it will be for the betterment of everybody."

Andrea continued her tale. "I am very careful to choose some people to go along on the voyage who I know we are going to lose. I know who is going to survive and who is not. We're going to settle somewhere but I'm not sure where that is. We have a lot of livestock on board, but I don't see any horses. There are some people on oars on the boat, but they seem to be banked. The wind is howling and it is just magnificent. We do have to battle and there are people lost. We settle somewhere and eventually it is wonderful, but I feel a tremendous guilt at selecting the people to go on this exploration, especially because I know some won't make it." Andrea became very thoughtful. Then she said, "I think I get these visions and I blank out. It's like going into a trance. I think I'm not really responsible when they happen."

Spontaneously Andrea continued with, "There is another lifetime where I have the sight. I'm absolutely fearless. My God, I am absolutely huge. I'm so strong, I can carry a double-headed ax and swing it over my shoulder. This is the time of William the Conqueror. William is an invader. I see a bridge and I know I'm killed. There is some kind of trickery." I asked Andrea to look further to discover what happened. She replied, "I have a brother and I love him so much. I also have a wife named Matilda and children. Women fought in those days and she is fighting with me. I am told she was killed and I lose control. Because I lose control, I lose my sight. I don't go with what my senses tell me. The rage. . . . Oh Lord, the rage. But Matilda isn't killed and the children aren't killed!

"There is a man I trust. He is one of my lieutenants. I think he is jealous. I think he wants Matilda, so he tells me she is killed, knowing how I'll react. He doesn't get her, though. Because of my rage, I just go in there and am killed and so are many others. Because of that rage, I just can't think, so I am just like a bull. We had been beating them. We had done such a good job, but when I lose control, I lose my vision and we lose all those people." Andrea began crying with sadness over such devastation and loss. I asked her to describe herself so that she could move on to the next stage of her session. She said, "I am just huge, just solid muscle. I'm a Saxon. I see scars all over my body. You know, I am crying then, too, because I know our days are numbered. I know all this is coming. You know we are accused of eating something that stimulates us so we are fearless in battle, but we aren't high on potents and stuff. That is wrong. I psych the men up for battle by talking to them. I do it with my mind."

I asked Andrea an important question. I asked her to see if the man who betrayed her is with her in this life. She gasped and said, "It's Anne, my sister." I asked her what her reaction was when Anne was born. She replied, "I don't like her. I don't like her the minute she is born. She did the same things to me in this life. She has this super personality, so I was always told, 'Oh, you're Anne's sister.' I actually hated her. She was so jealous of me then, but now I've had to swallow a lot from her." I asked Andrea how she thought this information would help her in her relationship with her sister. She responded, "I just won't compete with her now." Then she continued by saying, "I feel very sad that I don't have any of those qualities now that I had then. Actually I'm terrified of all those abilities because I don't know where they come from. I certainly can't *see* in this lifetime."

Once again, Andrea saw another lifetime very easily, belying her last statement. She continued, "I'm seeing Egypt. I misuse the power in that life. Oh no, I'm leading armies again. I see chariots and armies. It's not a good war, and I'm using my power to foretell bad times. I know what is going to happen, and I feel so alone. I'm scared to death of what I'm doing. I don't trust what I see. I try to use it for protection, but it seems I fail a lot of people." I asked Andrea to be specific about herself. She said, "I'm a woman and I am in love with this man. He trusts me and it is like a game. We have to plot and plan. I have to lead these people, but I am supposed to find people who are vulnerable and lead them." Andrea appeared very grave and shook her head. She went on to say, "I just want to go around peacefully, but it seems I am born into this responsibility. I keep seeing a woman who is prodding me. Oh, it's my mother in this life!" I suggested that she had at least seen the karmic tie she had with both her mother and sister in this life, and I asked her, "Why did you have to be born to your mother again? Was it to resist her? Have you let her win in this lifetime?" She replied, "Yes." I asked, "Will you let that happen again?" She said, "I don't know. I think I have to use the awareness that she is not evil, but just determined to have her own way. I must trust myself more. In that lifetime, we are expanding and I have to give all the directions. People don't know I have the sight and I have to keep it quiet for so long. Someone is in power and is using my information to manipulate the people, some of whom are very gullible. No wonder I don't want to make decisions for anything, but especially in my own life. That's why I let my mother and sister take over, in a sense. I feel so guilty about the things I did with my gift in those past lives. This explains a lot to me about myself. I simply have to learn to trust myself completely and rely on what I know is right to say and do."

Andrea's regression session confirmed what I had seen in her astrological chart. With Saturn opposite Mercury, she was still reacting to situations from past lives and blocking her ability to think and speak. Saturn is placed in her second house of financial matters, with Mercury in opposition in the eighth house of transformation. If Saturn was not blocking the mercurial energy in her chart, Andrea's greatest gift to humanity would be to give information to people, especially since Mercury rules her ninth house of publishing, lecturing, speaking. It is a co-ruler with Venus of the tenth house and describes an especially beautiful speaking voice and an ability to disseminate information with grace and charm. It can indicate diplomacy as well. But because Saturn is blocking all that energy in her chart, she resists her ability to be a decision maker. She is capable of finding solutions for people and giving out valuable information, but her inner voice dictates, "Don't make decisions or suggest to people what they should do. Remember the past when you suffered so much!"

Right thinking is the quality that sets up the conditions in this life and the one to follow. Rather than avoiding using that quality, Andrea, in her newfound decision to trust her thoughts, needs to analyze any lack of clarity in her mental processes to see why she would choose the negative aspect of the mind rather than the positive. Finally, she will learn to analyze and process data, making a decision or a choice in her life, rather than just reacting to situations and people in a passive way. She gained tremendous insight about the need to live her own life when she said, "I need to rely on what *I* know is right to say and do."

DESTRUCTIVE DECISION FROM THE PAST

Although Andrea's sense of "sight" and the decisions that were made as a result affected the lives of many people, Ted had a different view of how his decisions affected him. In Ted's astrological chart, Saturn is in opposition to Mercury. Saturn is placed in the tenth house of the father and career matters, with Mercury placed in the fourth house of home and mother. Saturn rules the sixth house concerning work patterns, so it is clear that Ted puts himself under a lot of pressure with his work and career. Mercury rules the eleventh house of associations and the second house of money in his chart. All those areas in his life would be under heavy restrictions. He would be very responsible and very diligent. However, Ted may not allow himself to be in a position to make decisions for groups of people, especially when financial matters are concerned.

Ted started his regression session by describing the Saturnian condition he was born into. He said, "My father is thirty-eight and my mother is forty when I am born. My mother couldn't have children so she thought she had a tumor when she was pregnant with me. Even though they haven't planned for me, my father is thrilled. However, my mother is feeling very inadequate. She is saying to herself, 'Oh my God, how do I take care of him?'" I asked Ted why he would pick such a family to be born to? His response did not directly answer the question. He said:

I feel heat and humidity, and wet, like a jungle. It's oppressive. It's not Africa, but more like Mexico. It's a rain forest and it's coastal. I'm very small and the forest is huge. I'm a male about ten years old. I almost wonder if I'm a person, everything around me is so big. It seems as if I'm from a place that is very dry... New England. I'm not a native, I'm white and I'm in this area all alone. I am taken to Mexico by my parents because we're moving. Everyone in the family is uprooted. I have three older brothers. My parents are very severe and very religious. I have wandered into the forest and now I'm lost. However, I think I have run away. My pain is that I just don't belong to these people (my family). They don't want me and I feel very much an outsider. The others are a whole unit and I'm just outside that circle, so I run away to change my circumstances.

It's midday and I just walk into the jungle, which will hide me. My parents make no attempt to find me. I'm not frightened. I eat fruit to survive, I think mainly bananas. It's warm and I'm walking to the ocean. I'm on a cliff that one can go down to the ocean and a beach. It's beautiful. I'm not hurt, and I find a job working around nice people. I work around the ocean. I can feel rope and chains, so it must be around boats. I'm not unhappy. I have no family and I live to be around fifty-six years old. The best thing is that I'm breathing and am free.

I asked Ted if he knew anyone from that life in the present and he said no.

I suggested that Ted go to a life where he might have had some karma with his father and where he might have been in a position of some prestige. He replied, "It's England around 1550. My station in life is upper class. It seems I'm the son of important people. When I look at my house, I see woods around it. Inside there are wooden walls, wooden furniture, and it's very spacious. It's not elaborate, but it's comfortable. There is a good relationship within the family. There is a mother, father and a sister and myself. We all really like each other. My father is in a position of authority. Oh, he is the same father I'm born to in this life! He seems to be a financial adviser to the court. It is possible that Queen Elizabeth is the ruler. I don't go to court, but I see it from the outside. I go to school and I think I am being groomed for this level of society, not nobles or within the court but a safer level of society...like high tradesmen...comfortable but not nobility. Perhaps to succeed, my father is working with financial matters.

"My sister is pretty and blond. She's very nice." Ted paused long enough for me to ask him what was going through his mind. He replied, "It just came into my mind that I have a thing for my sister...it could have been a physical thing." After another long pause, in which Ted was obviously searching for truth, he said, "I think I do have a sexual relationship with her. I think people know, but it's not acknowledged openly. People sweep it under the carpet. There's no disgrace...it doesn't exist for them. But I think it does something to me. She goes away to marry someone in the north. I'm terribly upset. We know she has to go, but..." I asked Ted if he could evaluate his pain on a scale of one to ten, how upset would he find himself. He replied, "About a four. After that I drift. Business doesn't interest me and I have lost some sort of reason or will to continue...not to live but to go on." Ted released a deep sigh of sadness. He said, "I do care. It's really about a level of a ten. I am doomed to start with. I decide to enjoy my relationship with my sister while I can, knowing our physical expression is going to end. I'm willing to let it go, but I am a changed person. I go through the motions. The light, the ambitions fade. I live to be forty-three. I have no guilt, but it changes my life. If I met her today, the love would still be there. So in that life, I am a failure." I asked Ted if he knew this woman in the present life. He replied, "No."

Ted volunteered, "Somewhere I was very important. I have been fighting that ever since." I asked where that might have been and what position he might have occupied. He said, "I want to say Egypt. I am a ruler. I have power and I'm a good ruler, but I am alone. I can see a lot of silver and gold. It's funny, I've been fascinated by Egypt all my life. When I was in the fourth and fifth grade at school, I would read about Cleopatra and Ramses. I'm comfortable there. I like the air and the heat. I made sure I visited Egypt as soon as I could in this life." Ted went back to his view of a past life. "I'm a pharaoh. I see lustrous golden fabrics. I've been born to this role and now I have assumed the position. I'm only twenty-three. Lots of people come and go, but it has a rhythm to it. There's such an air of tranquillity and peace. I'm not at all uncomfortable with my role. I've inherited a peaceful climate. All the wars are gone. I'm married, but I see myself alone. Oh, I'm married to lots of wives. I'm heterosexual in that life and I have twelve wives. They're different for different moods. I seem to have eight children. The fly in the ointment is, 'Can I keep it this way?' I have enemies. There is a lot of jealousy. My enemies seem to be the religious leaders of that time. If I am a divinity and they're divinity, it is very difficult. There is no war, no overt thing, but the priests want more power. I keep them happy with scraps of power. There is an element of danger that can't be removed, however."

Ted paused in his view of that lifetime and took a deep breath. "There is one man, third in line, who could be trouble. I see him in an orange robe and he is bald. He tries to poison me, but someone else dies. Oh, it's one of the women. It is much better not to confront this openly, however. I'm very upset. I decide I'm going to get him and I do! I make it look like an accident and I have him removed. I live to be about fifty-six, and my contribution is architecture and beauty. Order is my way of life. It's intolerable to have that level of consciousness and come into the restriction of this life!"

I asked Ted to review his position in the two lives he had just related. He said, "In England I ran away from responsibility. The two images in my mind are that in one life, I had power and responsibility, and in the other, I had a lack of responsibility. All my life I have fought a battle with myself not to assume authority and responsibility. I seem to hide from that, but I get it anyway. The big question is this: If I had done so well in Egypt, why wouldn't I have kept the same role throughout the thread of life? The image of the pharaoh is golden. In England, it is still sunny. But in this life, the direction has changed."

I suggested that we look more closely to see where the strongest guilt might lie. Ted continued, "I think in England I might

have hurt my sister. I didn't hurt her physically, but sexually...
not a rape, but I want to say something about a child. I think
there's birth of some kind, maybe a miscarriage. Some damage
was done to her, but not violently." Ted had a look on his face that
indicated the sight of something very painful. He said, "Oh, the
child is born and is killed. My father kills the child. It is a male
child and I know that boy in this life. He is an eighteen-year-old
boy who is the son of a friend of mine. I feel like crying. I defi-
nitely feel a responsibility for this boy. There's a lot of guilt from
England. It's amazing that I carry the shadows from that life into
this one.

"When I first said my pain was on a level of a four, it was just a
deadening of myself, so that I wouldn't feel. If I get in touch with
that feeling now, it will be total annihilation. The feeling that
emerges is terrible sadness that I poisoned someone with my
penis. In this lifetime, most of my relationships have been with
men. I like women very much, but at the same time, I feel as
though I am poison." I suggested that we rewrite the script of his
life in England. In other words, if we could recast his painful
experiences from the past life, then *those* would be the images he
would carry over into this life. I said, "How could you rewrite the
script from 1550?" Ted said, "We could have taken the child and
run away. We were weak. I didn't take responsibility for making
the right choice then. I was very weak, and there was a lack of
action. The reaction, as a result of taking action, scares me. I pull
back. I can see myself being pulled between being in the light in
Egypt and being shoved aside now. It is clear that I must remain
in the position where I make clear choices. I can't allow other
people to make my decisions for me. Evidently I just let my father
take over in the life in England, and do something that I'm still
suffering for. I feel so paternal toward this eighteen-year-old boy.
But it is not easy, because eighteen-year-olds are difficult. He is
the son of a woman who doesn't take responsibility for him. She
is my friend, but he is not my son in this life." I suggested that
Ted follow his instincts and trust himself to make the right decisions now. He said, "I certainly don't want to do anything that

will harm another being. I can see how dreadful the results are. I will just have to trust myself to have the right motivation. In that way, I won't hurt him and perhaps I can do some good for him in this life."

By the end of his regression session, Ted had also answered my question, "Why would you choose to be born to a family who weren't ready for you and were not necessarily joyous about your birth?" He had already recognized the karmic tie with his father, as his present-life father was the father in England. He realized he had to forgive his father for the decision he'd made in the past and also take greater control of making right choices in the present. In reviewing all three lifetimes, we see that in Egypt, he had a great deal of people around him and a large family. In England, he had a loving family but abused that family situation. In New England, he was born to a family who clearly didn't care about him and who couldn't really understand his level of consciousness. Finally, in this life, he began to climb back up to a level where he could have some kind of family ties, even though they were not very satisfying. As a result of his new awareness, Ted can begin to make decisions about the rest of his life as well as the lives to come. He may decide to set up conditions that will allow him to have loving family relationships once again, with the resolve that he will treat them with sacred respect. Most of all, Ted can begin to take on the ultimate responsibility in his life. He can climb to the true level of his career potential simply by choosing to assume a leadership role once again. He may even tap an ability to make financial decisions that might have been his career destiny in the Elizabethan life. He will allow himself the privilege of gaining more control over his own life by consciously making right choices. For, again, it is the conscious choices we make that set up future conditions.

In the regression sessions of both Andrea and Ted, decisions played an important part in the conditions of their past and present lives. Both Andrea and Ted have resisted taking charge of their own lives, allowing others to make the choices for them. Andrea's lack of desire to be the captain of her own ship was due to the pain of watching others suffer for what she knew was right for the group. For Ted, guilt over an incestuous relationship and the consequent death of his child, as well as the decision of having to remove a rival in self-defense, leave him reluctant to be in any decision-making situations again. Now aware of how important it is to learn to make right choices, both Andrea and Ted have decided to grasp the reins of their own lives more tightly.

CHAPTER EIGHT

Saturn and Venus

V *enus* is the planet that describes love, beauty, pleasure, tranquillity and art. It indicates activities such as theater, entertainment and social situations. It describes architecture, interior design and furnishings as well as clothing, beauty products, paintings and fabrics. It rules such things as jewelry, perfumes and flowers and indicates sociability, graciousness and charm. In short, Venus is connected to any situation, object or person related to pleasure in life. Most important, Venus describes the expression of love. When it is well aspected in a natal chart, an individual is blessed with harmonious relationships and demonstrations of love through touching and hugging and is easily able to express his love and affection as well. In its highest sense, Venus describes love for mankind or the desire for social justice and fairness for all of humanity.

Venus is one of the two "benefics" in the lineup of planets, Jupiter being the other. Therefore, the negative side of the energy of Venus is not destructive or bad. It is more often nonproductive. The person is not lazy in the usual sense of the word, but he may hesitate to take action for fear of disrupting the peace and harmony he has so far achieved. His need for pleasure, harmony and beauty in life is so pronounced, he may take the easy way out in many situations in which more dynamic action is called for. He can be overly adaptive, that is, he can adapt to others' wishes rather than stand up for what is fair and right in a diplomatic way. The now-passé expression of "cop-out" is a perfect illustration of this principle of passivity. He may be overly indulgent in his quest for pleasure and ease of living.

When Saturn casts its shadow over Venus, life can seem lacking in pleasure, relationships may not provide the demonstration of love that is desired, and harmony may be difficult to achieve. In general, affection and harmony may seem limited in some way. From a karmic point of view, there may be guilts carried over from past-life situations that prevent ease of living in the present. An individual may keep himself under tight rein as far as pleasures are concerned, denying his need for social expression and harmony in relationships. In many instances, a person may push away love on an unconscious level. An attraction to the very conditions and people who will not respond to his overtures of love may be a perverse way of satisfying his guilt over an unremembered past-life situation.

When there is a hard aspect between Saturn and Venus in a natal chart, it may describe a latent artistic talent that has never been acknowledged. Sometimes a client only needs encouragement through the reading of his astrological chart to allow him to develop that latent talent. He may deny much inner joy and self-satisfaction, until someone else says, "You can do it." One woman with a grown family and grandchildren confessed to a secret yearning to explore an artistic talent. She had never had the courage to join an art class. When such a talent was indicated in her horoscope, she dared to begin a new adventure in her life. After a short time, she was able to present members of her family with her original paintings. She had a deep psychological block about her artistry from a past life when she had neglected her family and ignored a political responsibility by devoting herself to art. In the present life, she had satisfied her need for duty and could then allow pleasure from her art to come into full expression later in life.

The description of this aspect in the horoscope may be different, depending on its placement in the chart. For instance, I may talk about the affectionate nature by saying, "You may have had a great deal of love, affection and hugging as a child, yet it was not enough." With this aspect, a person may feel safer with less demonstration of affection than with too much. It seems that along with comforting reassurance from another person comes the fear of deprivation. Perhaps karmic memories of the loss of a loved one overshadows a present need for affection in life.

With Saturn in difficult aspect to Venus, many times a woman marries a man she knows will provide material comforts, but later finds him unwilling or unable to make basic efforts to ensure harmony in the marriage. He may be too busy to spend cozy moments with her or refuse on principle to acknowledge her efforts to dress well or look beautiful. In such cases, the woman suffers deeply over the lack of love in her life, although she may have the outward manifestations of a luxurious, harmonious life-style.

The same can be true of a man with Saturn square Venus in his chart. He can marry a woman who appears to be someone he can feel proud of. She may be beautiful and a good hostess. Yet behind closed doors, she is less than affectionate and loving. One man was married for many years, with teenage children, when he suddenly acknowledged that his attraction to his wife was mainly due to an ethereal kind of beauty that seemed pure and untouched by any ugliness in life. At that late stage of his marriage, he realized that she was merely cold and undemonstrative. It came as quite a shock that all his efforts to capture the elusive quality she seemed to possess would always go unrewarded.

How could a person be so deceived in his expectations of a lifelong partner? The answer may lie in a look at past-life loves. We seem to attract the person we need to ensure spiritual growth, not someone we think we desire on a personal basis. Especially in the case of Saturn/Venus, an individual may feel safer with deprivation for fear of self-indulgence or as a way of punishing himself for love expressed in a past life.

Until a person takes a good look at the past-life indulgence or loss that may have preconditioned the quality of happiness in this life, he may unconsciously try to rectify the imbalance by depriving himself and rationing the flow of love. As well as punishing himself in his personal life, he may also hide from involvement in areas in which he could make a contribution in a higher social sense and thereby have a different kind of love flowing into his life. He can run from situations that promise joy, fearing that he will cause unhappiness in the lives of others or fail in his efforts. He may look instead to nonproductive, difficult or punishing conditions that somehow represent safety. But with a closer look at the origins of this deprivation of love, the person sees how harmony can be restored. It is by making a contribution and sending forth love, whether on a personal or humanitarian level, that the doors can be opened for the inflow of greater joy, peace and harmony.

Many times when Saturn is in difficult aspect to Venus, a review of a past-life situation will reveal that the individual has taken his own life. The penalty for suicide in one life is loneliness in another. The basic theory is that if one has taken himself away from others, he will be deprived of companionship in the future. But the deep wounds that may have led to a suicide can be healed by sending love to the self. For most people, self-love is the hardest kind of love to express. During a regression session with Paula (see Saturn-Neptune), her loneliness in the present, even in the prenatal stages, came from a memory of a past-life suicide. (Rarely does Saturn make only one difficult aspect in a natal horoscope. In Paula's case, Saturn is inconjunct Venus as well as conjunct Neptune. Since the Neptune aspect is especially strong in her life, I placed her recollection of a past-life situation in that chapter.) Paula saw that in a past life, she had left her husband and tiny daughter because the situation had seemed very restrictive to her. She lived alone, loveless, but was quite happy until she had a chance meeting with the daughter she had abandoned twenty years before. Her mother-love swelled in her heart, but it was too late for the relationship to blossom. In despair over what she had done, she took herbs that caused her to die. In this life, she was most fortunate to have that daughter with her once again. Yet her guilt and pain over the past-life situation tempted her to abandon her daughter all over again. She tried to abort her, but it was too late. She felt grateful to her daughter for forcing her way into this life. As a result, Paula can heal the past and her tendency to push away love, pleasure and ease of living in the present. Most of all, Paula needs to forgive herself for past mistakes and learn to love the true self within the shell of her present body.

MOTHER-LOVE

One young man recalled a situation that was just the opposite of Paula's memory. He reviewed an important, deep love relationship from the past that blocked all his attempts to have satisfying love in the present. Sandy had been married only once and had no desire to repeat the experience. Although his good looks and charming personality brought lovely women to his side, he seemed unwilling to form any kind of permanent attachment.

In a regression session, he saw himself living in Egypt in a very high position. He was married to a beautiful woman whom he loved deeply. She loved him in return, and life was simply beautiful. When his wife died, the devastating loneliness he felt without her physical presence was too much to bear. He saw himself dissolving into a purple light, and then acknowledged that he had committed suicide. He was born to that same woman in this life. He had never been able to communicate any love or affection to her in the present and rarely allowed himself to acknowledge how deeply he cared for her. When he saw that his ancient love could be recaptured in the present life, on a different level due to the change of relationship, he began to make new contact with his mother. By fully revealing and expressing his affection for her he freed himself to allow a love relationship to flourish in his personal life. He, too, had to heal the wounds caused by the searing pain of a former loss. Subconsciously he had said to himself, "I never want to love again if I am only to lose it eventually through separation." But he clearly saw that there is no real separation and therefore no need to deprive oneself of deep affection.

With all Saturn-Venus aspects, the deeper understanding of love is important. The individual must understand that the flow of universal love is constant. In personal relationships, that love is brought into a sharper focus, as though forced into a special beam or prism. The fleeting love or sense of attachment from one life carries with it the pain of separation. Yet it is still only a tiny refraction of the greater light of universal love. When relationships change from one life to another, the quality of universal love simply flows into another channel. We are able to experience love in mother-daughter or mother-son relationships or as siblings. That same love may flow in a man-woman, husband-wife vein. Nature's gift of changing relationships allows us to experience the different facets and prisms of the same love flow. Sometimes this change of relationship with the same person from life to life can present problems.

Ellen reviewed a past life spent in England. She was able to describe her house in vivid detail. She saw a beautiful tapestry on a wall next to a large, wood-carved staircase leading to an upper level. She saw herself walking up that staircase and knew that she was a young boy about twelve years of age. When she followed herself up that staircase (which she was able to do only with great reluctance), she saw a bedchamber rich with wall hangings. In the center of the room was a bed hung with draperies that were typical of that time in England. Upon that bed was a lovely young girl, whom she recognized as her sister in that life. She saw herself, as that young boy, making love to his sister as often as possible. They were deeply in love with each other. Unfortunately, or fortunately, the relationship between the brother and sister was discovered by their mother and father. Their punishment was separation from each other. Although Ellen, as a grown man, married in that life, he was never as much in love with his wife as he was with his sister. In the present time, the sister has returned as Ellen's daughter. With Saturn square Venus in her astrological chart, Ellen came into this life to work out negative considerations about love. Saturn rules her twelfth house, the one associated with karmic, racial guilt, whereas Venus is posited in the

fifth house, describing children, creative self-expression and romance. It is clear that any children Ellen might have in this life are
probably karmic relationships from the past, and expressing love
to them is an important issue. It became clear to Ellen that she
was not demonstrating as much affection as she felt for her
daughter simply because of her guilt from another life. She realized that in this life, her love was clearly channeled in a mother-
daughter relationship and she need have no fear of revealing her
affection. As a result, she finally felt free to be more demonstrative
to her child. A similar situation was recalled by Ted in the chapter
Saturn-Mercury. In Ted's situation the karmic block affected his
decision-making ability whereas for Ellen, it was an expression of
affection and love that suffered in this life.

UNDERSTANDING HOMOSEXUALITY THAT STEMS FROM THE PAST

Keith has Saturn inconjunct Venus in his chart. However,
Venus is conjunct Mars and Mercury, all posited in the fifth house
of creative expression, talent and romance, indicating a tremendous block or denial in those areas. Since Venus rules his ascendant, I chose to include Keith's story in the Venus chapter. Keith's
Saturn is placed in the twelfth house of the subconscious. Whenever I see this placement, I describe it as a karmic, racial guilt. In
Keith's case, I would describe it as a block to true creative potential caused by some situation in a past life in which he neglected
his group or shirked some kind of responsibility. It can indicate
karmic guilt of omission or commission in connection to responsibility of the highest order.

Keith began his regression session by describing the lack of love
and affection in his childhood. He talked about the state of his
family relationships when he was seven years old. "I don't have a
very warm and loving family. Everyone is living in their own little
world and they are very judgmental. I actually think they are all
crazy. I have strong ties to my family and I know some things they
don't know. Yet they can teach me some things I don't know. I go
away to play just to get away from them and to work off steam

and frustration. Everyone calls me a sissy because I dress up in girl's clothes and I dance. My brother is mainly the one who calls me that. I don't think I'm a sissy, but I am scared a lot. I feel a lot of isolation. No one is at home when I get there, so I don't have anyone to comfort me if I get hurt. I go to my grandmother when I need something."

Keith reviewed a memory of the separation of his father and mother. He said:

I'm sitting on my grandmother's lap in a courtroom. My sister is off to the right with my mother, and my brother is off to the left with my father. They ask each child who they want to live with. My brother and sister have already chosen and I'm left in the middle. When they ask me, I say my grandmother. The judge awards custody of me to my grandmother, and she picks me up and takes me out of the room. I think that's because I start screaming. I'm feeling such anger, and I feel it in my head. I'm angry mainly at my mother because she doesn't get along with my father. I think she could make an effort. I feel like I'm going off by myself. In a way, I'm disowning them. I feel abandoned, so I'll take the initiative and attack rather than get left out.

I have the measles. They put me on a porch and isolate me from the rest of the family. I see myself in a baby bed and I see my mother and father looking at me through the glass. It is an instant of realization for me that they are really rather stupid. I feel very different from the rest of the family. I feel connected to them only because I look like them.

Keith paused for a moment and then said:

I'm called a little bastard. I'm about two and I'm in the garage with my father. He says, "Go away, you little bastard." He actually accuses my mother of having an affair with someone else who might have fathered me. My mother screws around, but I am my father's son. I'm so hurt when he calls me that. It means to me that I don't belong to him. My father drinks a lot and there's a lot of trouble between my mother and father. I don't feel rejected, I just think, "You two don't know what you're talking about. Stop screaming so much."

We have an old washing machine in the garage. Sometimes my mother gets crazy and beats up all the kids over the Bendix. It is very frightening to have her put you over the Bendix and give you a few swats over the legs and ass. I remember one time when it was my brother and sisters turn to go over that thing and I started screaming to my father to stop hitting them. I was protecting them. So he stopped hitting them and gave me about five lashes instead. One time when he called me a little bastard I cried, so he threw me across the room.

Keith reviewed his birth process. He described the event as one of curiosity. He said, "It's like the first time you walk into a restaurant. You look around to see what's going on. I'm also angry because they have me by the legs. I'm cold, but I'm also curious. I have absolutely no identification with anyone in that room. Then I get slapped on the rear and I'm indignant." The prenatal period for Keith was upsetting because he sensed his mother's nervousness. He described it as a buzzing.

I feel like I'm stuffed up into a little bag. I don't feel rested. My bottom is sort of turned up and I feel like I'll be born backward. Periodically I feel a zzzzst . . . like a zzzzzst. It must be my mother's nervousness. She's not nervous about being pregnant, but there are things going on in her life that have nothing to do with me or being pregnant that cause this nervousness. I'm getting the backlash. I want to say, "Calm down." It makes me sort of irritated. Those jumps cause an eerie sensation and are very upsetting. Now it's time for birth. I'm pretty big and I'm trying to get my shoulders out. They have to use forceps to get me out and I have dents in my head as a result.

When Keith reviewed a past life, he said:

It seems I'm close to Jerusalem. (When I was there, everything was so familiar.) I see a black-headed boy walking through the streets. He is about nine. He's going home to a room on the side of the wall. He lives with his mother . . . Oh, the mother then seems to be my mother now. She has never been married, and she's too old to be married now. My father was a very handsome soldier, but I think she's alone now. The impression she gives is that of a witch, because she wears ragged clothes. She might be a young woman who has aged prematurely because of a hard life. I marry in that life, and have two kids, but it is an arranged marriage and there is no real love. It certainly was not a marriage with any kind of affection that would hold me. I think I had many male lovers then to compensate for the lack of affection with my wife.

I want to get to the point that I can understand my homosexuality. It could have started then when I tried to compensate for lack of love in my life with a lot of men. I was also a bastard in that life.

I suggested that we look further into his past lives to find a thread of continuity that would help him clarify the situation even more thoroughly. He described a scene of simple grandeur. "I see a corner terrace overlooking a garden. I'm young and a girl. I must be around eighteen. This life is very nice, very affluent. My father is my grandfather in this life. We are very comfortable, but I'm not interested in materialism. My parents are an older couple. It seems as though I teach children, for I see pencils and paper. I think I teach general subjects, not something special." Keith paused. "It feels like I am in love and waiting for someone to return. . . . Oh. . . . He is killed in the war. I've been teaching while I was waiting for him to return. After his death, I stop teaching because of my own pain. I could have made a more important contribution to the children if I hadn't been just biding my time, and if I hadn't stopped my work altogether because of my own pain."

I asked Keith if he recognized the person he loved in this life. He replied, "He is back with me in this life as my present lover. I think I never married then because I was so devastated that the person I loved was taken away from me. I guess we never lose people from our lives. It is clear that there is some karmic relationship between us now. I may hold back with my expression of affection because of that lifetime of loss."

Keith had one more life to view. In the present time, he is a dancer. He said he would like to know where that talent was developed. The scene that appeared before his eyes was one that

caused him to exclaim in wonderment. He said, "Ohhhhh...
Phew...I see a very exotic dancer....Ooooooooh...This is in
Egypt. I see myself as a woman, maybe a gypsy, dancing around
the fire. I am a virgin, but I sure do know a lot about the art of
sex and love. I see a lot of men around me. I am not married in
that life, either, but I sure do have plenty of chance if I want to
marry. I really do know how to dance." When Keith opened his
eyes, he was able to gain some perspective on what he had revealed to himself. He said, "I feel like the exotic woman inside
who danced so beautifully. I think the programming in this life,
being called a sissy, was difficult. I simply didn't fit into a mold of
what others expected of me. I think I understand a lot more about
myself now, especially in connection with the homosexuality." It
appears as though Keith will give himself permission to really
develop the talent he saw exhibited in his life as a gypsy dancer. At
least he was able to see the fiery, exotic part of his nature that he
may not have known was still within him in the present.

SENSE OF RACIAL INJUSTICE FROM THE PAST

Cynthia is a lovely black woman with sparkling eyes and a beautiful smile, complete with dimples. She is beautifully groomed,
very poised and charming. When she came to me for a reading of
her astrological chart, she was interested in some very practical
advice. She was involved in a major lawsuit with one of the big-
gest automobile manufacturers in the United States over what she
considered unfair hiring and firing practices. Since she had ini-
tiated the lawsuit, it was especially interesting to observe the
power packed in this small, seemingly gentle lady.

After we finished her astrological reading, however, I suggested
that she would benefit by a regression session, since Saturn is in
difficult aspect to many planets in her chart. She has Pluto conjunct Venus in the subconscious twelfth house and Mars in the
fifth house of romance, creativity and children. Saturn describes
her work and health, with its rulership of the sixth house. However, it is posited in the ninth house of publishing, promotional
efforts, legalities and higher education. Perhaps with the coura-

geous stand she was about to take, Cynthia would be able to bring about a bit more reform for people with like complaints. However, with Saturn overshadowing Venus in the twelfth house, she has what I describe as a karmic, racial guilt, tending to deny herself love, affection and pleasure in this life.

Venus is the ruler of the tenth house of career and public life for Cynthia. In the highest sense, Venus describes a sense of social justice. Since it is conjunct Pluto, the power planet in her chart, it is clear that her power lies in social situations or in connection with her sense of what is fair and right in public areas. She is especially potent when dealing with matters that require diplomacy and tact. The transformation that she can effect in areas of social justice are blocked only because of a karmic fear or restriction in those areas. During her regression session, the most disturbing thing to emerge was the lack of fairness in life, especially in *her* life.

Cynthia described the first time she became aware of a racial difference. She stressed over and over, "I don't know what *black* means. I have no concept of a difference." She told of the wonderful expectations of going to summer camp with her sister. It was a Girl Scout camp and she was to be gone two weeks. Since her home life was not pleasant for her, she was really looking forward to being away from the friction within her family. She described the experience. "We drive up to a big building and go inside, where my parents sign whatever is necessary. We are met by a large, fat lady wearing green short shorts. She has all this pink flesh hanging out, but she is a very pleasant woman. She takes us, my sister Rosemary and me, to our tent after we say good-bye to our parents. (There is no affectionate good-bye for us, and I probably don't expect a hug or kiss. I don't know that is what other people do.) There are four of us to a tent. Some men bring our footlocker, which we unpack in front of this woman so that she can make sure we have brought everything we were supposed to bring. I put my things in a metal cabinet and sit on the bed while the other girls finish unpacking. There are two white girls sharing the tent. I don't remember having any conversation with them. No one is talking to anyone else very much. Then it's time for dinner." A very ironic note crept into Cynthia's voice that telegraphed the event to come. "After dinner, someone has to stay behind and clean the table. I was the lucky one chosen. But I figure today is my turn so I don't mind. In the two weeks that we are there, only Rosemary or I stay behind to clean the table." I asked about the proportion of white girls to black girls. Cynthia replied, "All the girls at my table are white." She continued.

By about Thursday, we are supposed to do our cookout. We are then to visit whatever unit has the totem pole and then we will sing and roast marshmallows. But neither Rosemary nor I go to that event. We have to clean up the pit area and stay until the fire goes out. So we miss all the fun. We never get to that gathering because it takes a long time for the fire to go out and we're not supposed to just put it out.

I am really mad. I want to know who are the people who tell me I can go to camp and I can't do what everyone else is doing. I guess I'm mad at the universe, because I don't know about the white race. Why is it that *we* have to stay and do all the work? Rosemary tells me it is because we are black. She can curse and yell and get her anger out, but I just sit there looking at the fire. I listen to her, but I don't understand. It doesn't make any sense to me because I don't know what she is saying. At home when I am angry, I go and play the piano. Here I just sit and watch the fire burn. I can hear the other kids in the distance. Something is not right, something is not fair. I can feel the anxiety in my stomach. When I ask the counselor why Rosemary and I have to stay, she just says, "Somebody has to stay." I'd like to just put dirt on the fire and join the others, but if I do, I'll probably be sent home. At this point, I'd still rather be here than at home. If I take action of any kind, it will be worse than not doing anything at all. But then we're supposed to take a hike on Saturday and stay out overnight. Then we'll come back on Sunday when the parents come for a visit.

We get our stuff together and we are hiking about five miles to a farm or a barn. We are supposed to sleep outside in sleeping bags, but it begins to rain, so we're told we're going to sleep in the barn. I tell the counselor that I am allergic to hay. She says you either sleep in the barn or you sleep in the rain. Someone gets an upset stomach, so they go into the farmhouse and call the camp. A truck arrives to take that girl back to camp. I ask the counselor if I can go back with her, but I'm told I can't. I tell them I will be sick, but she says, "No you won't." Well, I can't breathe around that hay and I keep everyone up all night long. I make a lot of noise trying to breathe. It takes a lot of effort and is very tiring to try to get air quietly. I don't do it deliberately, I just can't help it. By five o'clock in the morning, the counselor finally gets up and goes to the farmhouse to call the truck. That same truck arrives to take *me* back to the camp. I'm put in the infirmary, so when my parents arrive on Sunday, they expect to take me home with them. The camp officials say I'll probably be okay on Monday, but by Tuesday, I don't get any better, so my parents come back up to get me. I was really sick. It went from the hard breathing into my lungs. That was the first time I had pneumonia.

Cynthia and I discussed the possibility that this was the only way she could vent her anger. She said, "No one will listen to me. I have no power, so looking at it now from an adult point of view, I suppose that was the only thing I could do. In 1967, I went to a new doctor for the asthma, so I learned how to control it. However, I now have a hiatal hernia. So my anger is just moving all around my body. That is very interesting. I hadn't related it to anger."

I asked Cynthia if she had ever heard that when one has a cold, it really means that you are crying inside. I suggested that the asthma attacks are also the inner tears that have no release. In her case, tears, anger and emotional reactions seem to be very bottled up, as her chart indicates.

Cynthia continued, "I know I made that woman quite miserable. She just wouldn't listen. It is always a source of frustration when I am not believed. I don't stand and argue with the person, I just walk away, but then I get sick inside. It's funny, but to this day, I'll pay someone else to clean my house. I don't like to clean up at all."

Cynthia then went to a review of her birth process. She described her awareness of not wanting to be born. She said, "It is a quandary, but I have left something unfinished and I have to come back to complete the task." From her past-life memories, it would become clear that Cynthia does indeed have something left unfinished. Cynthia continued:

I am fully developed. Inside the womb it feels wet. I'm probably ready to get away from there because I don't like to be cramped inside. I need light. I think I want to be born only because I don't like it when there is no light. I'm very impatient and frustrated because things are not happening as fast as I want them to happen. I just want the door to open so I can walk out, and it won't open fast enough. I feel a gnawing in my stomach, because my mother is holding me back. I think she knows what I don't know at this point, and that is my father really doesn't want me to be born. He claims no responsibility for my mother getting pregnant two months after they are married. He is a student at a major university in the department of languages and isn't able to continue because of me. My birth is thwarting all his plans. She subconsciously knows it won't be a bed of roses, so she's holding back, preventing my birth. She's protecting all three of us by holding off the inevitable. I am simply miserable. I don't want to be here in the first place and now I can't get on with it. I think I decided if *I'm* miserable, *you* should be miserable too!

I must have been a fighter a long time ago. I'm in a male body and I'm fighting for conditions to be right. I have a huge sense of fairness. It's in the 1800s and I seem to be fighting against slavery. I live in Philadelphia in a big house with a porch. I have a wife and three children. I'm a bit paunchy, with sideburns, and my wife is a bit dowdy. Oh.... I run a newspaper and I write articles that are probably inflammatory because they don't go along with the norm. I do them diplomatically and professionally, but I don't have a lot of friends because of this. I have a lot of broken glass from the windows of my house. It seems that people who disagree with me throw rocks. I'm white in this life. It seems to be before the Civil War, just as slavery is becoming an issue. I have a lot of land and property, so it must be an area outside Philadelphia. I think I have an underground railway station for runaway slaves.

Some people get caught before they get to me because of a lack of communication. That is very upsetting to me. Once they get to me, they are safe. I blame myself for not doing more to help. My business suffers and my children suffer. They don't have many friends and people call them all sorts of names. Everyone pleads with me to stop. Eventually I lose my family, too, at least on an emotional level.

I ask Cynthia if she recognizes anyone in that lifetime who has returned in the present. She said, "My brother, now, is one of my children then. And my mother in this life is my wife in that life. That explains a lot. She doesn't talk to me now and she refused to talk to me then. It's funny because my brother refuses to talk to me also. They're still holding a grudge because I make their lives miserable then and now! Most other people in that life sit with their tails between their legs, waiting for the tide to turn one way or another. So I am essentially alone in my fight. The angrier I get over the way people treat me, the more inflammatory are my articles. Even though everyone says 'please stop,' I have to do what I think is right."

Cynthia had described her father in this life as being very difficult to live with. He seemed to complain about everything and blame other members of the family for whatever went wrong. She talked about him. "I see my father as one of the people who lead the group of people against me. They are the ones who break my windows, or harass me in some way. He has the same personality today." Cynthia became very quiet. I asked her what she saw and she described a group of people in white hoods. "I am killed in that life by those masked people. They don't just go after blacks but whites too. They take me into the woods on my own property and shoot me. Hanging is reserved only for blacks." Cynthia let out a huge sigh. I suggested that she remove the hoods from the faces of the people who kill her and she said, "I can't." After a bit of persuasion, she said, "It is my father who shoots me. That would certainly explain why he didn't want me to be born, but it doesn't explain the whole relationship.

"There is another life in which my sense of justice seems to be connected with antagonists or protagonists in the Christian era. Again I'm in a white body and I'm a general. I set out to do what I'm told to do and then I say, 'That's not right.' I do what I'm supposed to do because of my sense of duty, but I know it isn't right. My father is the caesar of the time who makes me do what isn't right. A lot of people are killed because I don't stand up for what I know is right. Now that is a lot to think about."

When Cynthia opened her eyes, she expressed amazement that she had had such an experience. In the beginning, it had been a bit difficult to convince Cynthia to leave her rational mind aside for the moment. She had said, "But I am logical and rational." It became clear to her that her sense of justice is just as strong as ever and that she has returned to the present life with the same anger. However, the overriding guilt of first having gone against her conscience impelled her to rash behavior in the life of the 1800s, just as her Saturn aspects indicated. This time she must find the moderate, balanced method of achieving her goals. Clearly, with Venus ruling her tenth house of public life and Saturn square that planet, her destiny once again is to get on her soapbox. The placement of Saturn in that house of recognition can easily make her say, "Not again." Yet as she grows older and becomes more aware of her power, I am certain Cynthia will be a positive force for fair play, no matter what issue she chooses to attack.

In each of the instances related in this chapter, love, ease of living and pleasure were denied in the present lifetime. Sandy hesitated to allow love in his life because in the past, when he was deprived of the companionship of his wife, he chose to commit suicide. He was afraid to fall in love in the present for fear of what might happen again. Ellen hesitated to express affection to her daughter because of a memory of incest from the past. She learned about the continuation of pure love. Both people were fortunate to have that special love object in their lives again, this time to learn the nonpossessive qualities of universal love.

Both Keith and Cynthia have the potential to effect change on a social level, for Venus is the planet that describes fair play and the desire for conditions to be equal for all mankind. It is the planet that rules the lawyer or the diplomat, or anyone in a position to institute harmonious conditions that can better the lot of mankind. Keith is a dancer in the present and is in touch with his artistic ability. But in a former life, he could have upgraded social conditions simply because he was born to a privileged level of society. He acknowledged that he worked with children merely to be busy while he waited for his love to return. In that life, he was denied the pleasure of children, yet in the lifetime in Israel, he was not very concerned with the welfare of his children. Since Keith came back with what I term karmic racial guilt, he may need to work with children in this life to bring about more pleasure or encourage artistic expression when no other encouragement is forthcoming.

Cynthia, on the other hand, is expressing her concern for what is fair and right, yet throughout all her reviewed lifetimes, she set about that task with antagonism. Since Venus is the planet of diplomacy, it is through her charm and graciousness, with no ad-aptation or lack of strength, that she can best bring about fair and right conditions for all people. Cynthia recalled a life in which she neglected to do what was fair and right, not wanting to go against the will of her father, the caesar of the time. In that way, she adapted to someone else rather than following her own sense of justice. It may be that all the people Cynthia helped to escape, in her life as a newspaper publisher, were the very people she caused to die in her life as a general. The balance that needs to be re-stored in her particular case is that between her sense of what is correct and fair and her desire to be a fighter with no holds barred. When Cynthia taps her powerful ability to bring about a major change in social conditions, she will no doubt be in a posi-tion in which tact and diplomacy will play a large part in her life.

CHAPTER NINE

Saturn and Mars

he planet Mars describes many qualities of energy, but its most basic characteristics are action and initiative. The Mars quality of vitality is impulsive and instinctual, describing a kind of courage that leads to risks and exploration and taking a person into uncharted territory. Mars also describes romance and sexuality. It relates to a kind of zest that makes an individual want to win, for Mars, as the ruler of the first sign of the zodiac (Aries) indicates drive and ambition. The person with this energy wants to be first in all areas. That active quality of energy also indicates resourcefulness that can enable a person to solve problems and be a troubleshooter. It describes the adrenaline rush that is released into the system when an emergency arises. Particularly strong Mars aspects are found in the charts of athletes, explorers, mountain climbers and entertainers. All areas of competition demand a Martian fighting spirit that can lead to overall success.

Along with the positive qualities of Mars—ambition, courage, resourcefulness, drive and determination—comes the not-so-positive side of Mars. For when Mars has many difficult aspects in a natal chart, it describes anger, frustration, impatience and even violence. Therefore Mars can be associated with primitive, unrefined qualities of the survival instinct that may be unconcerned with the welfare of others. Since Mars was the god of war, Mars relates to the killing instinct as well as to the highest form of creativity.

Sometimes those Mars qualities are not exhibited on the surface of the personality. They appear to be nonexistent, yet they may be ready to burst forth in nonproductive ways at the slightest provocation. People may find very original ways to repress the rage they carry inside, even denying its existence to themselves. The problem is that hidden rage is just as potent and much less manageable than rage acknowledged and censored by the rational mind. When a person has a sense of his potential for violence or anger, he has a chance to think things through in an attempt to redirect and rechannel those feelings into productive activity or positive action.

In her book *Wounded Woman,* Linda Leonard says, "Rage can be veiled in many ways. One way is via addictions. With alcohol, the rage can come out when one is drunk, but without the conscious and responsible acceptance of it. Overeating may be another way of 'throwing one's weight around.' Rage is often hidden in the body. Many women suffer from hypochondria, experiencing physical weakness and illness that really cover pent-up energy. Headaches, backaches, ulcers, colitis, and stomach problems frequently disappear when anger is accepted."

When Saturn is in difficult aspect to Mars, a natural fear of free expression of those Mars qualities can prevent an individual from taking action. He blocks his initiative. That kind of hesitation is not cowardice but may be the result of conditioning from childhood experiences or from parental injunctions. The child may have been told not to be aggressive or ambitious. He may have been reprimanded for any expression of early sexuality. He may have been punished for getting into fights. In any case, he learns to repress his natural instinctual drive, which leads to many aggravations.

The inability to be resourceful when dealing with problems produces more negative results in his life. For the negative side of Mars represents delays, more inaction and lack of forward motion. On top of that, the Saturn part of himself piles on more cautious behavior, and a deadlocked paralysis sets in. A positive Mars part of himself says, "Onward and upward," but the Saturn part says, "Hold back, be careful." Together, these two planets express a push-pull effect. So when Saturn overshadows Mars energy, there is a perversion of ambitious drives, natural and healthy competitive spirit, and any pioneering tendencies. The paralysis may cause the person to misuse his energy in a cold, ruthless manner or simply not know how to tap his hidden ambition and resourcefulness. Repressed energy may be released only by a condition that stimulates anger, impatience and frustration. That can bring forth more destructive behavior, because the energy may burst forth in the form of cold-blooded rage or hatred. Inwardly there is a feeling of being pulled apart, and the person may not know how to deal with that inner rage. He doesn't know whether to go forward or hold back, whether to take action or simply sit still.

The Saturn overshadowing of Mars energy may be connected with past-life memories of guilts and fears. They may be associated with vague memories of violence, misuse of sexuality, sacrifice or betrayal. The individual may not know why he hesitates. He simply knows he is reluctant to take risks. When Saturn is conjunct Mars, ambitious plans may be born from an almost cold-blooded, gritted-teeth, clenched-jaw determination. It may also describe sadism, to some degree, but quite often the sadistic expression is turned inward, not outward. The individual may suffer physically and emotionally because he stops himself from taking courageous action that might be productive. He maintains harsh control over himself. He becomes judgmental about any kind of ambition—his own or that of others—in order to rationalize his own frustrations. Or he may be so determined to get to the top that he is unconcerned about whom he has to step on to get there. The results of his ambitious efforts may not bring pleasure but, rather, a perverse kind of satisfaction, since they were motivated by anger and frustration.

A look at past-life circumstances can shed greater light on these frustrated present-life conditions. With new insights, the individual learns to take action consistently and to find a project that will challenge him. He needs to develop a structured program of exercise to prevent any backup of Mars energy in his physical body. Only then will he be able to call on that adrenalin rush when an opportunity arises.

ANGER REVIEWED

Mary was born in Asia. She came to the United States and moved to a southern city, where she developed a valuable reputation as a massage therapist. She combined techniques of massage with the oriental methods of acupuncture and acupressure. Her recommendations about diet and herbal remedies proved to be very valuable in restoring vital energy and health to her clients. The fact that Mary made her way to the United States with small children showed her courage. Her special wit and sense of humor mitigated the obvious sense of dedication and responsibility necessary for her work. Mary made friends with her clients and never lacked for an interesting social life.

Saturn has a predominant position at the very top of Mary's astrological chart, placed in the ninth house of travel, international reputation, promotional efforts and philosophy. Saturn is conjunct the mid-heaven, describing career and public life, as well as conjunct Mars, sitting just on the other side of the mid-heaven in the tenth house. The tenth house also describes the career and public predisposition as well as the parent of the same sex. Since Mars not only rules the tenth house but is also placed therein, it is clear that Mary has a strong karmic tie with her mother and also a strong sense of responsibility for her welfare. She might tend to parent her mother but be angry with her at the same time. A sense of rejection from the mother is also strongly indicated by that placement. Saturn squares the ascendant in her chart, that ascendant being in the sign of Cancer. Mary came into this life with a resistance to being born. The most obvious cause may have been a strong sense of not being wanted by her mother producing hurt and anger, but she would have had just as strong a sense of duty toward her. Mary's regression session confirmed what, to me, was clearly indicated in her horoscope.

In the review of her present life, it was quite clear why Mary felt rejected at birth. Her entry into this life coincided with the approach of World War II. When she was a very young child, Japanese troops invaded and occupied her village. Mary was not given permission to be adventurous as a child because of the danger involved. She had to take on a great deal of responsibility for herself and for her little brother. She had to grow up in a hurry. She also saw her mother having many frustrated ambitions, feelings of restriction and anger or rage that had nowhere to go. She quite naturally took on some of these qualities herself.

One of her earliest memories was of living underground in a cave just outside the village, along with the elders and other very young children. It was essential that everyone be absolutely silent in order to protect the rest of the people. Some of the villagers acted as scouts when it was suspected that the Japanese soldiers were in the vicinity of their hiding place. Mary's mother was one of these scouts. One day Mary remembered hearing her mother talking to a Japanese soldier just near the entrance to the hiding place. Her mother was young and pretty, and it appeared that she was flirting with the enemy. The villagers were horrified that she would allow herself to be so friendly, asking for cigarettes and volunteering to run errands for him. Mary found herself in a position of defending her mother, even in her own mind, since no accusations were brought into the open. It was clear to Mary, as an adult, that her mother was terrified and used the only way she knew to distract the soldier in order to protect her friends, family and children.

Mary herself was the object of scorn, when she allowed her little brother to crawl out of the cave into the open road. Luckily for everyone, no damage was done, but she was severely scolded and punished by everyone for her negligence. Mary was only two or three years old and her brother a mere infant. Clearly Mary was forced to take on the parent role during her childhood. Later on, in puberty, Mary was the object of her stepfather's sexual interest.

She ran away from home at a very early age to get away from his advances. Once again, she protected her mother by never revealing what was threatening in the relationship with this man, her mother's second husband. (In her astrological chart, the stepfather is described by Pluto, which is squared by Saturn. Mary obviously had a karmic tie to be resolved with this man too.)

When Mary reviewed her birth, she used the same words that many subjects who have Saturn overshadowing the ascendant use. She said:

I am sensing that I just don't want to come here. I'm being punished . . . it is a punishment to come back. I really don't want to come in. I see myself as being very arrogant, even prenatally, and very powerful. I say to myself, 'This is ridiculous.' I know I can prevent this from happening, but something is not complete, so I have to come back. If they promise me a good challenge, I'll come back, but I'm not happy about what I have to do. It is a tough birth. I make it tough by being a very big baby. My mother is only sixteen and a very small woman. I make a mistake by being a big baby and I have to pay for it. I almost choke myself by having to get through the pubic bone. I don't dislike my mother . . . she is my best entrance into the world, but I still make it tough for her. I'm mad at everything, and at people. People are so ignorant. They are not doing things the right way and they are hurting themselves. They are going to want me to correct it for them. I get very angry over that, so I am born rebellious.

I feel good about choosing my mama, because she is a strong woman. I am born in a little house built over water. Water flows underneath for the paddy fields. The first thing I see is that water down below. A midwife delivers me. My father is also there. [Since Mary's father died when she was quite young, I asked her to describe him to herself.] He is a very stout man, short, about five feet four inches or five feet five inches. He's very muscular and strong, but he's very gentle. [Mary's father is described by Libra ruling the fourth house of home and natural father.] My mother is in a lot of pain and is too weak to even care about me. I don't think she is in love with my father, because it was a fixed marriage. She was engaged to him at birth. He is already an old man when I am born, thirty-two, whereas she is only sixteen. Mama is being punished by my grandfather for being a woman. He didn't like girls, but he had four wives and thirty-six girls. He only had four boys. He was obviously punished for not liking women. At birth, I accept the situation as best I can, but I'm already rebelling inside.

I asked Mary to go to a past life that would give her an explanation for the circumstances of the present life. She said:

I see myself at court. I'm standing in a courtyard with all these people asking me for help. I'm a physician, a woman. This is quite near China, but I'm not quite Chinese. My feeling is that it is in Tibet. I'm thirty-five years old and all these people come to me for help, but they don't do exactly what I tell them to do. I'm very upset that they won't follow instructions. So I don't want the job. I've been there for ten years, serving the imperial court, but all these people just cause extra work. They know they can come to me, and I *will* help them if they do exactly what I tell them to do. But they take advantage of me. I know I have the power to control them and stop them from doing stupid things, but I don't think I should hurt them physically, so I just let them go and do what they want to. I'm angry at them. . . . I'm really angry. I decide this is a little too tough a job for me. I'd rather not give them an easy out. I'd really like to get rid of myself, so they can't get any more help from me. So I take my own life by swallowing poison. [This part of Mary's regression was very descriptive of the sadistic quality of Saturn/Mars, turned inward on herself.]

I ask Mary to look around at all those people to see if she knows anyone who has come back to the present life with her. She said, "The first person I see is my stepfather. He is one of the soldiers of the court. I was summoned to do something and I rebelled against it. He reports me. Then I have to make up for it by doing extra work. I become very angry with him, but he is also very angry with me. I was arrogant, but he was arrogant with me in that life too. I had to come back to finish things up with him." I asked Mary if she could forgive him for what he did then as well as what he did to her in this life. She replied, "I have forgiven him. In fact, I'm going home this year to resolve a lot of my anger toward him from my childhood."

I asked Mary where her relationship with her mother began. She replied, "I think my mother and I have been mother and daughter for many, many lifetimes. We are sisters in that life in Tibet. There are seven of us, but we are particularly close. We are very mischievous. We just love to play. But then we cause someone some pain. I think we caused everyone some miseries. It's ironic; I saw my mother go through such pain in this life and therefore it was very painful for me too. In another lifetime, she hurt me very badly when I was her mother. I see her running away with a man when she is only sixteen. I have to hide it, because if I don't do that for her, then we're all in trouble. She is very naughty and almost costs me my life. I have a hard time keeping the village elders quiet. That was also in Tibet, but that time, I wasn't born in Tibet but in China. I ran away to Tibet as an adult. We have been related many times. The last life before this one, she is also my mother. The good time is the life in Tibet when we are sisters and have so much fun. However, I ran away from her by taking poison and dying. It seems we're always running away from each other."

Mary had talked earlier in her regression session about always being scared. That was not too surprising, considering the early scare of having her life endangered by the Japanese troops. I asked her why she felt she had to come back to these specific circumstances and what she was meant to do in this life to balance the scales. She replied, "I had to come back to serve people and do it willingly and lovingly. I'm still scared that I might be so powerful I will forget where to end; I stop myself. But what I know now is that there is a positive way of working, by just being more aware. I don't have to control myself by being scared anymore." Mary opened her eyes and said, "What a trip I have just been on."

Mary used the typical device of blocking her potentially destructive anger in this lifetime. The fear had had its beginning in her danger-filled childhood but continued into adulthood when there was no longer a true cause for that fear. Mary began to release a great deal of energy and happiness into her life as a result of her new awareness. Her work with acupuncture is a natural way to release Mars energy, because Mars rules metals. Each day Mary transmutes her frustration into the healing of others.

CONSEQUENCES OF IMPULSE

Linda started her regression session by confessing her fear of hurting people if she ever really let herself go. She saw herself as a very small child, already taking on guilt for anything that happened in her family, even though she was clearly not to blame. Her astrological chart indicates self-imposed control through the placement of Saturn and Mars in an inconjunct aspect. With Aries on the ascendant, Linda would naturally be quite an innovative person, with lots of dynamic energy, but the Saturn influence curbs that tendency and turns it into the opposite kind of energy. Linda commented that one of her problems was not following through with many of her plans. I had described it as the "push-pull" aspect in her chart, especially due to a sense of responsibility for any hardships her mother might have suffered, since Saturn rules her tenth house of career and mother. Saturn's placement in the second house of finance could have preconditioned Linda to worry about money, even unnecessarily, because of financial hardships she felt her mother had to bear. The overall effect would be one of cautious action, not aggression. She may have been in a big hurry to return to the world, yet restrictions or feelings of rejection would tend to make her serious, cautious, conservative and very parental or responsible.

The first incident that came to her mind during the regression session concerned those very feelings of guilt and responsibility. She saw a scene that brought near-tragedy to her family when she was only four years old. Her mother was going to the grocery store one Saturday morning, leaving the children at home with their father. Linda's little brother was only eighteen months old. As his mother was going outside to get into the car, he followed without anyone being aware of his absence. Linda saw herself standing in the garden when her mother was backing the car out of the driveway, but with her back to the scene. She knew her father was in the house getting dressed after just having finished breakfast. She said, "I don't see what happens, but I see my father run out of the house with his khaki army pants, an undershirt and his bare feet. I don't remember ever seeing my father with bare feet before. My father runs across the yard to the car. I walk over and look down. My mother is holding my little brother and blood is running out of his ear, and he's unconscious. It's as if time stands still and this is taking hours to happen, instead of just a few minutes."

During a regression session, it is sometimes very necessary for a person to review what he sees in greater detail. What seems obvious at the first look may hide the essential facts associated with the guilt. When Linda began to give me more details, such as fixing the time of day at 9:00 A.M. and describing what she had just eaten for breakfast, she became aware of the fact that she had indeed seen the whole accident. She saw her brother running to get into the car with his mother, without her knowledge. He fell, and her mother backed the car over him. Linda saw her mother put the car in gear, move forward and then get out to see what she had hit. Linda said, "Someone screams, because Daddy runs out of the house." After a very long time, Linda realized that the scream had come from her own mouth. She said, "I had blocked out so much of this, but I see clearly that I blamed myself for not watching him more carefully." With more discussion about the incident, Linda saw herself at four, being cognizant of the fact that even though her father was designated to take care of the children, she knew he was not really a responsible person in that area. She felt guilty because she knew beforehand that she was more capable in this respect than her father.

Her little brother was rushed to the hospital, but it was not until the next day that he opened his eyes. When he finally came home, months later, he was unable to talk. Linda revealed that for years afterward, whenever he fell down, he would have a convulsion. Her life was a living hell, because she felt she had to watch him all the time to prevent further damage. She also saw that her brother was aware of her feelings of responsibility for him and played on her guilt, sometimes really taking advantage of the situation. For the first time in her life, Linda took a look at how her mother and father must have felt about their own part in the accident. She had felt rejected by her family because at the time of the accident, no one took time to comfort or reassure her about her lack of caretaking. But it was obvious that her mother and father had no idea she was taking on the whole guilt load for her brother's accident and the responsibility for his welfare thereafter.

Linda then saw the circumstances surrounding the death of her grandmother, whom she loved very much. She was tiny when her grandmother had a stroke and became bedridden and paralyzed. Linda's mother went to take care of her own mother, and Linda herself felt great joy at being able to accompany her mother and do anything to make her grandmother more comfortable. When her grandmother died, she was never told. She just became aware that Grandmother was no longer there. She felt great anger that her grandmother would simply go away and not say good-bye, and at the same time, she felt she must have done something wrong to cause such an action on the part of her beloved grandmother. Once again, she took on unnecessary guilt for something that was not made clear to her.

From a rational point of view, it is obvious to Linda that her perceptions of her true responsibility are clouded and have been since early childhood. In the review of her birth process and the prenatal period, some of this became more clear. She described the birth process by saying, "It hurts my head. I'm trying to come out, but the doctor has not arrived at the hospital yet and my mother is very nervous about his not being there. But there has been more tension just because of the financial situation they're in. My father had planned to open his own business, but when my mother discovers she is pregnant, he has to abandon his plans. I feel very responsible about that."

Linda is aware that she is trying to help relieve the panic around her at the time of her birth by resisting the pressure forcing her into the world. She sees herself hanging on by hooking her forehead against the pubic bone, but then becomes aware that she is tired and just cannot hang on any longer. She continued with the description. "Both my grandmother and my father are there, because my mother is still in her room at the hospital, waiting for the doctor to arrive. Finally Grandmother sees my head coming out and says, 'Get the doctor!' I have to come out anyway because I can't hold back anymore. I'm born in the hallway outside my mother's room."

With Mars ruling the ascendant, describing the birth process, it is clear that Linda was in a big hurry to be born, but the Saturn overshadow describes the circumstances that prevent her quick entry into the world. Even with the review of her birth and underlying rejection of her parents due to the momentary circumstances of limitation, Linda was not yet in touch with the real reason for her overdeveloped sense of duty and responsibility.

I asked her to go to a lifetime that would give her an explanation of the circumstances of now. Linda recalled a recurring dream that she has had since childhood. The dream showed fragments of a military situation, but Linda had never seen more than that in a dream state. I asked her to describe what she saw in connection with that fragment of information and to place herself somewhere in the world. She replied, "I'm in France, just outside of Paris. It is in modern times and it seems to be during the war. I am a leader of a group. I'm a woman, and we seem to be part of some resistance group. I seem to be planning something when there is an emergency. We're running through the streets, being shot at by the enemy." I ask her to tell me who the enemy might be, and she promptly replied, "The Germans." She placed the time as the beginning of the German occupation of France. "I'm stopping to help someone, while the others run on. I think it is a woman who has fallen. Then I run as fast as I can to catch up with the others. It seems we're trying to rescue another group who are trapped in another part of the city. As I come around the corner, the army is standing right there. They shoot me in the stomach and kill me."

When Linda had a moment to digest this new knowledge, she said, "I can understand now why I don't want to take charge or take action. I have a very aggressive side, but I'm torn between that tendency and a very cautious nature. I think I was too reckless in that life. My lack of caution caused the whole group to be killed. No wonder I worry about hurting someone else, since I was the leader of the group in that time and was responsible for them. I must have died regretting my recklessness, because I came back being very cautious, but guilty in this life too."

Reviewing experiences from the past gives an individual new perspective about his automatic decisions in the present time. Linda was born in this country during the early years of the war, so she didn't wait very long to be reincarnated. If she had more time in a resting place between lives, she might have had a chance to heal or recover a bit from her trauma. But with such a shock fresh in her mind, she came back with the guilt about her recklessness close to the surface of her consciousness and chose difficult external conditioning that would force her to slow down. With her new insight, Linda felt she could begin to release the burdens she had carried so long. She knew it might take some time to repattern herself completely. She was determined to invest time in making plans that she would be capable of carrying out on a consistent basis. She decided to observe a tendency to stop herself before those plans were completed. With the awareness of her tendency to go forward and then to hold back, Linda expressed confidence in her ability to redirect more energy and latent ambition. It appears that Linda has quite an ability to fight for others, perhaps in connection with reform programs. Consistent determination to pave the way by her own action will help her resolve and rebalance her guilt over causing death to her group.

INCEST

There have been quite a few women who have come to me for regression sessions unaware of the kind of trauma that is ready to emerge from their subconscious in connection with their fathers. One young woman described the house where she lived at two years of age, and saw herself being very fearful of the basement. She saw herself going down those steps hesitantly, because she was being called by her father. She felt that her mother was in the kitchen just within reach, yet all-pervading fear flooded her body.

The basement seemed very dark and threatening. With a closer look, she described the washing machine and dryer, as well as other standard equipment of most basements, and then knew that her father was waiting for her at the bottom of the steps. It took quite some time for her to see further into the situation, but obviously this was a memory that had to be reckoned with. It seemed at first glance to be a quite ordinary day, but when she looked further, she saw that her father continually molested her when he could entice her down those stairs. She was horrified to learn of this shocking situation but also knew that she had felt guilty because, to some degree, she found the sensations pleasurable. She not only resisted telling her mother but, as most women do, she effectively blocked it out of her own mind.

The occurrence of incest between father and daughter is more frequent than one might suspect. Inevitably when memories of sexual molestation were revealed through a regression session, the daughter described a time in her life when she had made a complete break with her father and felt unreasonable anger toward him. This was true even when the conscious memory of the incestuous relationship was completely blocked. The description of how that rage manifests itself later in life with man-woman relationships was clearly indicated by Linda Leonard in *Wounded Woman*. She said, "Often when there is a great deal of rage resulting from a negative relation to the father, that rage is experienced also with one's lover. And frequently it is hard to handle ordinary anger. [Acknowledgment of the] rage can release the wounded woman, for her wound has a burning center that stings and hurts. Behind the rage are often tears. But underneath the anger is vulnerability and the possibility for tenderness and intimacy." One tragedy of these sexual advances is the helplessness the daughter often feels to prevent her father from doing what is distasteful and guilt-producing—she feels that in some way she must be responsible, since daddies are supposed to be all-wise and all-caring. Eventually, after the rage has been explored, forgiveness must take place.

Rebecca came to me for a regression session as a matter of

curiosity. She said she remembered very little before the age of twelve but knew she had had a happy childhood. The only problems she had encountered were bouts of asthma that periodically debilitated her. Rebecca was born in Europe but had lived in the United States from the time she was a very young child. The first childhood memory that came to mind was when her mother spent a month in Europe when Rebecca was twelve years old. Rebecca's grandmother was ill and dying, but Rebecca could not accompany her mother because it was during the school year. She was to remain at home in the care of her father.

Rebecca knew that she would be sad at the demise of her grandmother and lonely without her mother, but the emotion that accompanied the prospect of her mother's departure was total panic. It seemed quite an overreaction to the situation. After a long period of descriptions of the rooms in the house, her school activities and schedules in which she and her father shared the cooking and food shopping, Rebecca began to describe her bedroom. It was decorated in soft colors and was a pleasant young girl's room, yet she postponed going to her room at night for as long as possible. She was actually afraid of getting ready for bed. Finally she saw her father getting in bed with her each night and making love to her before allowing her to go to sleep. Rebecca's reaction was to deny the truth of what she had "seen" in her mind's eye. She couldn't believe that such a situation had occurred for the month-long period, yet on another level, she acknowledged that indeed that was exactly what had taken place. Finally she saw the intense relief that came when her mother returned. She had evidently held herself in such tight control that with the pressure off, she became quite ill with asthma.

Then she went to an earlier time and saw herself as a nine-month-old baby. Rebecca began to talk in baby talk, calling herself by her own name instead of saying "I." She saw that she spent a lot of time at that age with her maternal grandmother, whom she called Omah. She said, "Daddy is away. Mommy has to work very, very hard. Mommy takes care of other people's things and other people's houses. Rebecca goes to Omah's house." Rebecca described the apartment where she and her mother lived as being very gray. She didn't like being in that apartment. I asked her if she missed her mother while she was working. Rebecca replied, "No, because Omah loves Rebecca. Rebecca is a big girl at Omah's house. Rebecca looks very pretty. Mommy stays at Omah's house, too, but then she goes to work and Rebecca stays at Omah's house. Omah loves me, I can feel that." I asked Rebecca why she had picked the age of nine months. Had something happened at that age? She said, "Daddy comes home. Everyone much happier when Daddy comes home. Rebecca wants Mommy to pick her up, but tries to be a good girl and not cry. When Daddy comes into the room, he hugs Rebecca too." Then she said, "Daddy touched me, and I don't understand. Daddy touched me and I'm only a baby... Oh, no... Daddy touches me in weird places. You can't do that to me, Daddy." She began to cry softly. "I don't know why, but that seems to stick out in my mind." I asked her what she did about it. "I cry, and then he stops." She immediately saw herself as a baby having a very hard time breathing. I asked her if she was in an incubator and if she had asthma. She said, "I'm scared." Rebecca began having a very hard time breathing. Suddenly she screamed, "Oh, no! Who did that? Oh no, I'm two days old.... She didn't really mean it. She didn't mean to do that." When Rebecca finally stopped crying, she explained that she saw her mother pick up a pillow and hold it across her face. But with Rebecca's struggles, the mother took the pillow away. She continued, "She is all alone and she's so scared. I want to help Mommy but I can't. I don't know what to do. I'm just a baby. I want to hug Mommy and say, 'It's okay, Mommy, I love you.' Mommy is a very sad person. She's in a Catholic hospital and they have sisters. They probably don't understand Mommy for getting into a situation like this. Mommy is not that type of person. Mommy is a good girl. She loved Daddy, she just made a mistake." Rebecca described the period of her mother's confinement by saying, "Mommy makes things for people with a needle and thread. She is very happy when she's around people, but when she's alone, she's very scared."

Rebecca began to describe the birth process when I asked her how she felt about being born. She continued, "Mommy is in a lot of pain. I feel kind of scared. It's more than I can probably handle. But I'm strong, I can do it . . . but I don't know, it's kind of cold out there." She gasped, "I'm ready to be born, but I don't know if I'm not going to be born on the ground. I'm facing the wrong way. I feel like I'm sitting up!" I asked how long the birth process takes. She answered, "It takes thirty hours to be born. This sounds incredible, but I think it takes a long time because I'm not going to change. I think I'm going to be born sitting up! I don't want to give this woman a hard time . . . I love this woman and she loves me, and she doesn't deserve to be given a hard time, but . . ."

I asked Rebecca if she tries to help the birth process at all. She replied, "I don't think I know how to turn around. Oh, I can't turn around, because something got stuck around my neck. I guess I should help them. In true Aries style, I'm giving her a hard time. But I wonder if the cord is around my neck and I can't do much about it. I guess sitting up wasn't such a good idea after all. I'm pretty helpless. Maybe I can turn around, otherwise I may not make it through the rest of this life." I encouraged her to talk about her efforts to help the situation. It is my experience that the unborn child is totally aware of his part in the birth process, whether that is to hinder and try to prevent the birth from taking place or to try to help it along.

Rebecca volunteered her reason for picking this particular situation for her new life. "I picked this life for a . . . heck of a . . . I know why. I guess I'm tired of being where I was. I just want to do something different. This woman looks like she can handle it. I guess I have to learn it somewhere, so I guess I can handle it too." She released a big sigh. "I'm on my side now. I keep moving around. I don't think they know what they're doing. There's no doctor there. They're just kind of hoping it all works out. It must have hurt, but I don't remember. Right now I feel like sitting. I think I'm resisting coming in. I think I got more than I bargained for, but I'm a survivor." She continued her description by saying,

"This is ridiculous. There's no reason to sit around and give this woman hell. Okay, it's time. That hurts the head just a little bit, but we can do it. I feel the pain around the neck, I think the cord *is* around my neck, but they catch it in time."

Rebecca proceeded to correct her own birth time. She said, "It's 7:10 A.M. Mommy told me it was 7:00 A.M. but it's not. I see lots and lots of white. Mommy is happy it's over, because Mommy hurts." Then Rebecca changed her tone of voice and said, "Why isn't Mommy holding me? A person in white is holding me. They love me . . . they love people. They wash me off. Mommy doesn't hold me right away. Mommy is not sure. Mommy is not sure she wants to keep me. She doesn't want to hold me in case she decides to give me up. It hurts her. . . . I can feel that all the way over here. It is much easier to get along if she doesn't keep me, but I look a lot like Daddy, so she decides to keep me. She's mad at Daddy. Daddy should have been there and not made her go through that alone. I'm feeling her pain before I know what she's going to do. I'm a survivor, but I just wish someone would really want me. Poor Mommy, I'll take care of Mommy, if she doesn't keep fighting me." Rebecca paused for a moment to assimilate what she had been seeing. She said, "It sure does feel good to talk about it. I never knew how good it would be to let it out."

With further exploration, Rebecca discovered the truth of her prenatal life. She saw her mother taking some sort of drug and knew her mother had tried to abort her. She also saw the struggle her mother underwent in accepting her unwanted pregnancy. "She figures if she takes something, she'll get rid of me, but it's not going to be that easy. She doesn't know it yet, but I'm a very tough little cookie. The drug makes her sick and it makes me sick too. She's only three months pregnant." She felt someone punch her mother in the stomach and felt that punch herself. She finally saw that her mother had done that to herself and realizes that her mother continued taking different pills and then tried to kill herself. She described the scene. "She's depressed and she's drinking some kind of liquor. She toys with the idea of killing herself but she does it halfheartedly and it doesn't work. Finally she has to leave where she's working. She's very ashamed. Mommy has a lot of pride. Daddy went to live in America and then Mommy found out she was pregnant. Daddy didn't know anything about me. She doesn't tell him. I see him for the first time when I am nine months old."

With such traumatic prenatal experiences, it was important for Rebecca to understand why she would pick those trying circumstances. After a short period of time, I asked her to go to a past life that would give her an explanation for all this. She said, "I see a mean person. I am a man and I'm a mean person. I live in the woods, it seems like the German woods, and I appear to be about twenty-five. I'm married and I have two children. I'm kind of lazy, actually. I'm very grouchy and I drink a lot, and I fight a lot with my wife and children. No wonder I had to go through this life." I asked her to identify a time period and she said, "Eighteen hundred pops into my head." I then asked her to look at the people around her in that life to see if she recognized anyone from the present time. She said, "My wife comes up as my son in the present time. My father was one of my children. He was a little girl. . . ." Gentle tears began to flow from Rebecca's closed eyes. She whispered, "Oh, Daddy, I'm sorry. You were only doing what I did to you. I don't blame him for doing that to me. Poor Daddy."

Rebecca didn't have to explain what she was seeing. When she opened her eyes, she looked at me with great solemnity. "Now I just have to make sure it doesn't go on any further. My son is very beautiful. He was my wife then. You know what I'm saying, don't you?" I nodded and she went on, saying, "I was a lot meaner than my dad is. Poor Daddy. That means I can love him. That love may be born out of pity, but I can now love him." It became clear to Rebecca why she had had such violent acts perpetrated on her, beginning with her mother's attempts to abort her.

In Rebecca's astrological chart, the combination of Aries Sun with Aries rising (Aries ruled by Mars) suggests a very sexual, energetic, aggressive, ambitious person. But Saturn is also in Aries, in the twelfth house, conjunct the ascendant. This aspect represses and squelches the dynamic Aries personality and indicates stoicism instead. Saturn is also square Mars, which is placed in the tenth house of career, augmenting the block of Martian drives and describing her relationship with her mother. With this kind of placement, the individual comes into life not only feeling rejected and unwanted, in this case by the mother, but also feeling "paternal" toward the parent described by the tenth house. Rebecca confirmed this by her description of the birth process. "I'm probably going to give this woman a hard time.... She doesn't deserve it, but nevertheless..." It is clear that Rebecca feels compassion rather than anger toward her mother and wants to assure her that everything will be all right. Her frustration comes in not being able to help her mother early in life.

But Mars represents violence as well as sexuality. Rebecca revealed the second violent act perpetrated toward her when her mother tried to smother her with a pillow. Her natural anger at such an aggressive act was covered by understanding, perhaps because she was helpless to do anything about it. With the first meeting of her father she was helpless to do anything to defend herself from his sexual advances. During her whole life she submitted to her father's sexual advances without ever protecting herself or protesting. Her twelfth-house Saturn describes an inner guilt about her own Mars energy. This subconscious guilt was carried over into the present life, even though she had no conscious memory of having been a mean, sexually abusive man in a past life. She felt unable to do anything about the situation because that guilt paralyzed her.

Rebecca talked honestly about her relationship with her son, for incestuous patterning can be repeated, just as in the case of abused children who have not been sexually molested. Often, a child who was abused grows up to be an abuser of his or her own children. If such a condition exists in the present-day life, whether that abuse is sexual, physical, or simply some form of mental cruelty, the question should be asked, "What could I possibly have done in a past life that would cause such a terrible condition to exist in the present?" This question should be explored particularly if one feels helpless to do anything about the situation. Awareness of what that situation might have been can help to free one from the pain of inaction in present times.

MEMORIES OF VIOLENCE

Karen came to me for a regression session at the recommendation of her mother. She had been having difficulties at school and was escaping the ordeal by smoking a great deal of marijuana and drinking too much. Her mother's love and concern never took on the role of criticism, only a desire to help her resolve the underlying problems. Karen admitted that peer pressure was very hard to resist, and that she had begun smoking marijuana and joining her friends in drinking at the local tavern in an attempt to feel more a part of the group. After a period of time, she realized that she felt no more connected to her friends than before, and now that her grades were slipping, her panic was becoming unmanageable. She felt more like an outsider than ever before.

Karen's astrological chart indicated a need to look into the past through regression. Mars in her chart rules the twelfth house of the subconscious and is placed in the sixth house of work. Saturn is placed in the eleventh house of friends and rules the ninth house of higher education. When Saturn describes group activity and friendship and has difficult aspects in the chart, the tendency is to allow friends to exert negative pressure by real or implied threat of rejection. In Karen's case, since Saturn is inconjunct Mars, the fear of her own ambition, aggression and innovative, pioneering action may be connected to some memory of violence in her past. As her way of staying safe, she might choose friends who hold her back or who exert negative pressures. If Karen began to release her Mars energy through physical exercise, she could begin to repattern herself. She could release many of her ambitions, and she would be able to pave the way for everyone else instead of letting others take the lead for her.

With Saturn-Mars in this position, it is difficult to find an outlet for frustration because it exists in such completely hidden areas of her life. Every time an inner ambition begins to emerge, some little voice whispers, "Watch out, be cautious...remember your past." Mars can be associated with drinking and drugs, if it is in this position in the chart, simply because those are means to pour water on the frustrated aggressive, or even sexual, urges. In Karen's case, her choice of friends and activities could damage her health, yet it might be her way of avoiding and controlling her subconscious, karmic memories of violence from the past.

During the review of her present life, Karen acknowledged that she had been plagued with nightmares throughout her life. In looking at her childhood, she clearly saw the adventure of moving to South America when she was six years old, returning to the United States when she was twelve, and then living in Paris as a teenager. Although life was not dull, long-term friendships couldn't exist because of the many moves. With each change of country, she was even more of an outsider because of the language difficulty. She said she began drinking in Paris because she felt so different everywhere she went. She realized that she was a bit afraid of new experiences as a result of her early residential changes. She also saw that she felt the tension in her stomach. Drinking may have temporarily relieved the pressure and pain in that area of her body.

Birth memory revealed physical pain due to pressure around her head. She saw that she didn't want to come out into the world and began to tense her stomach in preparation for what she might find. The actual birth process took a few hours, and she saw her mother crying a bit as she was born, but felt they were tears of relief and joy. Karen immediately felt very comfortable with her mother. She decided that life would be an adventure and, although her brothers, and one in particular, were not too happy about her entry into the family, she would simply learn how to adapt to their wishes in order to get their approval. That survival decision obviously set the pattern for relationships with friends later in life.

When she went to a past-life situation for review, Karen saw herself in a Japanese lifetime. She appeared to be about fifteen years of age, pretty and intelligent, but under the control of some-

one who was always issuing orders. Family life was very traditional, and her father seemed to be placed in a very important
position, which meant that she was expected to do nothing more
than be a proper Japanese daughter. She longed to simply wander
in the woods, to explore and feel like a free soul, yet her apparent
compliance hid the part of her that longed to experience life more
fully. She saw that her every wish was attended to by servants; she
had a personal maid to dress her and comb her hair. Being a
dutiful daughter, she did what was expected of her, marrying a
man who gave her the same kind of pampered but controlled life.
She knew that her father loved her, but he was remote and a
disapproving man. The restriction she felt in that lifetime was like
that of a bird in a gilded cage.

Although that lifetime explained the aspect in her chart indicating her tendency to adapt rather than fight for what she wanted, it
didn't explain the level of violence and frustration I saw in her
chart. Karen has a generational aspect of Uranus conjunct Pluto,
with Saturn blocking that energy as well. That is the most potentially rebellious combination possible. The overshadowing of Saturn in opposition to that conjunction indicates an atomic level of
dynamic energy that is squelched or repressed. I asked her to find
another lifetime that might reveal why she harbored a fear of exploration and adventure in the present.

Karen said, "I have always been fascinated by the Mafia." Karen
described a lifetime in the early 1900s, when she lived in a very
elegant house somewhere outside New York City with her family.
She decided it was probably upper Westchester County. Her family consisted of a father, who seemed to have a very important
position and was once again very remote, a "sweetheart" of a
mother and a brother. Karen saw a scene in which she was sitting
with her mother on a sofa with her brother across the room.
Everyone seemed to be quite sad as well as worried. With a bit of
time, Karen realized that her father had been a member of the
mafia, and in fact had been a godfather. It seemed that he had
been killed two days previously and everyone was in mourning.
Although precautions had to be taken to prevent any further trag-

edy, no one seemed to be concerned about the safety of other family members. Karen never thought there might be danger around her. Suddenly she saw the door to the house burst open, allowing two men to enter. The men were holding machine guns, and before any warning could be given, they had opened fire, killing her mother, brother and herself, as well as other people in the room. In retrospect, she felt saddest for her mother, who was so beautiful and gentle. She felt no judgment about her father's life but wished he had taken more precaution. Karen's final comment was, "Safety has to do with being just like everyone else. Being different is going to get you killed."

Karen may have to work on a very high level of reform to transmute the power shown in her chart. She may be the very person to do battle against crime and violence, but in her own dedicated way, for Karen has the potential of being a new-age prophet as a result of her own experiences. She may first have to accept that she is indeed unique and a free soul.

SADISM IN THE PAST

One of the more moving experiences I've had in connection with a regression session began when Walter came to me after having had a reading of his astrological chart. Walter had embarked on a new life path within the last few years, for he is a recovering alcoholic. Along with his dedication to his own recovery came emerging spiritual awareness, for inherent in the disease of alcoholism is a sensitivity and knowledge of the spiritual life within. In many instances, alcoholics are unable to deal with the harsh cold facts of life, for they have an idealistic view of how life should be. When I met Walter for the first time, I saw tremendous sensitivity on his face, yet later, he told me he was thought of as being cool and always in control. He is an expert in a profession that demands a calculating wariness. He is at the top of his field because of his unwavering sense of duty and a lack of sentimentality that might color his judgment.

When Walter left my house after the reading of his chart, he made little comment, but I saw on his face that the information had not been taken lightly. He remarked at a later time that he said to himself, "At last, someone understands." I suggested that Walter would benefit from a regression session because he was born with Saturn opposite Mars in his natal chart. It took some time before he felt ready to uncover what lay behind his carefully controlled existence. He asked if I could help him interpret two recurring nightmares that plagued him. Those dreams were indeed dreadful, scary visions of the slaughter of innocence. In one dream, he saw a beautiful Palomino horse that had been given to him. He loved the horse so much that he kept the horse in the room with him. It was necessary to take the horse to someone for an "adjustment" before he could ride him, and it was with great reluctance that he gave his treasure into the care of someone he didn't really trust. When he returned for the horse, he discovered that it had been beheaded and skinned, and had shrunk to the size of a small dog. Walter awakened from his dream in total panic, with perspiration pouring down his body. He had been trying to find the poor animal who was hiding in agony somewhere in his room.

At last, Walter felt ready to look at a past life. He knew he would uncover something that might be frightening, yet he knew it was something that was necessary in order to feel whole. Walter had a difficult childhood because of an invalid in the family. He was forced to assume a sense of responsibility early in life because it was difficult to be frivolous in the face of the suffering of a relative. He had an unhappy marriage that ended in divorce and was now in an unhappy, nonfulfilling relationship in which sex was withheld from him. After a review of his present life, he saw himself in Germany during the war. In a very quiet voice, he said, "I think I am a German officer, a member of the Gestapo. I seem to be in charge of a camp... I don't think I want to see what I did." He went on to describe in vivid detail the way in which he selected his victims. With tears pouring down his face, he described his abusive treatment of the prisoners. He then talked about the people he murdered in cold blood, shooting them with his pistol, and about the women he had brutally raped. He recognized his ex-wife as one of those women. He said, "It is like I pick and choose certain people with a particular kind of sadistic cruelty. I am not arbitrary about whom I brutalize. I pick specific people. Finally, I think I am shot by one of my own officers. I am just too sadistic for them to deal with. I feel that I was tried and found guilty at Nuremberg posthumously."

After such a moving self-examination, Walter was noticeably shaken. I asked him to look at his childhood in prewar Germany. He saw that he had been orphaned and, as a sensitive young man, had been a prime target for the Hitler Youth. Without any family love to counterbalance the messages that were drilled into his head in his formative years, he took the injunctions too much to heart. Walter's awareness of the lack of family love in the early years of that lifetime helped him live with himself until further information came to light.

As is the case with many people who undergo regression sessions, the mind begins to release new insights even after the session takes place. Walter was profoundly open and trusting about information that came flooding into his consciousness in this way. Walter had volunteered to help with a project of mine, and so we saw each other again outside of a formal appointment. We were taking a break from work when we talked about the possibility of a past-life association between us. I told him that I could only trust my instincts, but I felt we were together in a Japanese lifetime. I described my fantasy of how he looked and the kind of clothes we wore. I saw Walter very clearly in a gray silk robe and knew he had been a man of great dignity and position. I felt rather than saw the delicacy of my own silken garments. The fabric was so gossamer, it was like an angel's wings. It felt like a kind of silk that I've never seen in my life. I knew that I was tiny and very delicate.

Walter contributed some of his own insights. He felt that we had been married. He said our relationship was very tender but didn't last for very long. He felt there was an element of danger around us that made our time together even more poignant. He knew that we lived a very elegant life, but that somehow we were apart and the quality of our life was not sustained.

I happened to be visiting a new friend the next day and told her about the conversation. She remarked, "Don't you remember my regression session? I was an infant in a room full of Japanese elders when a samurai burst in the door and chopped me in half!" With that bit of information, I burst into tears and said, "Oh my God, you were my baby, and I couldn't save you." She continued, "But you weren't even there and somehow you couldn't get to me."

This new friend and I had had similar experiences and associations long before I met her. In casual conversation, I would mention the name of someone in my life and she would have a story to tell. It was always, "what a small world," between us. So evidently it was not by accident that we felt a bond of friendship, even though we had recently met. My friend raised an interesting question. "How is it that I don't feel the same closeness to Walter as I do for you?" I said, "Because he wasn't there. He may never have seen you, in fact. There was some kind of political movement that kept him away. I think I was tied up when the samurai killed you and I don't think I lived very long after you."

When I spoke to Walter, I asked him if he wanted to hear our mutual fantasy and he said he *thought* he did. Walter heard my story and said in a very quiet voice, "I have always suspected that alcoholism doesn't develop in just one lifetime, that it must take many lives of drinking to develop an addiction. I think my disease began when I returned home and found that all my family had been murdered by my political enemies. I was so sad, I just sat and drank my life away."

There was one more bit of information that was needed to tie all the loose ends together. I asked Walter if he thought perhaps all the people he had so deliberately murdered during his time in the German army could have been the same people who had been involved in the massacre in Japan. He didn't answer me, but his silence was more poignant than words.

In Walter's chart, Saturn is placed in the eighth house of transformation. That house describes how one gets his or her needs met early in life and also the eventual turnaround that allows the individual to give his or her greatest gift to humanity. When Saturn is placed in this sector of the chart, denial of what one needs or wants can help at first to pour salve on open karmic wounds. Later in life, after this masochistic tendency is no longer profitable or productive, the person realizes that the greatest gift to others is to take on responsibility for mankind as a whole. In Walter's case, Saturn is not only opposite Mars in the financial house, it is conjunct Uranus in the same eighth house. Uranus describes a healing quality, and so Walter may need to develop his healing potential. Since Uranus rules the fifth house of romance and Mars rules the seventh house of marriage or partnership, the resolution of restrictive feelings about love and partnership can give way to a relationship in which both partners take responsibility for mankind on a vast level. When Walter has forgiven himself, he can begin to make a profound contribution.

In Walter's life in Nazi Germany, he was the perpetrator, not the victim. Owning the responsibility for what he had done could have been devastating, but instead, Walter looked like a new man. His appearance changed noticeably, for a real sense of serenity had emerged, giving him an air of confidence that was only a facade before. Walter has dedicated himself to the work of Alcoholics Anonymous. Although all AA members lend a helping hand to their fellow men or women struggling to combat addiction, it appears that Walter is especially potent in giving support to those in need. It may be that through his work in healing other recovering alcoholics, Walter will find his true partnership.

After Walter's regression session, he wrote me a twelve-page letter to describe his feelings about the new insights he had gained. He said, "I feel like we have traveled together on the most important journey of my life, and it is a journey which calls for a chronicle." With renewed courage to forge ahead on that journey, I feel sure Walter will find many like companions who will aid him and, in turn, receive comfort in the special and unique manner of Walter's healing ability. It seems as though Walter can now heal the very people he has hurt in the past, forgiving those who hurt him in the beginning.

• • •

All the Saturn/Mars regression sessions had one very important thing in common—the hesitancy to take action because of deep-seated fear or guilt in a past life. Mary had already found a way of releasing her anger, so clearly described in her regression session, but she knew her work would advance onto higher levels with the willingness to commit her time and energy in a more positive way. Rebecca's acknowledgment of her violent character in a past life can aid her in forgiving the violence that was perpetrated on her in the present life. After forgiveness and healing has taken place, she is free to go forward with her own life plan.

Karen's past-life memory of violence paralyzed her in the present, so that she allowed others to control her life. With awareness that accommodation is one of her overall patterns, going back centuries to a lifetime in Japan, she can begin to release her dynamic energy to fight for others who are trapped in the same level of inactivity. She might be a potent fighter against drug abuse, for instance, or simply learn to rechannel or develop her own ambitions. Walter was well on his way to the fulfillment of his life's work when he discovered his own underlying patterns. Now aware of his past, he can go forward with renewed determination and purpose in his work for Alcoholics Anonymous.

CHAPTER TEN

Saturn and Jupiter

Jupiter is the planet that describes joy. It indirectly rules religion, philosophy and expansion of the higher mind. It indicates enthusiasm that, when it is expressed to others, can be especially contagious. Described as the "great benefic," it is the planet of luck. The symbol for Jupiter, the centaur, gives us a picture that is worth a thousand words, for the centaur is half-man and half-horse. The horse's four feet, planted firmly on the earth, provide a base of security that enables the man part to aim toward his goals. In his hands, he holds a bow and arrow. He sights his goal and lets an arrow fly. In the Jupiterian personality, the need to have a goal in mind is extremely important. However, if he doesn't reach his goal, he is paralyzed and hesitates to sight another goal, for fear he won't reach it.

He does have a method for attaining his goals, however. The centaur has a quiver full of arrows. If he aims high and allows for the drift of the wind, he will have more of a chance to hit the target. And if he shoots many arrows, one of them is bound to hit the mark. Therefore, to avoid disappointment and the consequent paralysis, the Jupiter person must set many goals, knowing that he will hit the mark with some projects, while others may have to fall by the wayside. He must never doubt his ability to come up with new challenges for himself. With a Saturn shadow, he may hesitate to aim high and set new goals because there is hidden in his subconscious a memory of having failed in another lifetime. The penalty for his optimism or his striving may have been very severe—enough to teach him not to reach too high again. He develops stoic acceptance instead of fiery enthusiasm. He may have to uncover the karmic reason for his existence to allow that joy to have full sway again.

Jupiter describes a profound ability to teach. It also rules sales, for with his contagious enthusiasm, the Jupiterian person can convince others of anything, whether it be an item or an idea. Since goals are so important to this person, he may appear selfish or self-centered. But he is simply looking ahead. Once he has achieved whatever goal he set for himself, he can be bored. He wants new experiences, so travel is something that appeals to his sense of enthusiasm. He can also be an explorer of ideas rather than of territory, yet new vistas will help stimulate his imagination and enable him to visualize new conditions in his life. The person with this planet strongly aspected in his life appears unfailingly cheerful. You rarely know if he has a problem, for his attitude toward life is "*c'est la vie.*"

He may actually hesitate to set goals for fear that if he accomplishes everything he sets out to do, he will find nothing new to aim toward. This is particularly true if Saturn is overshadowing Jupiter in the astrological chart. In the deepest recesses of his mind, however, he may be searching to see if there is something new to activate him and fire his imagination once more. The sad but true fact is that when he has done something and done it well, he must have a new challenge to aim for in his life. He simply cannot keep doing the same thing, day in and day out.

If we look at the Saturn-Jupiter aspect from the point of view of reincarnation, we see that even a person's religious nature can be stifled. For instance, a person who has been tortured for his religious convictions in a past life may come into the present time fearing to display strong religious fervor. He may look back subconsciously and wonder if it was worth the pain he suffered trying to convince others of his way of thinking. He is not cynical but is concerned about expressing his inner joy or curiosity about the universe in an open way. He keeps things to himself. Outwardly he may appear conservative and cool rather than fiery and exuberant.

Perhaps an experience in my own life can illustrate this. In exploration of my own past lives, I saw a time spent in Rome. I knew that I was one of the people in the lion's den. I saw myself with many people, solemnly walking into the arena where the crowds were jeering and taunting and knowing that if I could keep my concentration on the light emanating from higher spheres and follow the teachings of the Master Jesus, I would be safe, as would all the people with me. I saw myself reminding those around me of that tenet and reassuring them that we would demonstrate what we had been taught. As I walked into the middle of the arena and the lions were set loose, I concentrated on sending loving energy and brilliant white light to the lions, reassuring them that we were creatures of the same energy force. Suddenly a Roman soldier banged a sword sharply against the wooden wall, and my concentration was broken. At that moment, the lion attacked me. As I was dying, I smelled his terrible breath and tasted blood mixed with the hair from the lion's head. It was a dreadful experience, and might give an explanation of my allergies to cats.

At one point, I was staying with my friend Susan Strasberg in New York, and preparing to travel to Europe. I was going to remain in Europe for a month and hoped I would be able to visit Rome during that time. I was not even thinking about my past-life memory. Susan awakened as I was finishing my packing and said, "I had the most incredible dream. I saw the two of us as Christian martyrs in the den of lions in Rome. You said to me, 'Keep the faith and the lions won't hurt you.' I did just that and they didn't touch me!" I laughed and said to her, "I've had that same awareness and I didn't follow my own advice." I often wondered who the Roman soldier might be in my present life.

When I got to Rome, I had a very bad feeling and decided to

leave after one day. To kill time, I took a bus tour, something I have never done before or since. When we passed a certain hilltop, I experienced such sickness that I thought I would have to get off the bus at the next stop. In a few moments, the tour operator said, "Most people think the Christian martyrs were in the Coliseum, which we're approaching now. But they were actually in an arena on the hill that we just passed."

Sometime later, I was doing a regression session with a young man who kept turning up in my life. During the session, he saw himself as a beggar woman in a lifetime in which I had been imprisoned. I had evidently helped him, and in that life, he, as the beggar woman, said to me, "I wish I could help you." I said, "It's all right, I'm reconciled to my approaching death. By the way, I forgive you for what you did to me in Rome." All of that came from *his* subconscious memory, not mine. He didn't know what he meant about the reference to Rome. At the end of his session, I explained what I had already seen in my view of that life. He said, "I was the Roman soldier that caused you to die, but you didn't suffer because your heart stopped just as the lion dove for you."

Saturn indicates a tendency to worry, the opposite of Jupiter's optimism. With my Saturn-Jupiter inconjunct, I have had to battle within myself alternate enthusiasm and discouragement. I'm enthusiastic about what I've learned concerning the workings of the universe, and I feel joyous about life and people. Yet at unexpected times, I can become very discouraged about the outcome of my ventures. They sometimes seem like an uphill battle all the way. On a conscious level, I have discovered that I must have a disciplined work program and a carefully regimented health program to enable me to live up to many of my own expectations and goals. (Both Saturn and Jupiter describe my sixth house of work and health, with Jupiter ruling that house and Saturn placed therein.)

I was brought up in a religious environment, and my deep feelings of awe and joy about the universe have always sustained me through tough times. However, I have rarely talked about my religious feelings and have always avoided the role of the teacher in my work as an astrologer. My fear is that I will once more leave myself open to unexpected attack. On a subconscious level, I worry that I will fail to evidently demonstrate, in my own life, what I know to be true and right. So it becomes clear to me that growth will come with the reconciliation of those two very different energies of Saturn and Jupiter. I have learned that I must take care of the practical aspects of life (Saturn) while aiming for new conditions and setting new goals (Jupiter). The final key to continued optimism is humor, another Jupiterian quality. With laughter and a sense of humor about the comedy in life, we can all make it what we want it to be.

Review of Selfishness from a Past Life

Janet is a very beautiful young woman with a special quality of serenity about her. She is a flower child, yet she has an elegance that shines through the simplicity she adopts in her external world and manner. In fact, she carries an almost imperious quality that breaks through her very charming, gentle personality. She is not a person to be ignored or taken for granted. She was born in a European country to an American father and a European mother. In the review of her childhood, Janet saw very clearly her reaction to the breakup of her family. She described herself as an observer. In one instance, she saw a scene where her mother and father were fighting. It was quite late, and no one seemed to notice that she was in the room. She was less than two years old, and her mother and father no doubt thought she would be unaware of what was going on. Janet saw herself being very quiet so that she wouldn't be noticed because she was fascinated by what was going on. She finally fell asleep and was put to bed. During the argument, she was not frightened but was curious about the way her mother and father spoke to each other. She identified with her father because her mother was behaving very badly. Her mother seemed highly nervous; she was obviously at the end of her rope and urgently wanted a change in the relationship. It was shortly after that argument that Janet saw her mother sitting in a bathtub, suddenly making up her mind that nothing was going to change

and it was up to her to leave. She witnessed her mother packing a
suitcase, having a final argument with her father, who became
very violent, and walking out.

Janet was not very perturbed about her mother's leaving, because her father was there to care for her and he was actually
much warmer than her mother. He had always played games with
her and laughed. Janet knew she could charm her father, whereas
her mother was impervious to entreaty. After a period of time,
Janet's mother returned, having seen a lawyer and set a date for a
court hearing. Until then, Janet's father refused to allow her to
take Janet elsewhere. He stayed home to look after her. It took
only a short time for Janet to realize that somehow things were
not the same with her father. He seemed to be drinking a lot, and
the comradeship he had always shown her when her mother was
there was dissipating rapidly. Janet saw that things were not or-
derly in the house as well. The food was not as well prepared and
her clothes were not as pretty as before. Everything seemed to be
degenerating. But most of all, no one seemed to consider her at
all. At first, that was not important to her, as she had always been
cared for. However, Janet knew on a subconscious level that one
day she had to wake her parents up. She saw herself playing with
a knife on the kitchen floor. She was trying to split a piece of
wood with the knife and she inadvertently jammed the wood deep
into the palm of her hand.

The blood and screams frightened her father and made him
realize that perhaps he wasn't capable of caring for Janet full-time.
After a visit to the hospital and stitches, she was finally handed
over to her mother. Shortly after that came the first big shock.
Janet saw herself being taken to a Catholic kindergarten when she
was two and a half years old. With no explanation from her
mother, she was left with the nuns, and she was terrified. She
said:

Going to that kindergarten is the first really painful experience in
my life. It is awful! I hate it! My mother takes me to the kindergarten because she is working. I'm by far the smallest child there. She

takes me there and she just leaves. I'm eating something and while I'm eating, she leaves without even saying good-bye. Suddenly I realize she is gone and I cry for hours. I'm in great, great pain. I really feel abandoned. I'm just sitting there screaming and crying for hours. The nuns try to comfort me, but they don't really know what to do with me, because I don't stop screaming and crying. The other children look at me with a lot of curiosity. Finally I must fall asleep from exhaustion.

I know what they do! They sit me at the table and give me an apple. They tell me I have to finish that horrible, brown apple before I can leave the table, and it takes just hours to finish that apple. I know that if I don't hurry, my mother will be gone, but I just can't eat any faster. She's in the office, but if I want to see her, I have to finish my food. I can't eat. It takes me half an hour to eat that apple, and I know I'll miss her. My throat closes. They know they'll get me with that maneuver. It's very tricky. To this day, I don't like apples.

When I run out looking for her and she's gone, something grabs me inside like a big iron fist. There's a big pain and incredible fear all over me. I think this is something I *never* expected to happen. I was too blasé. This is the first time they're both gone. I didn't think that they would *ever* do this to me. I'm too precious. I never took it into consideration that they could ever do something like this. I finally become angry. I'm mostly angry at her, but when I see her coming I don't care. I'm just so glad that's she's back. She doesn't give me any explanation. She's not too emotional about it. She just takes me home as if nothing has happened. Actually I'm amazed that she is so cool. Now I'm totally exposed to my mother. There's always been a balance between my mother and my father, and that gives me a lot of warmth. Now I'm a total victim with her.

We go to visit my father. My mother takes me there and leaves me with him quite often. He never comes to see us. I see him on a big bed with me, just hugging me, and I'm very happy when I'm with him. He shows me little tricks that he has in the kitchen. He's very inventive. I see him throughout my life when my mother feels like taking me there. There's something in me that is very secure. I'm like a little princess. There just has to be someone to look after me. I'm very surprised when I see what they can do to me. When I'm taken to those nuns, I hate it. Suddenly I know what can happen and now I'm helpless. Finally my grandmother comes to live nearby. She makes it much easier.

Janet saw another personality trait that developed very early in her life. She saw that she could always break through to her father with her personality and charming ways, but when she tried to protest about anything in connection with her mother, she was simply ignored. In addition, her mother made her feel very humiliated if she tried to protest or react emotionally.

I become very angry at myself if I do something that brings about her indignation. This is when I begin to be angry at myself if I'm less than perfect. It is impossible for me not to react to things like a human being, so I do it over and over again. I get reactions from other people, but never from her. She just makes me feel very stupid if I am not perfect. I learn not to show certain things. I seem to develop mental control. I learn to cut off my reactions by just freezing up. I cannot reason it out, so I have to cut off inside. Nowadays I can use my mind to reason, and if I understand things, I can let the wall down. I can be who I am and not worry about it. But at an early age, I decided I had to be perfect.

Janet went to a time when she was six months old. She saw herself in bed with her mother and father. Suddenly her mother picked her up and took her back to her crib. Janet said, "I'm totally bewildered. Obviously she wants to be with my father, and I'm feeling very shut out. I can't seem to accept their treating me that way. I just can't understand it. My pride is hurt. It's as if they don't know who I am. She puts me in bed with them in the mornings, but only on weekends. My mother never gives me an explanation for things. I'm just supposed to take whatever comes along without knowing why."

I suggested that Janet examine the first painful moment in her life and she said, "Birth." She described the event by saying,

Oh no, I don't want to do this again. I'm feeling so tired, but it is mental tiredness, because of the agony of having to go through all this again. The birth process itself is easy, but I've seen my mother become apprehensive during her pregnancy. At first she's very excited, but it is beginning to dawn on her that she will be trapped. It is not that I'm the problem, but already she's seeing different facets of my father than she had seen before. She's worried about her ability to be independent. When my mother begins to worry, it feels oppressive inside. I know it's not my problem so I have to protect myself, so it won't become my problem. My father is very jealous and possessive of her. She's a treasure to him, but that is not the way with my mother. I know I'll just have to surrender to the situation I'm faced with. It's not a positive kind of surrender. I'll just have to give in and I feel defeated to begin with.

Janet went to a past life to see the circumstances that might explain the difficult conditions at her birth. She said:

I see myself in India, in my middle twenties, and I'm very rich. I'm born to this wealth. I'm a man, and I seem to be dressed in white. This gown is beautiful. My life is very luxurious. My palace is very big, with huge columns and ornaments decorating the house. I see lots of women around me. I think they are part of my harem. I don't see a mother and father around. They seem to live somewhere else. They are very good people. I think there is some kind of treachery that forces them to leave. They lose everything. They are very poor where they are now, in China, I think, but they are happy. They are threatened on a political level, and somehow I could have warned them or stopped it from happening. But it is to my advantage that they go. I think power is the issue. It is also riches. I'm not an active part of their leaving, but by not taking action, I don't help them at all. My family have cause to resent me, but they are such good people, they love me in spite of everything. I could have informed them about this situation. I weighed the situation as to whether I should tell them, but then I decide I want them to go. If they are not there in physical presence, my conscience won't trouble me so much. I never see them again, and I manage to forget about them. I chose my well-being over theirs. I live very luxuriously, but I'm very bored. I find diversions to keep myself busy. Then I can keep them out of my memory.

I asked Janet what she came to resolve in connection with that experience. She replied:

This time I really have to deserve wealth or riches to be able to have them. I have to have them in the right way. I have to be put through tests in connection with what I get. I really have to be grateful. I have to remain modest. I know who I am, and I know my value, but I must humble myself while I retain a sense of expectancy and optimism.

I also see myself in China, again in a position of being well off, but not with such opulence. I have a sister. She seems to be my mother in this life. I'm the oldest, and there's a lot of jealousy and competition for the attention of our father. He's very fair about dividing his time and attention among us. I marry a man I know in this life. He is very wealthy and very handsome. I'm so jealous, I can hardly stand it. My sister receives a small amount of attention from him, no more than anyone else, but it makes me insane. She's jealous of me in connection with him too. She adores him. I manage to keep her away from him, but I can't keep everyone away. He's too attractive and too wealthy. He's so charming that everyone is attracted to him. He flirts too. I think I use magic to keep him bound to me. He loves me, but I have to be absolutely sure. I'm really crazy when he is too nice to other women. Of course, he does exactly what I don't want him to do.

I think my sister is a much better person than I am. I think that when I was born to my mother (my sister then), I was feeling very uncomfortable about it all. I think I want to get it over with as soon as possible; by that I mean the time I have to deal with her as my mother. I want to grow up as soon as possible. I think what I must do for my mother is take some weight from her, mentally, that is. I want to teach her how to have joy instead of burden in her life.

When Janet and I reviewed her regression session, she said that in the life in India, she was neither bad nor good.

I was not a very spiritual person. I lived very physically and indulgently in that life. I could have done more for my people. There was no organization. They were left to themselves and to the people around me. I didn't really care what happened to them. My father was there as my minister. He carried out the work I didn't want to be bothered with, but he didn't do a much better job than I did. I know I came into this life to take on some special kind of responsibility. I know I must give of myself and resist any temptation to be selfish or self-centered. I have tried in this life not to make waves. I just want to be left in peace. But now I know I must make a positive contribution by working to encourage people. I must teach and exhibit my positive energy to enable people to reach their goals. I can help them to find their chosen path.

With her last statement, Janet clarified the Saturn inconjunct aspect in her astrological chart.

Jupiter is posited in the tenth house, describing her career, her social life and her mother. It is clear from her regression session that Janet's mother is actually a light-hearted person who, because of the responsibility of raising her daughter alone, let the pressure of Saturn squelch her natural good humor and optimism. Janet was doing the same thing in her childhood, as long as she was near her mother. She couldn't lift her mother's spirits by laughter or joyous behavior because the burden of her mother's life restricted her ability to respond with humor. Therefore, Janet became very serious and made attempts at perfection, in order to please her mother and to avoid being more of a burden. Janet felt that any attempt to teach her mother that it is possible to enjoy life in spite of burdens might backfire. Ultimately she learned how to send joyous energy to her mother by having compassion for her.

Janet must do the same thing in her career. Teaching is a perfect tool for her to use, as Jupiter's placement in her chart indicates she has that ability. With Saturn ruling her twelfth house of the subconscious, Janet must clean out the karmic garbage of her own memories in order to make new decisions about her own goals and then take responsibility for the people around her. Janet has decided to begin a program of study that will help her do exactly that.

HEALING ANOTHER PERSON THROUGH A REGRESSION SESSION

Maribeth is a close friend of mine. Many years ago, she visited me in New York and stayed in my apartment. One morning she awakened to tell me about a dream she had. She seemed sad, as her dream had been very real to her. She said she saw herself standing on a hillside looking down on a group of people, tears streaming down her face. It appeared that these people were hungry or in trouble and there was nothing she could do to help. He inability to relieve their suffering was extremely painful to her, and when she awakened, the feeling stayed with her to a profound degree. She had described herself as wearing a green chiffon dress, and she felt the setting was Egypt. But she woke up before her dream could tell her anything more.

Many, many years later, she asked to do a regression session because she wanted to understand the strange and painful situation in which she now found herself. Her marriage had ended very unhappily, and her divorce agreement had been especially unfair. After some time, she found a job that was very fulfilling. She attained a very high position in a company where the employees were like a family. But something happened to cause a dreadful rift. She was dismissed from her job without explanation. Although she knew there was politics involved, she couldn't understand the manner in which she was fired. She had been extremely effective and efficient and had made a great deal of money for the company. So there was no logical explanation for her dismissal. Being out of a job was difficult for her financially and personally; her pride was badly damaged, and she went into a terrible depression.

Perhaps the most difficult part of the whole situation was that she had had a serious romantic involvement with the man who fired her. She knew the love had been reciprocated, so the wound to her pride and dignity was even more severe. She could never reconcile his love with his coldness and lack of consideration. To tell herself that he was cowardly or that she threatened him in some way was simply not a good enough explanation. The memory of the hurt couldn't easily be assuaged.

After a long period of spotty employment, she was asked to come back to the same company, but in a very different position and at a much lower salary. Because she needed the job, she swallowed her pride and decided she could manage as long as she had nothing to do with her former lover. So she kept a tight rein on her emotions and confined her concern for the overall welfare of the business to the hours when she was actually on the job. Maribeth's request for a regression session was an attempt to comprehend the strange behavior of the man she still loved. Also, she knew that someone must be hired to fill the job she had formerly done so well. The position had been vacant for several years and the company was suffering greatly as a result. She needed to be prepared for the insult she knew was about to come.

The review of her present life was not terribly painful. Her early years had not prepared her for the suffering she would experience later in life. Maribeth moved quickly to a previous life. She saw herself as an Egyptian woman, wearing the green chiffon gown she had seen in her dream of many years before. I asked Maribeth about her surroundings, and she began to describe the opulence of the Egyptian court. She saw huge marble columns and a parade of people asking for time to discuss matters with the ruler of the land. It seemed that a famine had come and very few people had enough food. Maribeth knew that she had taken matters into her own hands and had begun feeding many hungry people. She knew that she lived at the palace, but she was not sure in what capacity. With another review of the situation, she gasped and said, "I'm married to the ruler. I'm not sure if he is a pharaoh or a governor, but it is up to him to give the order for such a food program to begin." I asked her what had caused such a reaction on her part. She continued, "It's John [the man she loved in the present life]! He is just the same as he is today. We love each other very much, but there is great opposition from someone close to him, an adviser, I think, about starting to give aid to the starving people. I'm sure such a program will be instigated eventually, but my heart is breaking when I see people so thin and ill from lack of nourishment. I start giving them food from the palace."

I asked Maribeth to describe more of what she saw. Suddenly tears began to cascade down her cheeks. She couldn't speak for a moment, but when she could find words again, she said, "He issues an order for my death because I am defying him. It is just the same as today. Now I realize that I continually went over his head within the company, even if it was for his benefit. In Egypt,

I am being killed for humiliating him and taking his authority away from him. He issues an order that I am to be burned to death. I see a huge funeral pyre.... Oh, I can't look at this anymore." After a moment, I suggested that she finish reviewing the whole situation so that the haunting subconscious memories would be dissipated. After a moment, she continued. "It is breaking his heart to do this to me, but for the sake of his authority, he must treat me as he would anyone else who would go behind his back in such a manner. I don't think I actually suffer. I must die very quickly, but I think it is of a broken heart, not from the flames."

When Maribeth opened her eyes, she said, "That is really an incredible experience. I finally understand why he fired me in this life. I couldn't understand it no matter how much I thought about it before." Laughing through her tears, she said, "I was going to tell you that it is very important that I finish this session in time to do some shopping today, but I think that's out of the question now." I told Maribeth that we had a bit more work to do to heal the situation completely, but that she could keep her eyes open now if she liked.

I said, "If you could do it all over again, would you handle the Egyptian situation the same way?" She shook her head and said, "Oh no!" I continued, "What would you do if you had a second chance?" She said, in a very soft voice, "I'd go to him when he was alone, away from his advisers, and sit at his feet. I'd take his hand in mine and look in his eyes, expressing all the love I feel for him, and ask him if we can do this together." I asked Maribeth what his response would be. She said, "Of course he'd say yes, especially if we could work together on setting it up to avoid political problems. It was my defiance and impatience that was the problem before, not the program itself." Now I said to Maribeth, "Please look at this lifetime and see how you could have handled the situation with your job." She replied very quietly and with a great deal of emotion, "I would do in this life what I should have done in Egypt, that is, talked to him in a loving manner." Then I asked, "Is it too late?" She said "No." I suggested that she create a drama in her mind's eye where she would talk to the man she loved. She said, "I would ask him to use my talent for the welfare of the company, because it's wasted in my present capacity. I'd assure him that together we could reorganize things in a way that would be beneficial for everyone." I suggested that she might tell him how sorry she was to have caused the pain and hurt between them in Egypt. She proceeded to do just that by visualizing him in front of her and talking to him as if he were actually present.

The next day I had an urgent call from Maribeth. She said, "You won't believe what happened this morning. I was called into John's office very early this morning. You must understand that we have not spoken to each other since I've returned to work at the company. I knew this was the day they were planning to make some decisions about hiring someone new. I took my time getting some papers together, because my heart was beating so hard I was afraid someone else could hear it! When I went in to see him, he was with Greg, his other partner. They were both smiling and were very warm. I won't take time to tell you all the details now, but they offered me a job that is more important than the one I had before. In fact, I will be working just under John, and all the work must be approved by me before he sees it." I offered my congratulations. She continued, "I just can't believe it. Not only that, but all day long everyone has been saying, 'What happened to John? We all stay out of his way on Monday, as he can be very grumpy and hard to deal with. Something must have happened because he is all smiles.' It's true. He is like a new person." Not only had Maribeth healed her own reaction to the karmic debt between them, but also her work at the end of her session evidently reached John on a higher level, allowing him to offer her the perfect job. After several months, she confirmed that they were continuing to work side by side every day. The relationship is purely business, but the love flows between them within that framework. She reaffirmed that every day someone comments that he is a changed man.

In Maribeth's astrological chart, Saturn squares Jupiter. Saturn rules her house of work and is placed in the fifth house of romance, creative expression and the "gambling" impulses. With Saturn in that position, no matter what its aspects to other planets, caution, not recklessness, is the watchword. In Maribeth's chart, Jupiter is placed in the eighth house of transformation. That sector of the chart also describes the ability to get one's needs met and, eventually, to give one's greatest gift to humanity. With Jupiter in that position, her gift is that of encouragement, humor, optimism and the expression of contagious joy. As a result of her expansive feelings as well as her knowledge of how the company might best expand, great luck should come in the form of bonuses, income from residuals, royalties or commissions. On the negative side, Maribeth repressed her contagious humor and ability to encourage others with a Saturnish judgmental quality. With her new awareness, and especially because of the transformative eighth-house placement of Jupiter, she is now working diligently, behind the person she loves, to express constant joy and enthusiasm in the work they share. John has not been told about the regression session, but he has evidently benefited from Maribeth's review and healing of their deep karmic bond.

In each of these situations, there was a lesson to be learned and energy to be released through Jupiterian methods. For me, consistent humor and expectation help me to reach my goals. For Janet, the chance to expand her horizons through teaching seemed to be the way out of limiting, stagnant circumstances. Although Janet is not selfish in her present life, her selfishness from the past can manifest itself in an unwillingness to do things in the present that might cause problems for someone else. Therefore, she makes a passive contribution, not an active one. She has decided to dedicate herself to the study of a special subject that she will be able to use to help people achieve their goals. Perhaps she will teach that subject someday.

Maribeth has great generosity of spirit, for Jupiter rules that quality as well. She has had to learn not to dissipate all of her energy toward projects that may not come directly under her sphere of influence, and then feel discouraged if others are slow to take her up on her offers of help with expansive programs. In Egypt, she saw herself killed for being determined to set new conditions in motion without taking into consideration the feelings of the pharaoh, her husband. If she had used her enthusiasm, she could have enlisted his aid. She, too, must be willing to work behind others, encouraging them to do what she can see is in their best interest. In the meantime, her own goals can be satisfied by slowly working toward new conditions in her own life.

CHAPTER ELEVEN

Saturn and Uranus

ranus is the first of the higher octave planets. It describes a quality of electric energy that is very high in vibration. Therefore Uranus aspects lead to activity of a very special nature. Uranus describes healing, enlightenment and mental brilliance. It indicates a person who is humanitarian, individual and unique. Music, recordings and electronics are ruled by this planet. Special and unusual situations occur when Uranus is stimulated in the astrological chart. Those unexpected events lead to new awareness as a result of the breaking up of old patterns.

A person who has Uranus strong in the natal chart tends to march to the beat of a different drummer. He cannot conform to old rules and outmoded methods, for he is inventive and inspired. He may also be rebellious, high-strung and nervous. At times, the electrical energy in his body may not course smoothly through his system, and such physical conditions as allergies, rashes or asthma can occur. There is a great need for activities and conditions that allow for the release of this high energy; otherwise the nervous system can overload. The person needs to learn how to let off excess steam within his own system so that he doesn't damage his health.

Since Uranus rules the breathing mechanism as well as indicating the nervous system, tension may produce shallow breathing or a general lack of oxygen in the system. The meridians in the body may be reversed. (Meridians are the lines that connect acupuncture points in the body.) Reversed meridians may lead to what .appear to be learning disabilities. Actually the individual may learn so rapidly and be so far ahead of the norm that he tends to jam his own circuits by trying to slow down or conform to the methods of others. This is especially true if there are difficult aspects to Mercury or to the ruler of the third house of communications. In extreme situations, those difficult aspects may indicate a potential for dyslexia as a result of those reversed meridians.

In the interpretation of an astrological chart, when Uranus is very strongly placed (that is, on the ascendant, ruling the ascendant or aspecting the ascendant), I describe that energy as indicative of having lived in a "magic kingdom." By that I mean that the person had a previous existence in a place or level of awareness that is very high and magical. If one has lived with highly developed states of consciousness that allowed one to travel at the speed of sound and light, when one comes to the earth plane, the slowness can be difficult to handle. Not prepared for the obstructions he encounters, the individual can feel very limited and boxed in. The person with this illumination and potential for genius can want very much to run away to where he can operate once more with tremendous insight and rapidity.

Those Uranus aspects can indicate a suicidal complex. The desire to leave the earth plane is not maudlin but born of boredom. He or she may not be able to tolerate the highly charged electrical quality of his nervous system. It may prompt him to do something impulsive rather than just sit around waiting for an exciting event to come his way. He loves to live on the edge of danger and in the fast lane of life, so his suicidal complex is really an issue of "Please just stop the world and let me off." When events don't move rapidly enough for him there can be a feeling of loneliness and longing. That longing is not for earthly pleasures but for a faraway home. Home is where the vibrational energies allow him to feel attuned and safe, whether that be on another plane of existence or in special places on the earth where ley lines indicate an extra-high vibrational energy. (I am aware of several such places on the earth plane. There may be many more, but some special high energy points are the four corners in the United States where New Mexico, Arizona, Utah and Colorado meet; Glastonbury, England; Wales; points in Scotland; Ibiza; the Carpathian Mountains in Russia [formerly Transylvania], where the Carpathian monks reside; points in Bali; and Tibet.) Those higher vibrations are in tune with the nervous system—not only for people with Uranus strongly aspected in the chart but for everyone. However, such high energy spots seem to attract people who are unique or aware in some special way. Therefore, a person in need of high energy has a feeling of total freedom, exhilaration, and peace in such settings that he cannot feel in other locations.

When Saturn is in difficult aspect to Uranus, the individual may repress his special high energy and therefore deny his potential for genius. He is blocked by limiting circumstances or inner judgments, especially when he tries to conform to the rules and regulations of the restrictive conditions of his life. His karmic task has to do with the reconciliation of his desire to be free and to return "home" with his sense of responsibility to complete the task for which he was born. He may know on some level that the circumstances of life will entrap him rather than foster his Uranian need for freedom. Some souls are born ahead of their time. They may have to find artificial restrictive conditions on the earth plane that will force them to stick around long enough to find out what their mission is. When this person tries to be just like everybody else, he may stifle his genius potential, denying higher states of awareness even to himself. That can be hard on the nervous system. Periodically this person needs to release excess energy, letting off steam in a healthy, nonrebellious way. He may find that swinging in a hammock, tapping his foot, and swaying help to release the blocked energy that is causing an overload to his system.

Uranus describes a negative psychological state of "scare" as well as the potential for high vibrational attunement. It is like having a radio antenna in the stratosphere that may pick up static rather than the music of the spheres. Many autistic children exhibit a swaying syndrome. Perhaps, on a deep subconscious level, these children are living with a "scare" or a high degree of excitement that cannot be experienced by others. In the case of some children with learning disabilities or dyslexia, the energy going to the brain may be somehow mixed, causing the individual to reverse letters, read backward and generally be out of step with the earth plane. There are simple exercises that may help correct this problem. (They are described in the book *Touch for Health* by Dr. John Thye.) It is possible that these people are living on a sphere of awareness where their malfunction is perfectly normal. They may simply have to learn the rules of the earth plane and become attuned to lowered vibrational energy in order to function as others, on a practical, mundane level.

Uranian energy leads to high peaks of excitement and a desire to live in the fast lane. For someone with Saturn blocking that planet, the desire for excitement is there, but the karmic memory of having to pay a price for such levels of exhilaration or guilt about what he may have done is too painful for him. His individuality caused him trouble in the past, so it seems productive to deny its existence in the present. Since Uranus describes the limelight or fame, having been in a position of recognition in the past can cause negative feelings about attaining that sort of position once again. Lack of prominence represents safety. So the individual denies, to some degree, his ability to march to the beat of a different drummer and to live on a higher floor of consciousness. He may sabotage himself to avoid repetition of the pain that, for him, comes from being different or well known. One such woman was well aware of the pain she felt from the past in connection with special experiences.

PROMINENCE IN THE PAST

Laura is an incredibly exciting woman who exudes "electrical" energy. She has achieved prominence in her chosen career as a fashion publisher. But, though she is a prime force in the fashion world, Laura's reputation is confined to the fashion industry rather than extending to areas in which she might be an influence on a larger audience. In her regression session, she discovered a reason for this as well as a karmic relationship that needs to be resolved in her present life. In her chart, Saturn is placed in the seventh house of marriage and rules the fifth house of children. Laura's marriage ended painfully. She was left with the total support of three children, who rarely saw their father after the divorce. Uranus is the most elevated planet in her chart, posited in the ninth house at the most potent spot in the zodiac; that is, just before the mid-heaven (or M.C., describing the career potential). Uranus rules her sixth house of work, indicating a great deal of fame arising from work in exciting areas involving publicity, promotional efforts, publishing and international affairs. But as long as Laura allows the painful karmic memories of a past life to stop her, she will pick karmic relationships that give her an excuse to stop short of ultimate achievement. For instance, although Laura's children gave her a very strong motivation to succeed, she never traveled very far away from them because of her devotion to them. However, this may have caused her to miss opportunities to expand.

Before revealing an important event from a past life, Laura talked about an experience in this life. "I'm three years old. My mother has been gone for a long time. I'm told to sit still and wait for her to return. When she returns, I expect her to bring some warmth with her, but the room is still bare. This is a hotel room. (We came to the United States when I was only eighteen months old.) I see my mother but I can't touch her, because she's so removed. She's going through a lot of pain. She's trying to be strong, because my father has disappeared again. Actually he disappeared before I was born, so he hasn't been around very much. I'm feeling very sad about my father. No one has explained to me where he is. I don't understand why he's left me. He's very nurturing to me and I need him. It upsets me so much when he leaves." Evidently Laura's mother had left her alone while she was looking for work. Part of Laura's pain came from the fact that her mother was so sad and frightened.

She went to an earlier moment that was very frightening to her.

I see myself on the boat coming to America. The voyage is rough and I'm very seasick. It's unclear why I'm on this boat in the first place. It's turbulent and I don't like it. The room is down below and it's dark. I sleep a lot and I'm very anxious. My mother is comforting and protective on this trip, so it feels like the two of us against the world. I'm out on deck in a stroller only a few times. I look at the people and I like that, but I feel strange. I don't really want to get involved with them. I'm a bit indifferent, and I'm feeling a little bit superior. There is also an inner feeling of not fitting in. Outwardly I want to be part of the group, but something else is going on inside.

My mother is very frightened. She's hanging on to me. It's funny but I feel stronger and bigger than she is. I'm her security. She's frightened of what she's doing. I feel sorry for her and I'd like to help her if I could. It's very chaotic when we arrive. There's no sense of purpose, and we don't know anyone. She's reckless but also frightened, so I'm frightened too. I'm less patient, so I express my fears by crying. I'm feeling very unhappy. She's impatient because she has problems, so she starts to put up a plastic wall between us. When we arrive in the United States, she has no job and she doesn't have any money at all. She's running around everywhere, futilely. She's frantic. We go lots of places and look at things, but the tension is very hard to take.

After Laura's review of her birth, she looked at a past life that would give her an explanation for the circumstances of her present life. She said:

The people are poor. They have on brown tunics and rope belts, with cutoff pants and closed shoes. I'm sitting in a chair, and I'm wearing satin and I have a big round ring with a clear or gray stone. I'm a bit embarrassed at the ring. It seems gaudy and not a bit attractive, but it's supposed to be worn. My trousers seem to be a light gray or green. They are breeches, and I have on stockings. My jacket has buttons down the front. Obviously I am a man. I seem thin, but as I look down at my hands and ring, they seem gross to me. My body doesn't seem to fit my hand. There's some conflict with my wanting to be there. I'd like to be one of the women at the court because they are well taken care of. I don't like all the responsibility I have. It's very heavy and there's a lot to do. It's never-ending. The women sit around in pretty dresses and it's easy.

"I'm married, but my wife is just a fixture. There are some flirtations... but I don't think I want to look at them. Oh! I just had the wildest thought. I see the face of my daughter in this life framed by a hat. We have been lovers. But it is real love! There is anger and frustration, sadness and jealousy. I love her to pieces. She's one of the women at the court. At this particular moment, it seems a flirtation. She's very young... about sixteen. I'm thirty. When I look into her eyes, it seems as though I can see through to her soul. Ah... we're not lovers yet. I'm so bored with the people sitting at my feet, and then I look across at this young girl and I have an immediate attraction. I want to plot and plan to find out about her, and how to woo her.

I see her with me on a giant-size bed with a very ornate canopy. She's in a beautiful white nightdress. I've summoned her, and she's intrigued, but she is not here of her own free will. I asked for her and I got her. She has no choice, but she's intrigued. It is supposed to be just a young girl for an amusement, but when I look in her eyes, I fall in love. So I change from just wanting to make love to her to wanting to court her. I want to treat her kindly and with understanding. I don't make love to her that evening. I talk to her and touch her hair and comfort her. She's only a child and she's afraid. I take care of her. After she has been with me for a while, I call someone to take her away safely. The love develops slowly because she's the only one I could love. She finally falls in love with me, but more slowly than I. I see her many times before she's responsive. I care too much for her to force her.

I asked Laura to describe herself a bit more. She said, "I'm not handsome at all, but I'm strong and charismatic and very persuasive." I asked her what happened to her love affair with this young girl. She responded, "We do become lovers. For a while it is idyllic. Then the nastiness comes in. People are jealous. I get overly involved in the relationship and I don't see that people are taking advantage of me. In fact, there are a lot of things I don't see. Suddenly the thing that was so beautiful becomes a problem. My wife is very angry. She's not overly emotional about it, but she is angry and judgmental. It's an inconvenience to her. She doesn't understand that I love this person."

I asked Laura to describe her wife in that life. She said, "She's

Spanish, and very dark." I asked her if she recognized her in the present life. She replied, "Oh, it's my mother!" I then suggested that she look around the court to see if she recognized anyone else. She replied, "My boyfriend in the present is one of the young pages in the court. We laugh and giggle and have fun. We communicate very well. He's a nice friend. He is warning me to be more careful, but I don't listen. He's too young to be advising me. But he tells me that I have an enemy."

I asked Laura to describe the degree of danger this enemy represented. She answered, "It's dangerous to go to sleep at night. This man is waiting for the right moment to do something. He's plotting and planning something. He pretends to be a friend. He's older and experienced in the ways of the court. He knows protocol and he starts manipulating the people around me." Laura paused for a moment and then continued sadly, "He kills my young lover and therefore he has killed me too. I die because I don't want to live anymore. The dynasty passes to his line."

Suddenly Laura gasped, "This is too easy. My enemy is my husband in this life. He hurt my daughter all over again. She used to be afraid of him, but she's able to handle him a bit better now that she is older. I came back to get revenge on him. If I destroy him in this life, however, it will just keep on going. How can I forgive him for what he did to us then? I guess in this life, he helped me take some small steps upward, whereas in that life, he helped me to death. I must learn how to handle him and must refuse to get into games with him; I need to develop a positive kind of apathy. (By that I mean I must be attentive but not let him get to me.) Most of all, I must be aware of what he is capable of doing in this life."

Laura and I discussed the intricate web of relationships that exist from one lifetime to another. In this life, she had hoped to be well taken care of, as were the women in the court she had envied in the past. But circumstances forced her to take on the total support of her three children. And once again she is in a position of tremendous responsibility, for she runs a major corporation, with many employees dependent on her fashion judgment. At least responsibility and the pressures it brings are familiar to her. In the past life she described, however, she took risks with her personal feelings, allowing them to take precedence over her sense of duty. In this life, Laura is forced to take risks, but only those consistent with the level of responsibility she has accepted in her public life.

Since her husband has once again betrayed her, the first feelings that occurred to her were to get even, yet she is clearly unwilling to repeat the same patterns over and over again. If she forgives her husband, perhaps Laura will free herself to achieve the ultimate level of responsibility and fame that is indicated in her chart.

In my last conversation with Laura, she said, "At least I know not to grieve so much, because it is clear that we never lose anyone from our lives. It makes things very simple. I want to develop only good relationships, because it is no good having to pay off karmic debts the hard way and having to repeat difficult relationships." As Laura takes steps to broaden her career scope, she also gives permission to her husband and to her children to take the positive kinds of risks that will give them a sense of freedom as well. Laura has just enlarged her company to include an office in the Far East. She is finally allowing herself to travel and see the world and to accept an even higher level of responsibility for her family and her career.

PAST-LIFE BOREDOM

Patricia told an amazing story of escape from what appeared to be sure death and of a tragedy that could have tempted her to give up on life. Patricia was given a project that connected her with the government of a very remote island. Her husband was able to work in his own business, and together they moved to the island community for two years. While her sister was visiting from the United States, the three of them drove to a special spot on the island, high on a cliff overlooking a spectacular view. They knew this spot was dangerous because of the high waves that sometimes swept up over the rocks. Patricia was standing with her husband near the edge of the cliff. As she turned to walk back to her sister, a huge wave swept up over the rock where she had been standing with her husband. She turned to look over her shoulder and saw that her husband was gone. In the next second, another wave swept up, taking her backward over the cliff and far out to sea. Caught in a very strong undertow, she did the only thing she could. She held her breath and let herself be carried in this fierce maelstrom of water. As she related this in her regression session, she said:

> I know I'm going to die and that's okay. Suddenly, when my lungs are about to burst and I have no strength left, I feel a hand that's about the size of my body, or bigger, come from underneath me and lift me above and on top of the water. It seems to keep me there long enough so that I can begin to breathe on my own. I can only say it is like the hand of God. I don't realize what it feels like until later on. I just know that I am suddenly above the water. I am not lifting myself, and finally I'm able to begin treading water. I'm above the force that was pulling me down.
>
> I'm about a quarter of a mile out to sea when this hand lifts me to the surface. Then I can rest and get into an upright position. Since I had training as a lifeguard, I know certain survival techniques. It is important to tread water as long as you can. But I realize that there is quite a current where I am. (I am just outside the reef that surrounds the island. Boats cannot come inside the reef, except in certain places.) I can barely see the cliff where we had stood. I have very poor vision (I'm nearly blind) and my contacts are somewhere up on that rock. I don't know whether I actually see my sister or just imagine her still standing alone on that cliff. And I'm not sure I really hear her voice saying that help is coming. I keep treading water, knowing that if I don't, I will be pushed farther out to sea, and then I will really be lost. The island is very small, and I keep using that cliff as a point of reference so that my sister can see me, and so they can find me.
>
> This goes on for what seems an eternity, and I just keep having to decide whether I am going to keep on treading water or not make the effort. At one point, I become very angry because I am very tired. I'm angry at Peter, my husband, for not doing anything about it. He's not coming to rescue me. I'm enraged at him, and then in a few minutes, I know he is not coming because he is dead. It dawned on me just like that.

Patricia paused for a moment, and I asked her if she needed to cry. She said, "I've cried so much that I have no tears left now." She continued.

The other image that keeps coming to me is that of John F. Kennedy swimming all night in the South Pacific. (I had read his biography.) He swam for twelve hours or so when his boat went down. That's how he injured his back. Now I know firsthand that a person can continue dealing with the water.

I can tell that there is some action where my sister is standing. A person jumps into the water with a surfboard and paddles out to me. I have been wondering why no one had come to me, but I also know my sister can't leave the rocks to get help. It is a very isolated place. She must just stand there and wait for someone to come along so she can call for help. I also know it is very dangerous, and maybe impossible, to get to me. I expect it will be a Coast Guard boat that saves me but I know it will take a long time, because someone will have to go all the way through the jungle to call them, before they can come around to pick me up.

The man who comes out on a surfboard is an islander. This is really a very heroic thing for him to do, because the islanders don't swim. They will not go out in the open ocean, even in boats. He is really putting his own life in danger. And he loses his life jacket diving into the ocean because of the force of the water. When he comes, I hang on to his surfboard and then I get seasick. It's funny not to get seasick while I'm swimming, but during the time I wait for the Coast Guard boat to arrive, I'm seasick the whole time, about half an hour. I'm able to hang on to his surfboard, and I don't have to keep treading water during that time. Once on dry land, I continue to be seasick while we go to the hospital, which takes about half an hour.

Patricia described the fears she had while she was in the water.

It has been about three and a half hours. The waves have been about fifteen feet high, so I'm not just battling the current, I'm forever being deluged. I'm feeling the tension in my back. But the real problem is that my back has been bleeding and I've worried about sharks for some time. Finally the bleeding stops. I am having to control any tendency to panic because I know that's the worst thing you can do. I have only one basic underlying thought: "Do you choose to live through this?" Faced with that decision, I stay very cool.

When my sister comes to the hospital, I take one look at her face and know that Peter is dead. I see my sister's agony in the hospital and I cry as much for her pain as for my own. I've cried about that for eight and a half years. However, I know that if I begin to grieve for Peter at that moment, I won't make it. I need every bit of strength to survive.

When I asked Patricia about Peter's death, she replied, "My instinct is that he drowned immediately."

After reviewing this excruciatingly painful time in her life, Patricia described her early life as being somewhat drab—everything seemed to be shades of gray. She also knew she couldn't see very well. She had been born with fifteen more blind spots than most people, and everything she saw was just a blur. Describing her birth, she said:

> I'm watching. I'm not feeling like I'm supposed to do anything; I'm just looking on. Bewilderment is the word I would use. There's nothing threatening about being born, but I know I'm supposed to do something out there and if I just knew what it was. . . . Why doesn't someone come up and tell me what it is? I have no way to interpret the data, because there's nothing to interpret. I just go along for the ride. I'm not reluctant, but I'm going to be pushed. I'm feeling a hand again, behind my back, like, "Well come on!" It's a very gentle hand. When I come out, the impression I get is light. Everything is shadowy. What comes into focus are doctors with masks. They are being perfunctory. There's no emotion and there's no strong reaction from anyone. My mother is not even looking at me. She's just glad it's over with. My sense is that my father is out there in the waiting room. He seems worried. I feel, "Well, this is okay, and what isn't there is okay too." It doesn't occur to me to be upset over any lack. I don't even know anything is missing. My birth survival issue seems to be, "I'm the most curious of all to see what I'll do next."

Patricia then gave a perfect example of how Uranian energy manifests itself. She described the impulses that periodically led to adventures in her life.

> I have always found myself far more interesting than the world. I get these flashes—a switch goes on and I do what I feel led to do. I never know where these flashes or impulses come from. For in-

stance, I used to participate in science fairs and thought about being a doctor, but then I entered a Miss America beauty pageant. I have no idea where that impulse came from. Having observed these impulses all my life, I just know that all of a sudden, something becomes a dead certainty. That's where my curiosity comes from. Until that switch goes on, I'm stuck in those in-between places! I still wait for that switch to go on, but I don't like the in-between states where nothing is happening. I have such continual frustration with people and places that I am just ready to exit the scene. I don't have a problem with that thought. What I would like is to find something interesting to do while I'm waiting for that switch to go on. To this very day, there is nothing that can substitute for the aliveness that suddenly happens when the switch goes on.

Patricia had described not only the boredom that accompanies the aspect of Saturn shadowing Uranus (those unending waiting periods) but also what I term the suicidal complex... "Please just stop the world and let me off." This comes from having lived a former life where the intellectual and spiritual level was so high that it was like breathing rarefied air, a life where one could travel at the speed of light and sound. So the boredom that sets in on the earth plane (described by Saturn) is almost intolerable. One has a tremendous desire to live, once again, where all higher perspectives and desires can be quickly manifested in the outer conditions of life. Uranus indicates leanings toward science, but in all cases, it describes brilliance of intellect that may set an individual apart from other less adventurous souls. It certainly describes a person who is a risk taker. In this earth plane existence, however, there may be some karmic situation that prevents the "switch" from going on. Some grounding may be necessary to balance the individual energy and hold him to a slower level of existence. It may be that external blocks are necessary to prevent the person from running away prematurely, thereby missing his destiny because of lack of synchronicity with the earth plane. Certainly some karmic guilt must be resolved.

Patricia continued with her view of herself in another existence. "One scene I see is in Atlantis. I am exceedingly brilliant. I'm a philosophy teacher by the age of ten. I'm nothing but a super brain. I try to break out and explore other aspects of my life, but by the age of twenty-five or thirty, I am tired of that level of existence but unable to change or break the mold. I am too polarized on a mental level. So I go off to live on an island until the destruction of civilization is complete. I don't live to be more than about thirty-three in that life."

When I asked Patricia to describe her view of Atlantis, she said:

My life is a very ivory-tower sort of existence. My home feels like a university. It literally looks like a blazing white building with a tower, where I live. I'm female and blond. I'm very attractive. I think my mother has died in childbirth, from the baby born just after my birth. I have a father and four siblings, but I have been removed from their presence early in life. My siblings are bright, but not genius level. One of my brothers is a late bloomer in that life. He's the same brother in this life, and once again, he's the same late bloomer. Of course there's some resentment on the part of my brothers because I get a lot of attention. The role I have is not a female role, even in that society.

My brain is like a computer or I wouldn't be elevated to the role I have at the university. It doesn't occur to me until I'm in my mid-twenties that there is anything lacking in my life. I'm so intellectual that I have no one to talk to. There's a terrible lack of stimulation.

Referring to what Patricia had said about her early childhood in this life, I commented, "You see how far back the boredom set in." Patricia had seen her childhood as nothing but a series of grays, shadowy and not very stimulating. She had also talked about her poor vision. She commented many times that she was just not interested in what was going on outside her in the world. I suggested that nothing in her outside world was exciting enough to make her come out of herself and look around. Her lack of interest kept her looking within. Could it be that her blindness was a result of her disinterest in exterior events and people, or just the other way around? It appeared that the beginnings of the condition existed in Atlantis, when she couldn't easily relate to the people around her because of her brilliance.

I asked Patricia to describe in more detail what her responsibilities were in connection with the university in Atlantis. She said:

I teach and I write. But beyond a certain point, my work doesn't seem to have any effect. Early on, my bent is toward the mathematical and scientific fields. It's like quantum physics somehow combined with the concepts of the Tao, so my work becomes very philosophical. There's no one else who can go into the esoteric realms, so I'm there by myself. I'm lonely because I have no one to talk to. I become a resource they can't use anymore, so I take a boat to a nearby island. I live among the native villagers for about two years, until the destruction of Atlantis.

I see another life, but this time the colors are different. (I find it interesting that Atlantis was all white.) This life is in Italy. I'm not only intellectually bright, but I write poetry, design, and draw as well. It is clear that this is Florence. There is more of a tapestry of colors, very Renaissance. Until I'm of marriagable age, I'm encouraged to be involved in all kinds of artistic activities. Then all of a sudden, it stops. I'm not supposed to do anything anymore. I am supposed to be married and just sit around. I have a father and brothers. It is almost like a court family, but more like the third or fourth tier from the top. The name of the family may have carried down to the present day. I see a huge villa with courtyards and gardens. I'm beautifully dressed, with jewels and ornaments.

My sense is that my father tells me I'm to be married, with no forewarning. I don't have children, so I have to sit around where everyone is weaving and spinning and sewing: This is being female and I'm very bored. I'm frustrated about what to do with my creative energy, so I try to read my stories and get the people around me involved, but no one is interested. There's actually a lot of warmth within the family. Once again, I have no mother, but there is a second wife for my father. I don't seem to have any emotional involvement with my husband. He seems to be almost effeminate, so there's probably not a lot of sexuality in the marriage. The turning point in my life comes when my father tells me I'm to be married. All my free activities must cease. I die of suffocation, actually boredom, at thirty-five.

As I requested, Patricia looked at the people in that life to see if anyone came back with her into the present time. She said, "My mother, who died in that lifetime, is my sister now. We are extremely close."

When I asked Patricia if she had ever had a lifetime that was exciting, she replied, "There is one lifetime where I'm a shrouded old woman, an old crone, somewhere near Ireland or Scotland. I'm standing in the middle of the woods, wearing grayish clothes. The word that comes to me is *wisdom*. Someone is stirring a pot. . . . I must be a witch. It's like a cartoon. The woman standing with me is like an assistant. She is relatively young and she's stirring a pot. She's brewing something. It's late fall or spring, in the afternoon, and it's very pleasant. This is not actually an exciting life, but I have the wisdom to know it's irrelevant. I feel very wise and contented. The difference is that I'm not looking for anything in that life, so there are no disappointments. People come to see me, and I'm respected and looked up to." After a pause, Patricia said, "My assistant in that life is my sister again." Then I asked Patricia if there was an essence in that life that she could bring into this life. She replied, "I want to invite the energy of the old woman into my life now."

I felt at the end of Patricia's session that she had touched on the true essence of Uranus in an astrological chart. Her description of her life as a wise old woman showed that when Uranian energy is released into activities consistent with enlightenment, boredom ceases even though outer conditions may seem ordinary. Uranian energy can tap higher levels of awareness and intuition that can bring light (like electricity) to mankind. With Saturn blocks, it appears that one returns to the earth plane to integrate that high awareness with practical everyday living, without being pulled down into materiality. When the feet are firmly planted on earth, the mind is free to soar into the higher realms of inspiration.

In Patricia's case, the ability to act as an inspiration to others may be expressed later in life. Uranus is located in the eighth house of her astrological wheel and rules the fourth house that describes home life. (That house also indicates conditions in the third portion of one's life, which for Patricia should commence around the age of forty-five.) Saturn is placed in the tenth house of career and public life. That sector also describes the character of and the relationship with the parent of the same sex. Although Patricia didn't indicate having a heavy karmic situation to resolve with her mother, she did reveal a lack of mothering in her past lives. It would seem that she was deprived of nurturing on a very deep level, reaching way back and continuing into the present. Patricia might pick career situations that would represent a technical level of responsibility but might not propel her into the spotlight that would bring fame. She may unconsciously avoid peaks of excitement and honor because of the memory of loneliness in the past. For Patricia, different kinds of risks may be necessary to tap the true healing ability she recognized from her life as the old woman. It would seem that she came back to be a light and a beacon for mankind, perhaps on a wider scale than in her past life.

For both Laura and Patricia, the willingness to put themselves in a position where they can exhibit their own levels of enlightenment seems necessary once again. For Laura, it means learning to deal with the danger of risk, whereas for Patricia, it means dealing with a sense of isolation and loneliness. Yet the excitement that comes with expression of the true humanitarian, Uranian qualities can far outweigh both conditions. Both women have the potential to inspire others, lighting the way through their own special brand of genius and inspiration.

CHAPTER TWELVE

Saturn and Neptune

N *eptune* is the planet that is associated with high idealism, dreams and fantasies. It rules such activities as film, photography and therapy. Because Neptune's energy is conceptual and creative, it can describe projects that require vision, sensitivity and inspiration. It may describe the glamour world, poetry and prophecy. Neptune is the planet of faith, trust and hope. A person with a Neptunian outlook on life may see the world with special perceptions. He may be naive or simply have the expectation that other people are motivated by the same high altruism as himself. He may live in a fantasy world. However, he is the very person who can create the exact conditions he needs and wants in his life, simply because of his lofty dreams and conceptual ability.

But a Neptunian view of life may be that which only allows the person to see beauty and ideal conditions. If Neptune is strong in an astrological chart and has many difficult aspects, a person tends to put on blinders when ugliness, pain and sorrow come into view. He can have difficulty with confrontation, for a Neptunian outlook may describe an ostrich complex (hiding one's head in the sand). That attitude may be adopted at the moment of birth in order to survive a life that promises to have less than perfect conditions. Rather than be disillusioned, he simply won't look at the harsh, cold realities around him. Neptune can describe a kind of tyranny, however, for as gentle as the energy may be, there is an iron fist inside the velvet glove. A Neptunian person can say, "I expect you to be the way I see you and to live up to my expectations of you. Don't you dare let me down, for if you do, I won't be able to survive."

Neptune is a planet ruling the higher mind, and it describes right brain functions. Left brain, described by Mercury, deals with details, facts and figures, whereas Neptunian right brain is the creative conceptualizer. Neptune views people and situations through rose-colored glasses, tending to put people on a pedestal. The danger comes when those rosy glasses fall off and people are seen to be mere mortals. The resulting disillusionment can be devastating. Therefore, a Neptunian person finds interesting ways to avoid the possibility of seeing harsh, cold facts. Most of all, he may not see himself very realistically. Don Quixote, in his relationship to Dulcinea, provides the perfect example of how the Neptunian energy can work. In Don Quixote's mind, Dulcinea is a goddess, a woman to be worshipped and admired. In truth, Dulcinea is a prostitute, disillusioned with life and content with her debasement, for at least there are no dreams to be shattered. Don Quixote nearly drives her crazy in his attempts to make her what she is not. She screams at him, "Open your eyes, see me as I am or leave me alone."

During the Depression years, people flocked to the movies to escape the hardships and limitations in their lives. Hollywood glamour was at its height. Neptunian films presented an unrealistic view of life, for the hero always got the girl and they lived happily ever after. The generation that grew up watching those films longed to emulate their heros. They had been programmed in a subtle, subconscious Neptunian way. So boy met girl and they were married. Instead of the happy endings that were expected, the reality of day-to-day living brought about different scenarios. Disillusionment produced a high divorce rate.

Neptune has a tremendously important function in successful living, however. It describes the ability to create the exact circumstances in life that are desired through the process of visualization. In ancient days, men knew how to manifest the very things they needed for survival in life. Traditional Huna magic, for instance, taught the secrets of tapping the richness and resources of the universe. It is said that in pre-Atlantean days, man could simply visualize food or material objects and they would appear in front of his very eyes. With misuse of that ability, it was lost to some degree. We, in modern times, are beginning to learn once again how to tap the wellsprings of abundance by using the subconscious mind processes. The success of manifesting what one needs and wants in life has to do with the use of right brain fantasies and the subconscious mind described by Neptune. If one can visualize something strongly enough, he can have it. But he must be able to impress the sensitive subconscious mind strongly enough to bring things into reality. If doubt exists about the process, the subconscious mind hears doubt, and the conditions that manifest are the limited results of that doubt.

When Saturn casts its darkness over the high idealism of Neptunian energy, the person can see a glass as half-empty rather than half-full. He may develop a cynical approach to life as a protective device. How can he trust life and universal abundance when early programming has been less than optimistic and hopeful? One way to change that programming is to search for a past life where hope was suddenly swept away, leaving disillusionment in its wake. If an individual can trace the roots of his feeling of "what's the use," he may be able to regain his faith in the unremitting laws of nature and use them to his advantage instead of staying in his doubts.

HOPELESSNESS EXPLAINED FROM THE PAST

One young woman, who has Saturn conjunct Neptune in her natal chart, came to me for a egression session during a very crucial period in her life. Paula is married to a man she loved deeply for many years. They have a daughter who is healthy, bright and lively. To all outward appearances, Paula has an ideal family life. But her husband is a recovering heroin addict. During the years of his addiction, she worked very hard to keep the family life-style intact. Her profession enabled her to earn money and also provide loving compassion for him in his struggle to combat the addiction, for she is a medical doctor. Something happened to inspire her husband and lead him on the road to recovery. When Paula came to me for a regression session, he had been free of drugs for over a year. However, all the old patterns and pressures were catching up with them and it was time to make a decision about a new direction in their lives.

Paula has Virgo on the ascendant in her astrological chart. The opposite sign of Pisces rules the seventh house of marriage, so Paula would naturally be attracted to a man who is Neptunian, sensitive and idealistic. He might be a visionary, a prophet and a poet. Since Saturn is conjunct Neptune in her chart, however, she could attract a marital situation with a karmic shadow to be resolved. Her mate might bury or stifle those idealistic tendencies due to disillusionment sometime in his early life, or even in a past life. He may have adopted a "what's the use" attitude due to devastating eye-opening circumstances sometime in his past. He might look to alcohol or drugs as a way to bring back hope and bright colors in life, even without knowing that was what he was doing. Neptune is one of the planets that signifies possible addiction in an astrological chart, for it rules alcohol and drugs.

So for Paula, her own doubts and fears of disillusionment in life led to a marriage with someone acting out those qualities. The conjunction of Saturn-Neptune in her chart is placed in the second house of money. When Saturn is posited in that financial house, a poor complex can exist, in spite of the amount of money earned. By marrying a man with an expensive drug habit, Paula ensured that she would not have ideal financial conditions. The Saturn-Neptune conjunction also rules the fifth house in her chart. The fifth house describes her attitude and relationship with her daughter. That relationship would also have karmic overtones to be resolved. When Saturn conjuncts another planet, there exists a very positive opportunity to turn conditions around by taking on a different quality and level of responsibility. In Paula's case, hopelessness is not the only potential for the future. In fact, with dedication and a determination to reconcile and resolve guilts from the past, Paula's family life and relationship with her husband and child provide the very security she needs in order to live up to her financial and creative potential. The dream of creating an ideal life-style for the three of them can be a strong motivation indeed.

Paula began her regression session talking about an incident when she was a small child of two. She saw herself standing in a house that belonged to her grandmother. She knew she was moving to another house, but the way she saw herself dressed didn't seem to fit the occasion, for she was dressed in her nicest clothes. She said, "I'm very, very little and very clever. I can talk very well and I can even correct my baby-sitter because I speak better than she does. I'm aware of everything that is happening in the house. I see myself in a little white dress, white shoes and socks. Logically I wouldn't be wearing a special dress for moving. I see myself very much in control of the situation. I'm excited about a change. But then the lawyers come to see my grandmother and I'm very disturbed by that. I don't like those men. It's an awful feeling for the lawyers to come and ask for my grandmother. I blame them for taking the house."

Paula was born in a European village. Her grandmother, as the eldest, inherited a lovely house in the village, and her younger brother was given property and money to compensate. However, in those days, nothing was written down, and at a later time, the brother felt slighted. Paula's grandmother offered him money to balance the scales and he accepted, but again nothing was done legally. When the grandmother was fifty-two years old, her brother took her to court to get the house for himself and won the case. Even though she took the case to the highest court, the grandmother was forced to turn over the house to her brother when she was well along in years.

Paula's grandmother was the local teacher and conducted the school from part of the house. It would be easy to buy another house and start another school, so that was the grandmother's plan. She made enough money to buy another house, but just before the move, a servant stole the money. Paula realized that although her grandmother didn't show her feelings, she must have been devastated by the losses and the betrayal by her brother and a trusted servant. When Paula became aware that her grandmother had lost heart and never really recovered from the blow, she was shocked to realize how much it had affected her throughout her life.

Paula continued:

My grandmother is a major influence in my life. She is quite brilliant and very strong. There are no schools in the village except my grandmother's school, but the new house where we move is not as nice and is not run as well as the old house, so my grandmother must have suffered tremendously not to be able to open a school and continue her lifetime work. I realize at the age of two that the unexpected can happen quite suddenly and you can lose everything. I've always felt, "what's the use of building toward the future, when the future is so uncertain." I am a very intelligent little girl and young person, but I never feel I will get what I want out of life. I always feel, "Yes, I can try, but material things I will never get." When people talk about working toward the future, I feel, "What for? There is no future." I'm a doctor and yet I feel I will not succeed. Intellectually I know how capable I am, but I still feel that sense of defeat.

Paula talked about how the loss of her home affected her as a child and now. She said, "It's very traumatic and devastating for me to have to move. When I am two, I don't like the new house. It is a loss of prestige and a loss of friends because we are not in the center of village life anymore. I don't cry, but I know it is never going to be the same. After that, when I have to pass the old house, I can never just walk past the house, I have to run very fast. Now I would rather stay wherever I am than move. It's just too painful. I always think I can make my present home more comfortable just to avoid the possibility of a change, even if something else would be better. I almost feel, "What's the point of having nice things and having pleasure if it's just going to be taken away?"

Paula next saw herself at three months old. She said,

I'm very happy and content until my mother discovers she is pregnant again. Because of that, she can't nurse me, so she finds a poor woman who has a little boy just my age to be my milk mother. This woman is having a hard time, because she is not married. In my village, that is the same as being a prostitute. She's very gentle with me, but I'm very angry with my mother. I'm in this woman's arms and I'm thankful for her, but I'm out of place there. I know her child is there and I feel sorry for him, but not very compassionate, because I'm using his mother. I'm aware that she is a servant. I'm too angry to be compassionate and I take it out on my mother by ignoring her. I'm a very good actor, so she never knows it, but I shut myself away. I'm hurt and feeling abandoned by her. I don't think my father likes to see his baby with another woman, either, even though it is his fault. Everyone is angry with everyone else. I don't think my mother wants to be pregnant. She wanted to spend more time with me, but she pretends to be happy due to religious convictions. It's no wonder I have no faith in the future. This woman's milk is poisoned with defeat and hopelessness. She really has no future.

If my mother had only explained to me that it wasn't her fault and that it didn't mean she didn't love me and if she had said that the milk wasn't so important for our relationship, I would have understood and reacted differently. She doesn't think children should have any explanation for things, and I'm sure she doesn't think a three-month-old baby will understand. As it is, everyone is pretending, and everyone is acting. There is a real lack of clarity about feelings.

One manifestation of the Saturn-Neptune aspect is that anything less than crystal clear can be very threatening and disturbing. People who have this aspect in their charts don't like to deal with illusion and Neptunian hopes or dreams. Paula continued talking about the mirage that was created in her family. "It hurts when they try to act like nothing has happened. It's insulting. It hurts because they don't realize how angry I am. Later on, I hide behind pieces of furniture or behind draperies for the whole day. There's no way I can get the anger out of my system. It goes right into my heart. I close off my heart chakra. I still get angry when people don't explain things to me. It also happens with one of my brothers. He just presumes that I complain. Of course, it works the other way around too. I should have explained some things to my brother too. He's a bit blind, but so are my mother and father. Everything would have been so different if they had only explained things to me."

Paula described her birth process as something already experienced. The thought that came through for her in a very strong way was, "Here we go again." But that thought was replaced by a vision of a field on a mountain. She said:

It's grassy and seems like Switzerland. It is springtime and there are predominantly orange and yellow flowers everywhere. I'm waiting for someone, a young girl, and it's getting late. It's not a clandestine meeting but it is a little bit secret. I'm wearing a long dress, a bit like peasant women wear in Greece. It's a medium blue and I have something over my hair, like a cloth. It is in the last century, around 1870. I don't live in this village. I live alone. I think I'm a healer but I don't think I'm very compassionate. I am kind of a feminist. The girl who comes to meet me is blond with long hair. She has average good looks and she comes alone. When she arrives and before she says anything, I just know that she's pregnant and I offer to help her lose the baby if she wants. I have a knowledge of the herbs she could take and I know she is unmarried. She seems very familiar to me. Oh . . . she's my daughter! This is the first time I've seen her in twenty years. I left her with her father, because it was an impossible situation for me there. I think we meet by chance and I just know she is pregnant. Then we are talking and I know by asking her some questions that she is my daughter. I confess to her and she is shocked. She thinks this is all too fantastic that I would know that she is pregnant. She knows I left her when she was born and this meeting is traumatic for her.

The reunion is very sad. She feels very sad and she doesn't understand anything. I suddenly open up about my feelings for her. I haven't felt anything or thought about her for twenty years. I wanted to help her because of my conviction that no one should be forced to have an unwanted baby, but when I see myself in front of my daughter, it is something different. She doesn't really trust me so she doesn't take the herbs that would help her lose the baby. However, I don't think she has the baby after all. When I see her, I regret having ever left her. I was leaving the situation, not her. The father is very serious but a bit boring. He seems to be an artisan of some sort, maybe working with leather. As a younger person, I am of average good looks, physically, but I feel that I have some special powers that I can't show to people, because they won't understand. My family died when I was very young, so the marriage is one of convenience. Although the man is very gentle, I discover my powers and I feel I have to leave.

I am actually quite happy living by myself. I know I can read people's minds and help them, but I don't use my powers. I almost hide them altogether. Then I see a lot of sadness and I know I begin to use those powers, but not for compassionate reasons, but more for idealogical or political reasons. When I see my daughter, all my feelings turn on again.

Paula paused and with some astonishment said, "Oh . . . it is my daughter in this life. She doesn't look the same, but I know it is her." Then with sadness, Paula continued very softly, "I think I kill myself when she rejects me. It isn't very difficult with the herbs."

Paula talked about her present situation.

Now I don't have to hide from anyone, but I have to hide from myself. With the healing aspect in my present life, I can't seem to get it all together. In that life, it would have been difficult to stay with my husband, but if I had to do it again, I would have stayed. I could have dealt with my situation by transmitting my powers to my daughter in a very gentle way. I would have tried to teach her with love, keeping myself silent to other people. In a way, I deprived her of my love, but more than that, I deprived myself of love. I'm still punishing myself from that lifetime a lot. I deprive myself of the real satisfaction of love in this life. If I had talked to her, she would have forgiven me, and the man probably would have understood, too, if I had just taken the time to explain. It was too late to explain anything when she was twenty.

Paula also has Saturn square Venus in her chart, which describes the lack of acceptance of love in this life. She continued,

The problem is forgiving myself. I was lonely and I suffered in that life. I have paid for it, but I have to forgive myself for not showing love and compassion, and for cutting it off and not allowing myself to receive that too. Even now I tend to give love, but I'm not very ready to accept it. When friends do me a favor, I almost resent it. I don't let the love flow. In this life, I cut off the love from my brother by not explaining things to him. I just expect him to understand. A lot of my resentment covers the love I feel unable to express.

You know, I even felt the loneliness in the womb. I have felt very lonely in this life, too. It's ironic, but I tried to have an abortion when I was pregnant with my daughter. I got as far as having the anesthetic and the doctor said it was too late. I don't think it was too late; I always thought she was just so strong, she wouldn't let it happen. I never showed my guilt about that, but inside I felt really guilty. I have talked to her about this and I have explained it to her. Babies deserve to be treated with great respect and they are not too young to know what is going on. The wonderful thing is that she refused to let me go this time. Now we have another chance.

Paula took a very brief glance at another lifetime, where she knew her husband in the present time. She saw the relationship as very different from her current life. She said, "I think I knew my husband in a lifetime that seems to be located in a Mediterranean country. I see a lot of beautiful beaches. I think I am a male and I am a lighthouse keeper. I never married in that life, and although it was a lonely kind of life, I had the companionship of my mother, who seems to be my husband in this life! I think that explains a lot of my protective feelings toward him. If he mothered me then, it seems to be my turn to express those same feelings toward him. He is very important to me, and luckily I don't feel only mothering in my relationship to him now."

Paula has been through a great deal of therapy in order to understand the patterns in her life. After her session, she told me that she knows her new insights will help her therapy continue in an even more positive direction. She admitted that the hardest job is to remain open and trusting that the future holds bright promise, not more struggle and lack of hope. The courage she watches in her husband's life gives her additional strength to fight any dark feelings of defeat she wrestles with from her distant past.

PROBLEMS OF HEIGHTENED AWARENESS

Susan has Saturn conjunct Neptune in her natal chart. The placement in her case is in the sixth house of work, with that conjunction ruling the ninth house of travel, promotional matters, public relations and the higher mind. The conjunction also rules the eleventh house of friends and associations. The interpretation of that aspect, in her case, might lead me to point out a karmic guilt about friends and associates from a past life that would cause Susan to limit herself in the present. Susan might pick the kind of occupation that has the potential to bring recognition for her special brand of inspiration. But in some way, Susan might find an excuse not to work or to work too hard in nonproductive areas, possibly causing lowered vitality. In either case, she would be prevented from living up to her potential. She might take on such a heavy load of responsibility with work connected to advertising, promotional efforts or group situations that she would have to get sick to get out from under the pressure. She could work on such a technical level that her creative abilities might be stymied. These methods of overload are wonderful ways to avoid her destiny of inspiring her special group. Susan's regression session illustrated this aspect in her chart in a most profound manner.

Susan was born to a family who lived an interesting international, rather exotic life-style. The first memory that floated into her mind was that of being left behind when she was four years old. Her mother and father wanted to travel through the south of France and found a wonderful children's camp in Switzerland where they could leave their two daughters without fear for their well-being. Susan was told that her mother and father had to take care of some business matters when they left the girls at the well-run camp/hotel. However, Susan's mother couldn't bear to be away from her daughters without at least checking on their welfare periodically, so about once a week, they would visit the site and peer from a distance to be sure the girls looked healthy and happy. Susan's sister was only two years old and was perfectly content, but Susan had a different reaction.

Once I saw my mother and father looking at us from the woods beyond the play area and another time I saw them peering from behind the windows on the dining room doors. I asked someone if that was my parents come to visit, but I was told no. I knew very well that those shadows on the other side of the door were my mother and father, but the people denied it. [She continued talking to me in the present tense as I requested her to do.] I feel very betrayed because I know it's them. I want to say, "Don't go down so low. Have some respect for the truth. It's useless, wasteful . . . no consideration . . . It's the wrong game at the wrong time. It's just so dumb. Why do we have to lie to each other?" [Susan was visibly upset at this memory. She continued.] There's no one to talk to about it, because my sister is perfectly happy. I feel a lack of respect for my mother and father because there's no purpose to it. I feel very frustrated and helpless. I'm four, so I can't do anything on my own. I have to sit there and take it. I would have been in total agreement with them if they had just told me the facts. When they lie to me, or there's lack of clarity, it's like being in fogland. I don't like to be in fogland. I'm just overwhelmed by the experience. It's their right to travel if they want. I simply tune out so that I can handle the situation. I take long walks in the mountains so that I can work out a few things for myself. My telescope is going very deep into my emotions, trying to understand them and why they did that. I could have had a lot of fun if they had just been honest with me. It's all very confusing because I love them very much. This attempt to understand them is much more important than going to swing on the swings, for instance. This goes down to my basic human purpose and evolution.

I asked Susan what happened when it was time for her parents to take them home. She replied: "When they come to get me, I'm just so happy to see them, but there is resentment. I show the resentment by becoming secretive. I keep things from them." She volunteered:

This is going to sound terrible, but I know I'm a more evolved human being than they are and I'm just going to have to bear with them. That's hard. They are extraordinary in their own way. My mother really has potential, but she'll never live up to it. These are things I know at four that I will have to live with for a long time. I've already hit some realities that are not very pleasant for me. I'm very aware very early that it will be a long time before I can come out and express what I know. I have such high psychic energy that I can read people's minds. I know exactly who is going to walk in the door. It scares me because I feel very alone. Then I think, "Maybe I'm really weird." There's no one to share it, so I have to be silent. I'm going to have to wait for many years because I'm going to be considered a kook, and I'm not! I'm one of the sanest people I know.

Susan continued to talk about the way the deception affected her. "It's like I have to be on my guard with them. I can't quite relax. I trusted them 100 percent, so it's hard to take the disillusionment. I just feel paralyzed. I understand much more today why they did it than I could at age four. I just have to bear with the problem. I miss them very much, but something is broken between us." Susan recalled an incident when she was only nine months old. She knew that her mother was very sad because of the death of a favorite aunt. She commented, "I can't understand why they're sad. This woman is fine. I can't pay much attention to them, for they're just being silly." Susan's insight about death was already setting her apart from her mother at this early age.

When we looked at the birth process, Susan saw once again an incident where the people around her were behaving in a ridiculous fashion.

I can't be born. My mother is very tight, very nervous. She's so scared. I want to say, "Relax, lady." The walls give so much pressure that I'll suffocate unless she lets go. If I have to come out, let's do it once and for all. I begin radiating energy within her so she can relax. She needs to be reassured, so I'm reaching her mind by sending her white light. The whole womb is radiating light now and it seems to warm the entrance a little bit. Now I'm born and it feels great. Oh! They've just spanked me.... What a dumb thing to do. I'll have to be tolerant in this life. Now my mother sees me and she's just in ecstasy. I'm happy to be born to them because there'll be a lot of love.

A review of the prenatal period brought forth a description that was unusual among my clients. She continued, "It's wartime. My parents meet and fall in love. When I'm created, there's a lot of wonderful energy being given by both of them. I'm created during some very exciting lovemaking. But I say to myself, 'Why me? I don't want to go through this again. Why not somebody else?' It's so beautiful where I am. Being born is like going back to primitive times. But I have this debt with the universe and I have to volunteer my services. I might as well do it now and get it over with. I just don't want to face what I have to do in this life."

I asked Susan to go to a past life that would give her an explanation of why she had to return to earth. She began a description of a sad time in history. She first saw a tomb. She said, "It's in Peru in very high mountains. It's Machu Picchu. The tomb is very plain with only a stone to identify it. I wanted it that way. I'm an Incan, a man about thirty-four years old. I have long black hair and the same nose as now. I'm the head of a tribe of 1040 people. I'm a prince." As Susan began the description of what led to her death, her face took on a look of great sadness. With a deep sigh, she continued.

Someone is trying to persuade me to talk. My tribe is being overrun and hurt. Men come by horse from very far away . . . from the other side of the ocean. They want to take all our gold. It's another waste, because there's plenty of gold for all. All these gold items have no value for us other than the symbolic value. Our values are only concerned with one another. These people have values for the very low. I've never seen anything like these people. They eat and drink ostentatiously, far beyond their body's needs. They drink something that is very destructive to the body temples. They dress differently. They're doing things that are wrong and once again I'm helpless to do anything about it.

The feeling of helplessness and disillusionment is very indicative of the Saturn-Neptune aspect in Paula's chart. She went on to

[279]

describe the shock of seeing people behave in a base manner. "These men have no respect for human life. They only want this metal. We use it because it is a noble metal. It's the purest metal . . . it bends easily and it shines in the sun. We only extract it when we need more. There is one man who understands our laws, yet he is going to torture us until we tell him where all the gold is hidden. For now, I'm being kept apart from my tribe. There is one man who dies for me. They think I will talk by torturing him. They're stretching him by ropes on the ground. There is a wheel to turn the ropes. It's outside on the desert. We've already decided that we will not talk. We suffer because of the physical torture, but we're aware of the spiritual side, so we'll be all right. I'm going to die anyway."

Susan began to describe the people in her tribe who she knows in the present time. She then described the ornaments that she wore.

I have a beautiful necklace that is a symbol of my rank. I have something around my head and a very beautiful bracelet made out of a special herb which has been dried in the sun and dipped into special oils which my skin absorbs. It does something for my body energy. I have belts of leather and I'm barefoot. There is turquoise and amber. I'm wearing a loincloth and ankle wraps. I'm not tied up, but I have to sit and let all this take place. I feel so helpless. Once again, I'm very aware and I have to suffer for it. When my friend dies, I feel such anger about the ignorance and stupidity. We cannot do to them what they have done to us, because we can't lower ourselves to their kind of laws. We can't eliminate them because when you reach another level you respect life. Therefore we have to vanish . . . *vanish* to give them the example. It is going to take centuries upon centuries and generation after generation for them to learn by our example. We have to disappear, just like Atlantis.

Susan was visibly agitated and upset. It seemed she was watching a terrible scene of destruction right before her eyes. She went on to say more. "Yes I am tortured. Something is put around my neck. It's like a leather piece with something they keep on turning.

They stretch my mouth in different ways. It's painful, but I just leave my body. They kill about five hundred and twenty-five people. They don't find the gold, because I have given the order for all the Indians from Mexico to Peru to stop extracting the gold and to hide what they have. Whether these people have the gold is not the issue. With more gold, there will just be more greed."

When Susan described her birth process, she had noted terrible pressures around her neck, as if something were wrapped around it. I had asked her if the cord was around her throat, but she said, "The pressure hurts my throat. It could be that my chin is being forced down to my neck. The blood gets stuck here in my throat." Evidently the pain of the torture was still with her in the same part of her body, centuries later. In the present time, Paula finds that her throat is a very sensitive area in her physical makeup. (Paula has Taurus on the ascendant, the sign that rules the throat.)

Susan has more than one heavy Saturn aspect in her chart. She also has Saturn inconjunct Mars, describing the karmic memory of violence. Amazingly, she has Saturn in a sextile (positive aspect) to Pluto in her chart. Pluto describes power. Susan had much to say about the issue of power. She said, "If I could relive it, I would send out an alarm instantly. I have deep guilt about my naïveté. I don't want power now. However, my greatest fear is that I won't use my power. Having to lead a tribe is risky and I might make a mistake again. But I would certainly be more protective if I could do it all over again. I'd make my tribe invisible. The invaders wouldn't even see us." Susan was not guilty about her power but her innocence in assuming that the strange people were highly evolved and good people.

Susan continued with her description of that lifetime. She said, "I see you as an Incan child. You are a young boy. Your father has been killed and your mother is very close to me. I have so much love for her. I think she is my sister, so you are my nephew. After your father's death, I take on the parental responsibility of caring for you until I die."

Susan's identification of me as a young Incan boy was no surprise to me. Some time before I met Susan, I had a profound and moving experience where I saw myself in the same situation that Susan described. Susan went on to describe a rebellious trait that I carry with me to this day. She said, "Your mother is so sad because you are also killed. Although you are very young, you have the consciousness of a thirty-seven-year-old man. You are very brave and you want to do something to save my life. There's a stampede or something . . . a rebellion. It's born from frustration. A few people get away, including your mother, but you rush into battle with these people and are killed. If you had lived, you'd have been the leader of the tribe. You'd have been a good leader but you couldn't live with yourself unless you did something to defend your mother and your tribe. Your mother loses her brother, husband and child. She is not physically tortured but suffers a different kind of agony. She sees you being split in two." She then said, "Your mother, then, is your daughter now."

Some time earlier I had met a wonderful Indian woman who conducted workshops to teach people about crystals. I had always been fascinated with the healing power of crystals, and presumed that interest came from an Atlantean life that had been spent in the temples. I had been aware of being a priestess and working with many devices, such as color and crystals, to bring about healing. At the end of the three-day workshop, this lovely Indian woman talked about the plight of the Indians in the northwestern part of the United States. She said she would pass a bag among us. If it was possible to drop in some coins, they would be appreciated, but if that was not possible, we were simply to breathe a prayer into that bag, wishing for a peaceful end to a difficult situation. She began to play her guitar. At that point, I saw before my eyes such a terrible scene of destruction, torture and slaughter that involuntary tears poured down my face and I simply could not stop crying. The episode was embarrassing because the people in the group tried to comfort me, but no comfort was possible. The Indian woman said to me, "What are you seeing?" (not "what is the matter with you?"). I replied very spontaneously, "You know." She said, "Yes. It is as if it is all taking place again before our very eyes." She then quietly began another song and announced to the group, "This is a song about a young Indian boy who proves his manhood by fighting the enemy." I began to feel better about the scene before my eyes as soon as she sang her healing song.

That scene was exactly what Susan described in her regression session. I knew I had been a young Incan brave at the time of the Spanish invasion of Peru. I also knew my daughter had been with me in that lifetime as my mother. Contrary to Susan's concept that my mother had not been tortured, I saw clearly that her suffering was what enraged me so much that I entered battle against all odds. I do not have Saturn in hard aspect to Mars or Neptune in my chart, so with a review of that past experience, I would do the same thing again, but this time earlier and in a more effective way. My daughter does have Saturn conjunct Mars in her chart placed in the twelfth house of karmic memories. No doubt she remembers that torture on some level of consciousness.

Susan went on with her description of Atlantis. She said, "I knew you in Atlantis. We're about to blow apart and we know it. It's all aquamarine colors. We wear tunics and pants that are very comfortable. I'm a woman and a scientist. We're being picked up very shortly to leave Atlantis. I push the button [to blow up Atlantis] because it will be worse if we don't. Knowledge can go into the wrong hands. We go to a moon of Venus in a spaceship. The spaceship is gorgeous. It has sonic waves that are very healing. The lesson of Atlantis is that we didn't do enough, soon enough. We must learn to act the minute we become aware of a problem. If we don't, there are more problems created."

Once again, Susan described something I had been aware of. Although I had not been a scientist in Atlantis, I had left by way of a spaceship. I had run away from a powerful responsibility, but I knew, at that point, there was nothing I could do to solve the horrible situation in Atlantis and so I traveled to Venus to escape the devastation that was in store for the inhabitants of Atlantis. This awareness had come to me quite spontaneously, but I had never known where I had gone in that spaceship until a psychic woman in California had said to me, "Do you know that you used to travel to Venus?" I was able to confirm Susan's impressions of our departure from Atlantis when she had completed her regression session.

Groups of people seem to reincarnate at the same time in history. The next memories that came forth from Susan's subconscious brought into play another dynamic karmic situation that had already been hinted at by Connie in her memory of Elizabethan England. (See Saturn-Sun and Saturn-Moon, chapters 1 and 2.) I asked Susan if there was another past-life memory that was important to review for help in her present life. I actually said to her, "Was there a lifetime when you were supposed to be born and resisted that birth?" She answered immediately, "I was supposed to be born in 1535. In fact, I was to be born to Jennifer." (Jennifer was a mutual friend of Connie and Susan. Although Susan had heard about Connie from Jennifer and Connie knew of the existence of Susan, neither one had met in this life. I was the link between all three of these women.)

Susan continued, "What comes back to me is England. I am a male. Jennifer is dressed in a very fancy dress. She is married to a *very* strong man, but she is a very strong woman too. She keeps everyone on their toes. She is very, very ambitious, and wants to push me into power, no matter what the consequences. I'm just not made for that. I am a poet and a musician. She wants me to be king. She would have pushed me and would have destroyed me. I probably would have destroyed her too. She wouldn't have wanted to accept the fact that I only wanted to be a gentleman. She is much stronger than I am, however, so I leave. I see the light as I'm being born and so I leave. I'm not born dead, but I die just after birth. Queen Elizabeth is my sister." With that revelation, Susan opened her eyes. She commented, "Oh, Jennifer cried her eyes out. She didn't get her king. I think I stayed around her in spirit form for a long time. I tried to get close to Elizabeth but she was closed off. I am sorry I caused Jennifer so much pain."

I had already conducted a regression session with Connie during which she saw herself as Queen Elizabeth, and subsequently did a regression session with Jennifer on Connie's recommendation, for Connie had seen Jennifer as her mother in that lifetime. Jennifer revealed a great deal about her lifetime as Anne Boleyn. Now Susan completed the picture with her memory of birth into that period of history. For my own information and for confirmation of what had been revealed by the two other women, I asked Susan if Elizabeth is incarnated in the present time. She replied, "Yes, she's alive today, but I don't know her in the present. By the way, I would have been called Richard."

Historically, we know that Anne Boleyn was desperate to bear a son for Henry VIII. In fact, her life depended on it. After Henry's passionate and stormy courtship of Anne, the marriage finally took place, but at great cost to everyone. Henry had to defy the Catholic Church and the pope, risk making a terrible enemy of Spain (for the king of Spain was his ex-wife's brother) and chance the revolt of his subjects, for Queen Catherine was loved by the English people. Indeed, the only justification for his marriage to Anne was the possibility of producing a male heir to the throne. Henry claimed that he sinned in the eyes of God because he married his brother's widow, and that God's punishment was to deny him a healthy son. Therefore his divorce was the will of God, and Anne was the chosen mother of the future king.

When Anne became pregnant, it made the urgency of the divorce and marriage clear, and it forced the issue. But when she produced another girl child, Elizabeth, Henry's ardor was already cooling. Therefore it was imperative that she become pregnant again. She was able to accomplish this after much anxiety, but lost the male child prematurely. Anne wanted to name him Henry, but Henry VIII wished him to be called Edward. It is possible that one of his names might have been Richard, as was Susan's memory. It is obvious that Anne would have been extremely compulsive about everything in her life at that time, and her character fit the description Susan gave in her regression session. Anne was sentenced to death when Elizabeth was only four years old. After her beheading, Henry was free to marry again and try for a son with his third wife. He did have a son, also named Edward, by Jane Seymour who died giving birth, but Edward was not very strong and died quite young. Eventually Elizabeth was crowned queen.

We reviewed the thread of Susan's memories by seeing that she was in Atlantis in a very powerful position. It was up to her, among a few other scientists, to decide what to do with the advanced knowledge of crystal power. With the other scientists, she decided it was better to blow up Atlantis rather than let the power go into the wrong hands. She was then in another powerful position as the leader of the highly evolved Incan group. In that life, she was devastated by her own naïveté in assuming that the invaders from a distant land were highly motivated. She died with tremendous sorrow and guilt about her leadership and power. She decided in Elizabethan England that she had had enough of the expression of power and returned to her true home rather than be born into that position again. She returned in this life as a result of a debt owed to the universe, which she described by saying, "What I feel now is that my energy has been very thin and etheric [a good description of Neptunian quality of energy]. I can switch it on and off. By going to the source of that etheric energy, I'm in total control. My doubt seems to have faded away. By simply thinking about people in a positive way, I can change them and their energy. That is the real power. It is still up to me to act immediately and not be either naive or doubting of my ability to see things in true perspective. As a four-year-old, I knew I was right. My mistake was that I worried about whether I was really right or not. Now I choose to use knowledge and love in a constantly creative way. I will trust myself because I know I have divine guidance. All I want is that we all accept divine grace and live in unconditional love." Susan spoke like a true Neptunian prophet and poet.

Susan is an architect and has confessed that she has been involved in many projects that were momentarily satisfying but that much time could elapse between these projects. Susan said in her session that she doesn't want to face what she has to do in this life, so it would seem that she subconsciously picks work projects that will not bring the honor her talent might warrant. Having been in a position of authority, perhaps having been revered, she may not want to be on that pedestal again. She would be devastated if she let anyone down. She commented, "Having to lead is risky. I might make a mistake again." By forgiving herself her naïveté and trusting that she has divine guidance, Susan can allow herself to express the vision and poetry of her soul. Then she will be able to be a prophet in her own way and automatically attract ideal conditions into her life.

In Paula's case, she has confessed that she doubts her healing ability in the present. As a doctor, a special insight into her patients' problems can be a valuable tool to augment her practical skills in restoring the balance of health, for healing takes place on many levels. It may be that she must first forgive herself for not using her vision in a compassionate way in her previous life. Self-punishment in the form of doubt can keep one safe from making a mistake. It may take consistent practice to incorporate the higher Neptunian concepts into the work that Paula is capable of doing.

For both women, clarity was important for them to feel on safe ground. In childhood, they were not given information that would allow them to be noble and rise to the occasion, exhibiting the idealistic part of their natures. In adulthood, it may be necessary for each one to ask for information, to get everything "in writing," and clarify matters each step of the way. In that fashion, they can feel a sense of security. Working with Neptunian energy is much like focusing a camera. If one learns the technique and practices until the photographs look like what appeared in the mind's eye, one develops security with one's skills. Then the technique supports the conceptual, intuitive part of picture taking. Otherwise, if the individual is disillusioned over the finished product, he is likely to say, "What's the use? I'm just not a good photographer." That analogy can be applied to life and to the specific occupations involved when Saturn is found in difficult aspect to Neptune in an astrological chart.

CHAPTER THIRTEEN

Saturn and Pluto

luto is the planet that describes the ultimate in power, effectiveness and potency. Plutonian energy is very magnetic and charismatic. It is the planet that describes the greatest transformation in life, for it represents transcendency and a cosmic, universal quality. The growth process involved in that transformation is not a slow, steady upward climb but a drastic change from the depths to the heights. That change may come through traumatic conditions that force new awareness of a higher cosmic order. The struggle involved is somewhat like Moses wrestling with the angel on the mountaintop. Cosmic fire begins to purify and burn away lower, less elevated feelings such as revenge. Manipulation gives way to a concern about the welfare of everyone concerned. Forceful behavior and compulsions that keep the individual bound to the wheel of karma are transmuted into actions that beckon everyone to attune themselves to the highest constructive energy. It is the energy represented by both the serpent and the eagle.

The negative side of Pluto describes evil, destruction and danger, for Pluto was the god of the underworld. That energy might be used for black magic or to force matters into place by sheer willpower. Pluto rules plutonium and, indirectly, the atom bomb. The effect of that power can be devastatingly destructive or, if it is used for a different purpose, highly constructive. The force of Plutonian energy is never neutral or passive. It can be likened to the pull between good and evil. It is a smoldering fire that burns brightly for the highest cause or one that sweeps away anything that lies in its path.

The child ego state, in terms of transactional analysis, is particularly apt to describe this form of energy. The child who is secure in his position in the family structure and feels that he is the center of his particular universe grows up to exhibit an innocence that is especially appealing. He attracts people and conditions to his side like a magnet pulling in iron filings. But the child who has been traumatized develops a cleverness that can be especially deceptive. He gets what he needs by playing one parent against the other. He grows up playing games that vary from simple attention-getters to more complex systems of manipulation. Eventually, if his actions backfire, he may become self-destructive in the face of defeat. Nevertheless, his underlying motivation is "I want what I want and I'll get it any way I can." It is with only the greatest pain that he begins to develop the higher motivation of "I only want what is *right* for me and for the welfare of people around me." He finally learns to use his power to uplift mankind rather than only to satisfy his personal desires.

Saturn/Pluto aspects describe a potential for politics. In a positive sense, the individual can work with powerful people or groups and never lose his own sense of identity. Group dynamics or work with important organizations give him a sense of purpose. He enjoys being an important cog in the wheel of progress. But when Saturn is in difficult aspect to Pluto, the individual can have a deep fear of power. He may fear misusing his power or becoming involved with people who will misuse him. He may dislike crowds, for instance, for fear they might turn into a mob. He will then be especially averse to politics. If this aspect is viewed in the light of reincarnation, we can more easily understand this deep-seated terror. The terror is born from a memory of being manipulated and of an involvement with politics that carried death as the penalty for being on the wrong side.

The placement of Pluto in each of the twelve houses in the chart describes the area of life where an individual is most powerful and potent, and where the greatest transformation can take place. For instance, if Pluto is placed in or is ruling the fifth house of creativity, the person will be especially talented and potent in expressing his talent. He can reach masses of people very effectively. With high motivation, he can lift and inspire people through his creative works. He may have children who exhibit the same potency and magnetism. But if there are many difficult aspects to that planet, he may not be aware of his creative potency and may use his talent as a way of thumbing his nose at life or at people he feels misused him in the past. He could sink to the depths of depravity, or utilize such vehicles as pornography or gambling to release this atomic energy from within. Manipulation can be his way of getting even with life. His offspring may be manipulative or cunning, and perhaps unaware of their effectiveness. If the placement of Pluto is associated with the first house of personality, it is even more obvious that the level of magnetism is so high that the individual can knock people over with his intensity, pushing them away instead of magnetizing them to his side.

One of the most interesting placements of Pluto is in connection with the twelfth house of the subconscious. If Pluto is well aspected, and is ruling or placed therein, the individual's subconscious power is limitless. A quality of universal attunement is possible. The individual with such a high state of consciousness may be one of the chosen few who can act as an instrument for the awakening of mankind. He has obviously developed this state of consciousness from a past-life situation. He may have dedicated himself to his inner growth so completely that he comes back for the sole purpose of helping mankind evolve. He can then heal people around him on such a cosmic level that he changes their consciousness without saying a word or doing anything overt. However, if Pluto is badly aspected and is in this position in the chart, the power is there, but negative motivation and a desire to get even with life can be destructive. The individual's inner need for revenge may be transmitted to people around him on a subtle level. Ultimately that revenge only damages him, for Pluto acts with a boomerang effect, bringing back to the individual what he sends out.

During one of the health conferences I produced in Ibiza, Spain, one facet of Pluto was beautifully illustrated. A young woman came to the conference who said she had known exactly what I would look like. She told me she kept a journal and would like to show me what she had written about a particular dream. Before we did that, I took her into the town of Ibiza to buy some sandals. As she was trying on shoes, I said to her, "You have very narrow feet! I have a friend who thinks this is a special mark of elegance or elitism." She laughed and said, "Wait until you read my journal." Later, during the conference, we were discussing her chart and I said, "You know, with Pluto in the twelfth house in your chart, you have a dynamic subsconscious ability to reach people. Very few people have *only* positive aspects to Pluto, and with a few difficult aspects in your chart, you may have to be careful always to be highly motivated and to use your subconscious power wisely. I don't like to say this out of the context of reading your chart, but you may have been...(and I hesitated) ...a witch in another life." She laughed and said, "You must read my journal now."

When she returned with a thick bound book, she turned to a page and thrust it into my hands. She had told me that she had a dream many months before she even knew she might come to Spain (and certainly before she knew about the conference) and was told in her dream that she would attend an astrological conference on an island off the east coast of Spain. At a later date, she had another dream, this time after she had heard my name from a friend. She had written, "I saw a woman in my dream who had a very smiling face. She looked down at my feet and said to me, 'You know you have witch's feet.' In the dream we laughed together. For the first time, someone had acknowledged a part of my body that I hated because of the significance. I think that she was the astrologer Jeanne Avery." Naturally I was quite astounded at what her subconscious had revealed to her long before the facts were known. It was as if she were pulling information out of the cosmos, for I was not even sure, at the time of her dream, that I would hold another conference. With the acceptance of that facet of inner power, it is important to make a conscious choice about how to use the subconscious information that can be revealed. When Pluto is in that twelfth house, it is as if a bridge has been built from one building to another, so high above the traffic and noise it is quite easy simply to skip across this bridge without any obstructions. It can take years and perhaps many lives of total dedication to reach this state of power and consciousness. Clearly anyone who is very powerful on either the positive or negative side of the line is a person quite evolved in his inner growth. Therefore it is even more important that he be aware of his impact on the world around him.

The conflict comes when a person knows his inner power but is afraid of what he might do with it in this life. He may have seen a dark quality within his soul and be terrified of his own potency. He may worry that he could inadvertently misuse it; therefore he sits on that energy and tries to control it. When Saturn is overshadowing Pluto, the person has brought forth a karmic struggle concerning the repression of power and the need to express the positive qualities of that power. In his attempts to ignore that inner quality, and if he puts himself under too much pressure to repress it, it is possible that the energy could erupt quite unexpectedly, causing him to do or even *think* things that frighten him all over again. He may not know that his very thoughts affect the conditions around him.

The transformation of Plutonian energy in a person's life takes place primarily with the letting go of games, revenge and manipulation, even in the most subtle forms. This requires constant monitoring of all actions. One of the ways of working toward a more cosmic perspective is through meditation. The individual can begin to trust that the universe, or the higher self, can find the right solutions to problems. St. Germaine wrote about another technique in *Intermediate Alchemy*. He describes the transmutation of lead into gold, or the raising of the Saturnian consciousness (lead) to a golden Plutonian state by seeing a person or situation in a cloud of white light. The phrase "Let go and let God" can become a practical course of action in the transmutation process. With that letting go, manipulation gives way to a fierce desire to have only the things, people and situations that belong to one. The universe has an infinitely more exquisite way of working things out than we can possibly conceive by ourselves.

My interpretation of positive Saturn/Pluto aspects is that they indicate the ability to deal with politics. It may not be governmental politics but the politics of associating with potent, powerful situations or people that lead to the transmutation of world conditions. For instance, if Pluto is well aspected to Saturn, an individual will naturally gravitate to a very productive form of activity, functioning on an international level or in connection with major corporations. He may then be able to effect change in areas where his dedication to a project of magnitude will filter down for the benefit of humanity. He takes on great responsibility, but has such a sense of joy that he is like a free child: effective, magnetic and dynamic.

Since Saturn describes the lowest common denominator, if the individual has Saturn overshadowing Pluto, he may work on a lower level of effectiveness, denying his power in order to go along with the status quo, instead of trying to raise consciousness. He may fear working with major corporations or on a potent level because he might be lost in the crowd. Deep down, however, he may have a karmic memory of having been trapped by political manipulations or a political "machine." He may be afraid of masses of people. Positions of power may put dread and terror in his heart. He may overburden himself or trap himself by associating with people who maneuver him into positions of overload, preventing any possibility of power in this life.

Finally, the key to releasing Plutonian power and learning how to handle the atomic force of Pluto is through right motivation. If a person meditates constantly on his inner motivation, he can relieve the pressure of such inner questions as, "Should I?" "Is it the right thing?" He becomes a channel for world growth, working for the benefit of all sentient beings, not just for himself. He then places the decisions firmly in the hands of his higher consciousness, tuning in to a will higher than his own individual will.

THE DREADFUL CONSEQUENCES OF POWER

Suzanne is a vibrant, attractive woman with a quality of grace and elegance that cannot be ignored. Although she has a charming and modest manner, she exhibits a dynamic quality of energy from within. Suzanne has Pluto in the twelfth house in her chart, but Saturn opposes that position from the seventh house of marriage. That seventh-house position is intensified because she has Cancer on the ascendant with the Moon in Cancer in the first house, with Saturn ruling the seventh house of marriage as well. Suzanne is therefore enormously sensitive and vulnerable, especially in connection with partnership, and would be likely to attract a very powerful karmic relationship to be resolved in this life.

Suzanne was married to a man from a northern European country. He is dynamic, attractive and very powerful himself, but from the description in Suzanne's chart, this magnetic man may have karmic guilts of his own that would cause him to deny his true power, either stifling it or manipulating situations out of fear or insecurity. He could become the judgmental partner. Rather than "playing" together, he could put Suzanne under dreadful pressure by rejecting her or expecting her to be perfect. Rejection might be the tool he would automatically use to manipulate Suzanne's insecurities. She would therefore allow herself to fall totally under his control.

From Suzanne's description of their marriage, that was very much what happened in their relationship. Although she is now divorced from him, he recently persuaded her to live with him and try again for a united family situation. He gave her expensive presents and charmed her with security and stability for their children. The temptation was too great to resist, so Suzanne gave up a fabulous position in the United States, a powerful spot where she was able to build a strong sense of self-respect, and moved to Europe to be with her husband once more. Quite soon after she arrived, he informed her that he had changed his mind and would be traveling with his girlfriend. He told her that she could live in his house as long as he was away, but she might have to move when he returned. The subvertive manipulation of Pluto, ruling the house of children in her chart, worked again, and Suzanne found herself in an untenable position, for her husband had used the children to subjugate her more than once in her married life. Her insecurities instantly rose to the surface as she found herself totally trapped and dependent on his whims.

Suzanne came to me for a regression, not at all sure that she would accomplish anything by the session. She began by talking about her life at age five. It seemed that her father was involved with another woman. After some time, her mother demanded that he leave the house so that she could restore some balance to the family situation and have peace of mind. Her father left for a short time, but finally her mother relented, for the sake of the children, and allowed him to come back to be reunited with the family. Suzanne had always blamed her mother, not her father, for the difficulties at that time. She suddenly realized that she was repeating her mother's patterns almost exactly. However, as a result of the trauma (ruled by Pluto), Suzanne said to herself, "I'll never trust a man again," and "Life will never be the same." With the awareness of the repeated patterns, she said, "I understand my mother now. I have a lot of compassion for her, but I didn't five minutes ago. I'm living with the exact same situation." Tears spilled down her cheeks.

Suzanne then viewed herself at two months old. She saw that her mother developed a rash on her breasts and was unable to hold her, much less feed her. She said:

> She can't cuddle me. The breast-feeding has to stop. I see myself in a crib with teddy bears on the front. It seems to be in their room, and it is very dark. I don't like dark rooms. My stomach is uncomfortable, like I'm still hungry. I feel alone and dissatisfied. If they'd explained it to me, I'd have felt better about it. But my mother has the rash because she really doesn't want me.
>
> Mother is frightened because it is the time of the depression and

my father's business has just collapsed. She's worried about starting all over again. She could be more supportive of him. I'm shoved into a crib and put in a dark room. Oh, I wish I weren't born. I develop the attitude of "Nobody cares how I feel." I don't think my mother would have wanted me no matter what. She feels a little guilty about not wanting me, so when it is all over, at birth, she's momentarily excited about me. I feel so sad about coming in. I grit my teeth throughout the birth process. It's so cold outside. The passage is so small that it is very difficult and I can't breathe. That's funny, because I don't breathe normally now. When I'm scared, I shut off my breath. At birth, I feel like I might suffocate. My panic is from lack of air. I just can't get out to get enough air. Then when I'm born, I feel so cold and lonely.

I asked Suzanne what her birth survival decision might be. She replied, "I say to myself, 'I'll make you proud,' but that is said rather defiantly. I wonder why I don't just cash it in?" I then asked Suzanne to look at a past life that would answer that very question. She said, promptly, "I see a person on a horse, holding a flag. The man is about forty. The flag hangs down from a cross bar, like a Crusader's flag. It's white with silver around it. I think the man is me. I have on a Flemish type of hat of burgundy velvet. My waistcoat is the same velvet of the same color and I seem to have knickers, like jodphurs, and high boots. I'm riding a chestnut gelding with gold trappings." I asked Suzanne to tell me what position in society she might occupy. She said, "I feel like a priest, because there's a purpose about this. It feels like the northern part of Spain, toward the west. I'm a clergyman, but I think I'm the bishop of this corner of Spain." In answer to my question, she said, "It may be 1518. There's some sort of protest going on. Lots of people are involved. The protest is within Spain. It's a question of power and authority. It is related to the power of the church, but it seems that I'm responsible for a lot of people. I'm protesting against something...like the king of Spain is doing something that threatens the church. It feels like a rally.

"I want the king to pay attention. I feel absolutely driven by this cause. I'm trying to stop him from doing something very unfair politically. He doesn't listen. I'm strong, but not strong enough, so he puts me in prison. Whew . . . it's below ground and it's cold and dark." I asked Suzanne to tell me how long she/he was kept in that prison, and she replied, "I'm here for twenty years, until I die. I pray a lot and I grow on a soul level of consciousness. The tragedy is that I have led people to protest and they get killed. I have an enormous amount of guilt." I asked Suzanne to give the king a name. She replied, "Carlos? Or Charles." I then suggested that she look at his face to see if he is with her in this life. She volunteered, "The magistrate who sentences me is my father. I would have succeeded if I had planned better and persuaded the king to listen. I got carried away with a cause without thinking it through." Once again I asked her to look at the face of the king. She took a swift breath and said, "It's my husband in this life. It's just the same now. He has imprisoned me."

When Suzanne opened her eyes, we continued the discussion. She said, "I have the potential to fight for what is right. I was a reformer then and I have the same predisposition now. But I have a tremendous resistance to showing any power now. I've always let my husband just walk all over me. But our real problems started when I began to assert myself. So now I don't want anything to do with politics." We talked about my description in her chart of having a karmic racial guilt and she confirmed this. "I caused so many people to die in that life, I don't want to be in a position where I can influence people. The king should have listened to me, but I could have found a better way to approach him. With my husband it is the same. I only want what is fair and right now, so I will have to be wary of threatening him on a level of a power struggle. I must really approach him unemotionally and with some logic. Most of all, I must convince him that what I want is in his best interest. Therefore I must only ask for what is best for both of us in this tricky situation."

When I saw Suzanne later on, we discussed the possible benefits of the regression session. She said, "On one hand, I see my present-life patterns so clearly. It had never occurred to me that I have been living my mother's life all over again. But it is difficult in the situation with my husband, for after all, he did put me in prison before." We talked about how she could convince him that she only wants what is fair and right again. I suggested that she be aware of a possible guilt on the part of the king in a previous life. She said, "He had none." In the present life, her husband is a very heavy drinker. She acknowledged that it is possible he is trying to drown the memory of having used his power for detrimental causes in the past. We agreed that the regression session is not a magical cure-all but a tool to be used as an indicator of constructive decisions in the here and now.

I then told Suzanne that I had recently read an interesting book about the period of history around 1518. It seemed that Charles V had attained the office of Holy Roman Emperor as well as maintaining his position as King of Spain, after waging a war against the Vatican City in Rome where the pope had been captured and imprisoned. Many bishops and priests were murdered and tortured. That coincided with the period of history when Martin Luther was preaching the reformation of the church and Henry VIII was trying to divorce his Spanish Catholic wife to marry again. Although I knew little about the protests within Spain or about what their king was doing to the Catholics in Italy, it seemed likely she was viewing a historical event that could have taken place just as she described.

It may take some time before Suzanne is willing to acknowledge the power she still possesses. However, after glimpsing that past-life situation, she cannot ignore her effectiveness in fighting for what is right. Only time will tell how Suzanne chooses to use her power in the here and now.

PAST-LIFE IMPRISONMENT

Marianne had been subjected to several devastating events in her life, any one of which would have been enough to cause a major depression. She is a therapist and quickly took advantage of anything her colleagues might be able to offer in the way of help, simply to get through a very rough period in her life. She decided to have a regression session to see if any of the events could be explained by a past-life situation. One of the very difficult problems had to do with her relationship with her mother. She was born to a family with a great deal of property, and since she was her mother's only heir, she presumed the family estate would belong to her on her mother's death. She had plans to open a new-age health center that would be a haven for people in need of therapy, rest or information about their physical, mental and emotional well-being.

When Marianne's mother died, she learned that the estate had been given to charity instead of to her. She was naturally quite devastated to learn that her mother would reject her in such a blatant manner, especially since she was no longer in her early years. She had one course of action that might reverse the will, but she knew she would do nothing to contest her mother's wishes, even though she would lose so much by her inaction. We had already discussed the Saturn conjunct Pluto aspect located in the twelfth house of her chart. In Marianne's case, it was clear that the rejection had brought on a paralysis of such a deep subconscious level that rational thought could not explain it. She felt totally powerless to do anything about her dilemma.

In the review of a past life, Marianne saw herself in a male body, heir to a throne. Her father had died and her mother was the ruling queen. It was expected that sometime in the near future, Marianne, as the prince, would be crowned to take over her father's position. It was clear that political manipulation was rampant in the kingdom. Marianne saw herself standing in a room with heavy wooden furniture, with sunlight streaming in through large windows. That sunlight seemed to fascinate her, and she talked a great deal about her memory of that light. She saw that her mother in that life was her mother in the present life. It seemed she was trying to discuss the ascension to the throne in a rational way.

Marianne acknowledged that her mother, as the queen, was unwilling to relinquish her power. She was under political pressure to do so, and the only way she seemed to be able to resolve the problem was to get rid of her son. Marianne described in detail the terrible dilemma that she was now presented with. It was a power struggle to the death, it seemed. Either she killed her mother or she would be killed by her. She was not willing to die, but she was also unwilling to betray her mother, the queen. The feeling of family loyalty seemed to be uppermost in her mind.

It took quite a while for Marianne to allow the scenario to progress beyond the painful discussion in that room. After some time, she saw that she was in a dungeon. Political factions persuaded the queen to avoid having blood on her hands, so she had her son, the prince, imprisoned. It seemed that Marianne remained in that dungeon for the rest of her life. She saw one tiny spot of light, however, that allowed her to be released from consciousness. She used that light to travel out of her body to develop on a higher spiritual plane. She had no reason to forgive her mother, because it had been her choice to allow death or imprisonment rather than to have the crime of matricide on her conscience.

In this life, she once again had to deal with a power struggle with her mother. She was her father's favorite daughter. When he died, much of her family loyalty went with him. She could not force herself to be deceitful, pretending to be friends with her mother, when they both knew they were enemies underneath. In remaining loyal and true to her inner sense of values, she could not compromise her principles. She had not been able to do so in the other life either. Although she had been imprisoned, she had grown. She had prayed for the welfare of her people and, as a result, came into this life with a great power to heal people.

When Saturn and Pluto are conjunct, the aspect is easier to resolve than when it is an opposition or a square aspect. With determination and dedication to avoid any compromise of principles, an individual with such a potent aspect in the twelfth house of the subconscious is able to become a dynamic instrument for the awakening of mankind. So it finally became clear to Marianne that she didn't need her mother's property to become an effective force for the growth of others. She was able to forget the hurt and the sense of having been manipulated. Her willingness to let go of the whole situation, brought about through a great deal of therapy, resulted in incredible offers and opportunities for workshops and group work throughout Europe and the United States. In this life, Marianne has become a prince among princes as a result of her dedication to the principles of true power and her willingness to forget the past and go forward.

POLITICAL MANIPULATION FROM THE PAST

Allison is another very dynamic woman with a very successful career in the field of design. She lives in New York, where her originality in the creation of elegant apparel for women has brought her renown. Her work is featured in major department stores and shops around the United States and in the most prestigious fashion magazines. Allison has Pluto in the seventh house of marriage and partnership, with Saturn conjunct that planet. Since her ascendant is Capricorn, with Saturn as its ruler, she has an additional rulership of Pluto describing her personality and effectiveness. There is no question about the dynamic, quiet power that exudes from this exotic woman.

Allison came to me for several regression sessions. The first session was so clear and had such a dynamic impact that she returned to clarify and gather further information about the period of history that she saw in her mind's eye. Allison has long dark hair and has been described by one artist as a replica of all of Goya's women. She fully expected to see herself as an artist's model of that time. When she had her first session, she was romantically involved with a man who attracted her but also confused her. She mainly wanted clarification about their relationship.

After reviewing the painful experiences in this life, she went to the time of her birth. It was clear throughout her description of the present life that her guardian angel was her grandfather, who died when she was entering puberty. The love she felt for him was evident. His death was a great loss for her. She saw that he was very much a part of her life from the moment of birth. She said, "I see my mother in the hospital. She's dressed in a pretty nightgown and she's holding me. My grandfather is there when I'm first born." I asked her to look at herself to see what she looked like. Allison replied, "I'm cute, and with all those people there, I feel better. I'm scared when I first come out. I think I'm scared of my father. I don't want to be with him. He must have been someone in a past life that I was afraid of. I see myself as being really scared, saying 'No, no!' I see myself by a tree, like a little cherub, before my birth, saying, 'No, I don't want to do that, I don't want to be born to him.'"

Allison went easily to a past life where she saw a beautiful formal garden next to a palace. She could see herself standing in this garden as a little girl, holding the hand of one she presumed was her sister. She said,

> I'm three years old and I'm wearing a very heavy dress that is black and white. A man comes out of the house and takes me by the hand. He seems to be a servant. He takes me into the house. My sister stays outside...It really isn't my sister at all. It seems to be a part of me that I leave outside. I see her turning to stone. It's like part of me turns to stone at this moment. I'm very scared, as the servant takes me into this very grand palace.
>
> Next I see myself crying. Someone is screaming. I see that it is my mother who is screaming because my father is dying. I see myself in a hallway. I don't know what is going on and I'm scared and confused. I'm crying because of that. There's an air of hysteria. There are a few people around, but not a crowd. Now my mother is yelling, not crying. She is evidently hysterical. I don't like her. She looks like a witch. I don't know her in this life. Now I see my grandfather in this life. He is smiling and is very happy. Oh, he is my father in that life and he has just been released. He's very happy.
>
> It seems that I am now to be queen. I'm only three when my father dies, so I have someone who makes the decisions for me until I come of age. No wonder part of me has turned to stone. I leave that little girl part of me in the garden. Now I must become very serious about my duties.

I asked Allison if she needed to review anything else about the time of her father's death. Then I suggested that she move forward in time to see what happens later in her life. She said, "It seems to be the time of my wedding. Now I can see my father in this life. He seems to be standing at the bottom of a grand staircase, waiting for me to come down. I'm in my room at the top of the stairs getting dressed, but I don't want to go downstairs. I'm sixteen years old." I asked Allison to describe the clothes she saw in that scene. She replied, "My father is wearing red. He's young, and seems like an uncle. He's wearing a lot of medals. I think he is my adviser. I'm in a wedding dress, very lacy, but it is a soft dress. I'm carrying a large bunch of flowers. I'm just in a state of shock."

With very little prompting, Allison continued her story. She said, "Finally I go down the stairs to the man in red who is waiting for me. I'm holding on to him very tightly. He comforts me and we go into a big ballroom. It's in the afternoon, but there are huge crystal chandeliers and big windows, so the light is lovely. Lots of people are dancing, going around the room like in a waltz. The women have very big skirts. I'm coming into this room very reluctantly. I see my brother in this life. He seems to be a friend who protects me...another guardian, but not a legal guardian. He's making me feel better."

I asked Allison how she looks. She describes herself, "I have very long dark hair, very thick. I look similar to how I look now. There is a man who is very large, built something like my present boyfriend. He is wearing a dark blue suit with a very fitted jacket and lots of medals. There is a ribbon going across his chest. He has white breeches and boots. Now he's standing next to me. I don't actually see a wedding ceremony. I think I'm more afraid of the future and the unknown than anything specific. Now we're kissing each other, and a big celebration is beginning."

I asked Allison to describe her husband in that life. She continued,

He's very charming. He also seems very conscious of his image. Women seem to flock around him, not at the time of our wedding, but I know he's very attractive to them. Married life is generally ...well, I see us fighting. I'm crying, and he's screaming at me. He has on a uniform and has a sword attached to a belt. I think he's going away somewhere. He wants to be the head of the army. He wants more power and he wants to do battle. I want peace. He wants to conquer new territory and he's trying to control me. He gets very angry and leaves. I see myself as being very weak, but when it comes down to the most important decisions, I won't let him win. I'm about twenty-nine years old. I've just awakened and I have on a white nightgown. I seem to be on the verge of madness. I seem to be killing my husband by not giving him power. His hands are tied. There's a battle going on somewhere and I just want to keep him with me.

I don't see myself as being very powerful. There seems to be someone else, like a regent. I think that's my father in this life. My husband is ruling with me, however, but it seems the regent has all the power.

Allison became very quiet. Her face took on another look altogether. After a moment she said:

I see myself escaping with my child. I have a boy about ten years old. I'm going into a carriage with my son. Someone is driving us to another place. My husband wants me to go away where we'll be safe. I know I won't come back to the palace. Oh . . . my husband is killed. I see myself alone with my son. He's tall and lanky, with dark hair. We're very close. I see us alone in the countryside. I really miss all the festivities, all the beautiful clothes. I'm really depressed about my husband. I'm almost like a pauper now. No one seems to care about what happens to me. I see myself now as an old woman. I seem to die depressed and having lost everything. What a political mess. Most of my life was in a state of frustration over power. I was born with the memory of growing old and being rejected and ignored.

After a pause, I asked Allison to ask herself why she came back into this life. She replied, "I came back to be with my father. He was so nice to me in that life, but he was very jealous of my husband. In that life, he didn't defend me or support me. Really, I was just a political pawn in his hands. My family took over everything in that life. The situation would have been different if I'd been stronger. I think I killed my husband indirectly." After Allison had a chance to assimilate much of what she saw, we discussed how the review of that time could help her now. She continued, "I came into this life not wanting to be in a powerful position. It costs too much. But I must realize that I still have that power, so I mustn't let other people spoil it for me or take it away from me. I have to take control. I can't let things out of my own hands."

I was curious about Allison's mother in this life. I asked her if she saw her in that period of history. She said, "I think my mother was my personal maid or lady-in-waiting. She always takes care of me. She is so nice." As Allison opened her eyes, she continued, "I need to keep my eyes open at all times. I can't give over the power now. I was so manipulated then. They just got rid of me. They made me feel weak, as if I couldn't make decisions. I should have stayed in control." Then, after another short pause, I asked Allison if she knew her name. Without thinking, she said, "Isobel." Then her hands flew up to her mouth and her eyes grew very, very wide. She said, "Oh, I'm Queen Isobel."

Allison called me the next evening to tell me that she had made a very important discovery. She said, "I was so captivated by what I saw yesterday, I had to go to the public library to see if I was correct about some facts. I couldn't believe it when I read that Isobel's father died when she was three years old and that she was married at sixteen. It is not the Isobel who sponsored Christopher Columbus, but another one. I think she was called Isobella." Whether or not the regression session was beneficial for Allison in her business cannot really be known. However, she told me repeatedly that in her world of fashion, copies of original designs are made all the time. She said, "I'm always hiring people who leave me to start their own business, using my designs and ideas. I still have to keep my eyes wide open!"

THE FEAR OF MOBS

Jackie is a very psychic woman. She told me that she had many spontaneous memories of past lives, but that when she had flashes of previous existences, she was not always able to see as many details as she'd like. Therefore she wanted to do a regression session that would help her fill in missing facts. She began her session by describing some of the present-life phobias that she felt sure were rooted in the past. One of her deepest fears had to do with rodents. She said she was deathly afraid of mice or rats, and it didn't matter whether they were dead or alive. If she saw or even suspected that a mouse or rat was in a room, she couldn't walk into that room. She laughed and said she knew the Freudian significance of that animal, but it didn't seem to have any bearing on her fears. She volunteered that she had often thought she must have been in a prison where there were many rats crawling over the inhabitants. In fact, she suspected that she had been in a French jail awaiting execution at the time of the French Revolution. That suspicion was augmented by the fact that she was terrified of crowds, but she had not been able to see more than that on her own. She also volunteered that as a child, she was very musical, playing the piano and singing, but that she had such stagefright it was torturous to perform in school productions and at music recitals. She said her knees shook so badly, she could hardly go through with her commitment. On the other hand, she was drawn to theater and performance. She said she thought her fright was almost a self-punishment because of a past-life situation.

The first scene Jackie saw when she viewed a past life was herself in a room full of people. She said:

I seem to be singing, but I think I'm singing bawdy songs and getting great response from the room full of men and women. Everyone is dressed in silk and lace, even the men. This seems to be a very elite group of people, even among the members of the court. There is so much gossip and intrigue that it is very tricky to stay abreast of the politics of the group. One day one person is in favor and then that person is out. I seem to be able to juggle all that very well, but I absolutely hate it.

I seem to have a place to escape to. I think I participate in this raucous activity, flirting and playing the role with the best of the ladies, until I simply cannot take it anymore. When I'm in danger of blowing it all, I run away to my country house. It is like I have two distinct personalities. As I see myself leaving the scene of debauchery, I want to thumb my nose at everyone and never return.

So I'm compromising my principles every day. I don't think I'm royal, but I've been elevated to a very favored position by someone. It could be the king, but I think someone has sponsored me at the court and I've become a favorite. I see myself with a lover waiting for me at my house, so I don't think I am someone's mistress. However, all the luxury I have and like is dependent on being in favor. So I play the game.

When I am in my country home, I'm very happy. My love is tall and very handsome, and he never goes near the court. No one really knows of his existence. I keep him in a separate life, it seems. He wears a uniform, so perhaps he is in the army. He has the rank of captain. We are very, very much in love. I suppose he tolerates my time at the court because he can't do anything about it and he certainly can't provide the things I like on his small income. My house is just beautiful. I can see it in minute detail. It is very cozy and warm, with lots of very elegant touches. It is so painful to have to leave my love and my home and go back to all that pressure and intrigue. I have to be on my toes all the time.

I think the people around me in the country are very hungry. I seem to feed people from my kitchen. People like me, and I bring as much extra food as I can to give to my neighbors. One day I see a mob gathering at the rear door to the house. They seem to be people from quite far away. I think they have heard that I have food and they are demanding that I give them something to eat. I am sick about the situation because I don't have enough for everyone. I don't know what to do, so I shut the door and ignore their pleas. I hide inside my house, but I feel devastated about the situation. I want to cry about the waste at the court, but I feel so helpless to do anything at all.

Now I see myself coming out of a doorway, absolutely running down a small flight of stairs to a waiting carriage. This is somewhere at the court. I think I've been warned about the coming danger and I get away. My heart is pounding. I'm wearing a dark cape over my clothes, and as I leave this place, I'm looking over my shoulder to see if I've been noticed. I'm afraid someone will stop me from leaving. I get into the carriage without detection and hide as far over in the corner as I can. There seems to be great danger around me. The carriage heads due west, it seems, to a straight road that leads to my house. We almost make it to the safety of the house when a mob stops the carriage and demands that I get out. I don't move, so they are beginning to rock the coach and tear at the door. I'm just terrified. Suddenly, just as they are reaching for me and I'm half out of the door, my love rides up on a horse and manages to save me. I think we have some connection with the common people as well as my connection with the elite of the court. I'm really playing both sides against the middle.

The person who warns me seems to be a courtesan who never gets to the court. She is a favorite among the royal gentlemen and trades information, like pillow talk, to the revolutionists. When my lover identifies me as a friend of hers, the mob lets me go. But I'm so scared I don't leave my house again. When my love goes away, for necessity, I am taken from my house and there's nothing he can do for me now. I never see him again. I'm taken to prison and put in a cell with other women from the court. I think we have a degree of freedom, that is, to walk around in a courtyard, but we're all pretty resigned to dying. I think I perfect my needlepoint sitting in jail. I see myself a very sad, wiser person. My sadness is for the royal family. I think Marie Antoinette is a very close friend of mine and my heart aches for her. Louis is not very strong. He's a bit of a dolt.

I see one scene where I'm walking down a long corridor, resplendant with mirrors and tapestries. All of a sudden, I see the king coming my way and I'm furious with myself for not being able to duck out of sight more quickly. I have to smile and flirt as he's walking toward me. I pretend to be happy to see him, but I can't wait to get away from him. He's just so ineffective and weak.

As Jackie paused to think about what she had seen, I asked her to look at the other people in the court to determine whether she knew anyone in the present life.

"Oh, I can't believe it. Half the people I know, including members of my family, are in that court." She named many people and then identified the man who sponsored her at court as well as the woman who warned her of the approaching danger. Then she grew very sad. Tears began to pour from her eyes as she described the scene before her. "I'm standing in a line waiting my turn on the scaffold. I'm so frightened that a deadly calm has set in. But then I see something that rips my heart out. It is the young daughter of Marie Antoinette. She is led to the guillotine before my very eyes. I think we've been great companions. She's much younger than I, a mere child, but we've been together so much, it's like she's my own little darling. I can't believe what is happening. She's so innocent."

It was clear that Jackie was experiencing something very painful and frightening. I asked if she wanted to go on. She replied, "I want to see it all and be rid of the terrors that have haunted me all my life. I used to see people who had lost limbs and it scared me to death. I was so afraid as a child that I might lose a limb. I think it is a throwback to losing my head. As I watch so many people I know being guillotined, I almost go into a catatonic state, but when I see this child, so fearless and regal, it does something to shock me into a different state of mind. Now I want to die. I don't want to live among such evil and injustice. If she can be so serene and majestic faced with her death, I only want to get it over with and join her. The actual moment of death is not as painful as the anticipation."

We discussed the significance of Saturn opposing Pluto in her astrological chart. Saturn is placed in the sixth house of work, ruling her seventh house of marriage. Pluto is exactly conjunct her ascendant, ruling her fifth house of creative expression. Jackie vouched for the fact that her work is a way of avoiding power and politics. She said:

> If I work really hard at tasks that are boring and limiting, the drudgery keeps me from getting into trouble. I don't trust myself to be part of that kind of society again. All my life I've been involved with very dynamic, powerful people. Social situations have been presented that are far from what my background would indicate. So once again, I've stuck one toe in the water, but I'm terrified to plunge in. I fall back on the necessity of work. I also have a deadly fear of politics. I want nothing to do with intrigue.
>
> I also think that I deny a lot of my talent, because I misused my ability before. I can identify with the suffering of poor people to the point of debilitation. When I was younger, I couldn't face the fact that people, especially children and animals, might go hungry. I would cry over the plight of mankind. Perhaps I must now make a contribution that will enable people to learn how to take better care of themselves. I think we create our own conditions to a large

degree. But I also know there's a part of me that would love to be almost irresponsible, like a child. I've never let myself acknowledge that part, however. I'm afraid of what I might do!

Some time later, Jackie made her first visit to Paris. She called me on her return to tell me what had happened to her there.

I was due to leave for Paris on a Sunday. All day Saturday I was so sick, I didn't think I could make the trip. My throat hurt so badly I didn't think I could pack. Moreover, the pain was not up and down but across, like above the soft palate. I told myself that it was ridiculous and I knew it was all psychosomatic, but it was debilitating all the same. Finally I was able to put some things in a suitcase and get to the plane. Once I was en route, I was okay. When I got to Paris, it was like going home. I made friends immediately and had some crazy and wonderful adventures. When I walked in the Tuilleries, I knew every inch of land. It was so familiar. I identified buildings that I later read about. I saw the prison where I was held and even found the section of Paris where my family lived when I was at court.

Then I decided to go to Versailles. I wanted to find that doorway from which I escaped. I almost didn't get there. I finally arranged the trip the day before I was to come home. When I arrived, I had a bit of a letdown. The building was the wrong size and the wrong color. It was very familiar, but I couldn't find my doorway. I did have a revelation when I went into the chapel, however. I knew that we had prayed fervently when things began to go wrong. I'm sure I developed on a spiritual level because of my fear. Then I took a walk to Trianon. That was very familiar, but still not the building I saw in my mind's eye. I felt very strange. It had seemed so real. Suddenly I was walking toward Marie Antoinette's little hamlet when I saw my road! Now, a road looks like a road, but I knew that was the road where the carriage took me to my house. My knees were so weak, and I felt that if I continued around a hedge to the location of Le Petit Trianon, I would see my doorway. I thought I might faint. I gathered myself together and walked a bit farther. There was the exact doorway and circular stairs that I had seen in my mind's eye. I can't recall ever seeing a photograph of Le Petit Trianon, and I certainly didn't know that Marie Antoinette had built a theater just beyond.

I asked Jackie to describe what happened next. She said, "I discovered a wonderful book about Marie Antoinette when I returned home. I learned that she had a very select group around her at Le Petit Trianon, and it caused much jealousy among other members of the court. It was clear to me, then, that I was indeed her best friend. Then I felt very sad again, because in the end, she was so alone. She was very misunderstood. She would never have said, 'Let them eat cake.' The tragedy is that none of her friends was with her to help her through her terrible ordeal, including me."

For each of the people who reviewed the issue of power in their past lives, there was a specific lesson to be learned. For Suzanne, her compulsion to fight for a cause that was very important to her led to a head-on collision with a man in a position to imprison her. In this life, she is faced with the same situation. However, with a look at how she might have persuaded the king to desist from his warring plans, she can have clues about her relationship with him in the present. Suzanne may also need to acknowledge the level of power she brought into the present times, so that she can again find her particular cause and recognize her ability to transform conditions around her, directing her own energy into the right channels.

Marianne has been faced with the same manipulation in her present life, where her mother pulled the rug out from under her. In the past, she felt helpless to do anything about the situation. However, during her imprisonment, Marianne raised her level of consciousness to a very high degree. With total forgiveness of her mother's actions, she can rise above any seeming limitations to soar like an eagle, showing others the way through her own transformation and through her work as a therapist and healer.

Allison has had to be willing to accept the powerful position she lost in the past. Awareness of having left matters to other people, whose motivations were not in her best interests, has taught her a valuable lesson for her present life. She seems to be very ably taking matters into her own hands this time.

Jackie became entangled in a powerful political situation that cost her her life before. For Jackie, the resolution to be true to herself and never compromise her principles can bring her to a potent position again. She might have been able to anticipate danger in the past, giving her a chance to alert her friends in time. In this life, she may have the opportunity to save her friends again under the conditions existing in her present life.

For each person, acknowledgment and acceptance of a higher octave of power is the key to letting go of nonproductive people and situations. In that way, each individual can soar like the eagle, totally in tune with universal consciousness, which works for the welfare and awakening of mankind as a whole.

III

Techniques for Tapping the Subconscious

CHAPTER FOURTEEN

Techniques for Tapping the Subconscious

DEVELOPING INNER DIALOGUES

The basic premise of my work with past-life regression sessions is that every problem has its roots in the past. We are the writers of our scripts in the theater of our individual lives. But sometimes we neglect to look carefully at the results of acts we commit. We may not be aware that every action or choice is like planting a seed for the future. The plant will grow in exact proportion to the seed that is planted. So the first step to take in connection with a review of past lives is to acknowledge that no one but ourselves can be responsible for the present conditions of our lives. It is no good to blame our parents, or life, or outer conditions. People around us are merely other actors, performing their roles according to their own scripts and life drama.

The intricate interweaving and deciphering of relationships and events can be one of the most fascinating subjects for review in one's whole life. For if your life is out of balance or events seem out of your control, that is the time to ask questions of yourself to see where such a condition had its very beginning. In a regression session, a person learns how to ask questions of himself and listen for the answers. In essence, he learns how to have a dialogue with his own subconscious mind. He learns how to sustain that dialogue and retrieve information from his subconscious storehouse.

If he becomes proficient in this technique, he has access to that part of his mind whenever he needs more information about himself and life around him.

There are many techniques one can use to tap the subconscious and retrieve the information stored within. Some people use hypnosis for past-life regression; Shirley MacLaine has written a book about facilitating past-life awareness through the means of acupuncture. In the regression sessions I have described in this book, however, everyone has been able to tap into hitherto hidden information in a completely natural awake state. These sessions usually last about two hours and reveal enough information to reach a decisive point that will clarify present-life conditions, relationships and patterns. Naturally, one can do many sessions and continue with the unraveling process, but once the key to unblocking the hidden matters becomes clear, a person may discover that the information reveals itself at exactly the right and appropriate time in life.

I stress that the sessions are not conducted in the hypnotic state because I feel that if one can learn to reveal this information naturally, he has no need of setting the conscious mind aside. I feel the conscious part of the intellect plays a valuable part in assessing the information that is revealed and therefore should *not* be set aside, especially if one is aiming at new psychological awareness, not just a momentary and perhaps titillating cursory examination of past-life adventures. In fact, I feel a regression session is viable only if it is conducted with the serious intent of examining psychological patterns for the purpose of gaining a better quality of life as well as improved relationships and eventually a better world.

It is important not to be concerned about whether the information that comes forth in these sessions is accurate. If it is part of a person's fantasy, it belongs to him and therefore is valid psychologically. In the case of people who revealed past lives that could be confirmed historically, the accuracy of that revelation is equally unimportant. First of all, we cannot prove that historical accounts are totally accurate in the most minute and personal details, and therefore whatever emerges from a person's subconscious may be his or her special perception of what really happened. Also, memories are flawed as time elapses, even in the present life. And finally, it doesn't matter if the person was not actually the historical personage he sees himself as being. If that characterization explains his life to him, it is extremely valuable. By saying this, I am not in any way invalidating what people have seen; I mean only that we must develop a proper perspective about it.

What is important about all such memories is how they relate to events in the present. If any such revelation gives explanation to or clarifies matters, it becomes a productive experience. Therefore, I stress that I'm not trying to prove anything with historically correct data. For a person to find corroboration of what he sees in his mind's eye simply confirms that he is skilled in bringing forth meaningful information.

The akashic records contain information about each person's thoughts, actions and deeds throughout all of history. Students of metaphysics are familiar with the concept that everything has been recorded, almost magnetically, in the akashic records. These records exist on some sphere or energy level not readily available to everyone. However, the entire history of human collective and individual activity exists there, to be tapped whenever someone finds the key that fits the lock. There are no secrets in the universe! But, mercifully, we have little access to those records until we have developed the sense of responsibility and wisdom that must go hand in hand with possession of this knowledge. We are blissfully unaware of what we may have done in the past until the day when we can handle that information without threat to our survival. For this protection, we can be thankful to the left brain, which allows us to accept only what we can see, touch, taste, hear, smell and measure. Otherwise the knowledge (perhaps the same knowledge of good and evil described in the Bible) might be more than we could cope with.

At some point in our psychological/spiritual development, the "overself," or soul consciousness, causes us to become curious about unseen matters. We want to know more about life in general and about our own lives in particular, especially that part of it that forms our circumstances and inner patterns. We begin to look more deeply into the nature of things. We may see the patterns of our friends and develop more self-awareness by using them as our mirror. We may develop new concepts about the continuation of all life, sentient or otherwise, by observing the patterns in nature, such as the never-ending cycle of seasons. We may learn about life through observing plants or animals. Eventually we make a correlation between what we observe in our own lives and in all manner of life around us. Our curiosity begins to take us on a journey that can exist only on the level of mind. Curiosity about patterns of thought and behavior leads to questions that cannot be readily answered. Many times the journey is begun because of pain that we cannot reconcile or understand. We cannot find a teacher, psychic or religious leader who can give us all the answers, so we are forced to fall back upon ourselves. We learn to meditate, which is really the process of stilling the left brain, so valuable in protecting us from truths until some inner signal tells us we are ready to know more.

On our inner journey, it is the left brain that asks the practical questions, observes and assimilates knowledge. But the right brain has many answers stored that come forth only in the stillness necessary for listening on a higher level. Learning to have a dialogue with the subconscious is as simple as learning to ask the right questions and listening for the answers that come from within. Clearly, an individual who has practiced meditation will have an easier time, simply because he has developed more control of the left brain. However, there are other ways to by-pass the critical left brain. Anyone who has experimented with the I Ching or with a pendulum knows that the information obtained through such means is merely a reflection of inner knowledge. They are not merely fortune-telling devices, but tools that can be used for growth. Kinesiology is another method of obtaining information —emotional reactions and the accuracy of subconscious patterns can be verified through muscle reactions and health patterns. This technique is described in *Touch for Health*, by Dr. John Thye.

Some people seem to have easier access to subconscious information than others. In certain regression sessions, the information pours out. I am almost totally silent, simply listening while the individual in front of me relates his experiences. In other cases, I must work very hard to facilitate the flow of information that seems trapped or buried inside. In either case, my prime function seems to be to keep the person on the right track by asking him questions that will lead him to his own answers. If the person begins to wander off the focal point of the regression session, he might never get to the main point. So in doing a regression session alone, it is important to keep a dialogue going inside and not let the mind wander too aimlessly. I have discovered that after about two or three hours, the person can become tired. (The time may vary considerably when you're conducting your own session.) It seems that length of time is just right to allow a particular amount of past-life information to emerge.

It is important for the individual to let out only what he or she is able to deal with at the moment. In this regard, the practical left brain serves a valuable function. For that analytical part of the mind acts as a guardian to the door of the subconscious. It becomes the protector of the mind, doling out only what the total being can assimilate. That's why I stress to every client that he should trust the function of his left brain, knowing that it will release only what is appropriate at the moment. He can rest assured that his own mind will protect him and guide him to the pertinent information stored within the right brain.

If one thinks of the mind as a file cabinet with a combination lock on the outside, he can understand how the process works. The left brain processes the combination on that lock, which opens the door to the file cabinet. The files stored inside that cabinet are analogous to the information within the right brain, or the subconscious, intuitive part of the mind. However, the last secretary to put information into that cabinet left a mess. She put the files in scattered order and forgot to file some very important documents. In a regression session, the individual is simply looking inside to retrieve all the pieces of paper that will complete the picture. With that look, he begins to rearrange the data and locate any missing material. Once that rearranging job is finished, he has easy access to everything in that file cabinet and can open the door whenever he wants. When he closes the door and sets the combination lock, the information is safe once again. However, since he glanced at all those odd scraps of paper (receipts and duplicates, old deeds and addresses, etc.), he has a pretty good idea of what is contained within his family records, or his own mind. His thoughts are now uncluttered because the file cabinet is in order, and he can express much more of his mental energy in a productive way.

I also use the analogy of knitting to explain the process. Imagine knitting a sweater. As you are working on the twenty-fifth row, you suddenly realize that you've dropped a stitch on the eighteenth row. Your sweater won't be a very good sweater unless you go back and pick up the stitch. It is my opinion that in traditional therapeutic practices, the work you do is similar to picking up a crochet hook and weaving that dropped stitch into the whole sweater again. It is then necessary to pull and stretch the knitting around that dropped stitch to integrate it into the weave of the sweater. Sometimes that stitch shows and the pile isn't very smooth. It may be necessary to go back once more to pick out that stitch and try once again to blend it into the whole garment more evenly.

A regression session can augment the therapy process because in the regression process, a person unravels the *whole* row of knitting, or many rows of knitting, to pick up that dropped stitch. After that, the yarn begins to knit *itself.* By that I mean the regression session has lasting benefit for untold number of years, because information begins to float up to the surface for a long period afterward, without any prompting from the individual. The process of integrating this information into daily life begins as soon as the session is over, and in the case of an individual undergoing therapy, many pieces of the puzzle of life fall into place more easily with the deeper perspective obtained through regression.

The most important thing that changes in one's life after such a session is perspective. Before the regression session, decisions that were made during moments of trauma, loss or pain cause a person to see things out of proper perspective. This causes aberrant behavior. But as the new perspectives blend into outer consciousness, the patterns and data that have been rearranged in the regression session cause the person to live his life in a different manner simply because he begins making different kinds of decisions.

REVIEWING A PAST TRAUMA

Here's an example of how all this would work. Let's say that a child has been protected, loved, well fed and well cared for. He is secure within his environment. One day he is taking a nap when the family dog runs out of the house and is hit by a car. Mother runs out of the house to rescue the dog. She leaves the door open so she can hear the baby but she goes next door to see if her neighbor will take the dog to a veterinarian. Meanwhile, the baby, perhaps sensing something traumatic, awakens early. He cries, to alert mother that she is needed, but she doesn't respond as she usually does. He cries a little louder, but she doesn't come. Finally he screams and Mother can hear him from the neighbor's house. She runs home to get him, leaving the dog in the neighbor's care, but it is too late for the child. He has now said to himself, "My mother left me! She doesn't love me! I can never trust her again." Moreover, her attitude when she picks him up is very different. He can sense the difference, but he can't read her mind. He can't say, "Mother why didn't you come for me?" and she, being concerned about the dog, doesn't realize that the baby needs an explanation to help him feel secure once more.

The relationship between the two has changed. The baby now sees his mother as someone he can't completely trust. She only knows that formerly he was such a good baby. Now he cries when she leaves the room for just a moment. She becomes annoyed and tells him not to be a naughty baby. The pattern that has been set in motion is very different from the pattern of the loving, trusting relationship that existed before. Now the child begins to pull away from his mother. He has decided in a shocking moment of awareness that Mother is not really there to give aid and comfort when he needs her. He decides he'll have to take care of himself from now on. He doesn't trust anyone. As a protective device, he puts up a wall and becomes very independent. Mother feels unwanted and unneeded. She respects his apparent need for solitude and leaves him alone. He feels even more neglected. So a wall has arisen between them. Although this may seem like a trivial example, it is just such forgotten experiences that can cause lasting repercussions and need to be reviewed in a regression session.

During a solitary regression session, when the person reviews that moment in time, he can start by asking himself, "What was an early moment of trauma in my life?" He may simply see a small baby lying in a crib. He doesn't see any significance in that vision and is ready to dismiss it as unimportant. But if he asks himself simple questions like, "What am I doing in that crib?" he may get an impression that he is crying. He may then ask himself, "What time of day is this?" The answer... "Three o'clock in the afternoon. Oh, I've just awakened from a nap." Perhaps he's stuck for the next step. If he can look around to observe the colors in the room or the objects that seem to be there, he may suddenly see that he has awakened early from his nap and is crying because he is frightened.

Now his left-brain logic can take over and ask the next question: "Where is my mother?" The obvious answer is, "I don't know." Then, "Well, where might she be at three o'clock in the afternoon when I'm taking a nap?" The answer may come: "She isn't in the house; that's why I'm frightened." Now, where to proceed next. "Is she usually in the house while I'm napping?" The answer, "Yes, she is a very attentive, loving mother." Next, "Then why isn't she here today? There must be some kind of emergency." After a minute, "What kind of emergency could take her away from me?" Then the answer: "It feels like she ran out into the street for some reason. Oh! I see a car and I see a dog lying on the ground. Oh! It's my dog. I'm very upset because my dog has been hit. My mother is trying to help him, that's why she is late coming to me when I call for her." Then a query: "But why doesn't my mother reassure me and tell me the dog will be all right?" And the response, "Because she doesn't know I'm even aware that something has happened to the dog. She thinks I'm only a baby."

Finally, after a moment, comes the really important realization. "Oh, my poor mother. This is the moment when I decide to punish her for neglecting me. From now on, I begin to treat her so badly. I won't let her leave the room. Then I won't respond to her overtures of affection and I tell her to leave me alone. I feel so dreadful. My mother was only trying to help my dog." It is at this moment that the relationship between mother and child begins to heal.

BASIC GROUND RULES

Before you begin your own regression session, there are a few basic ground rules we need to cover.

1. It is important that you review the past in the *present tense*. When the events and questions are discussed in the past tense, you tend to be somewhat removed from the situation. Present-time language keeps you emotionally involved in the scene and is extremely important as part of the combination to open the file cabinet of the subconscious mind.

2. Trust whatever pops into your mind, even if it doesn't make sense at the moment. Leave the judgmental mind aside ("Is what I'm seeing or thinking accurate?") and trust your intuition.

If you feel you need help with your answers, invest in a pendulum. You can usually find such a pendulum at bookstores that carry astrological or metaphysical material. If you cannot purchase one, you can make a pendulum. Buy an unleaded crystal at a mineral and gem shop or a museum of natural history and tie a string around one end of it. Practice working with your pendulum by asking questions that have provable answers. Observe which way your pendulum swings for yes and which way for no. The pendulum will accurately reflect what's going on in your subconscious mind and may help you trust the answers that come to you in response to your questions.

3. Delete the word "remember" from your vocabulary, for remembering pushes things into the past again instead of keying you in to the present.

4. Describe events to yourself in as much detail as possible. Describing events in detail is important because it keeps your left brain busy so your right brain can release the information you need. Let's see how this works in everyday life.

When you are driving in heavy traffic, you must concentrate fully on the road conditions. You must observe traffic lights and keep track of the cars around you. However, after a long period of such intense concentration, your mind begins to float. Observing traffic becomes automatic; but another part of your mind—the right brain—is very busy. In fact, some people have observed that they do their best thinking while driving to and from work. During that journey, the left brain is so busy concentrating that it is tricked into allowing the right brain to have a moment of freedom.

In a regression session, the seemingly unimportant questions you ask yourself, such as "What time of day is it?" or "What color is the house I live in when I'm three years old?" keep the left brain busy. Soon the right-brain relaxes and determines that it is safe to release some valuable information that has been stored inside. In essence, the left brain has been tricked into allowing this information to come forth.

Let's say you review an incident that happened when you were three years old. You know that you fell off your bicycle and skinned your knee. You could easily tell yourself that the incident was unimportant because you remember it quite well. You know that you were taken to the hospital and had a few stitches. You're aware that you received extra comfort and attention from both Daddy and Mommy at that traumatic time.

However, with a deeper review, this is what happens. See yourself at the beginning of the incident. Describe to yourself what you're wearing. Pick a color for the dress or suit you're wearing, and then ask yourself what time of year it seems to be. Next, pick an exact date that just springs into your mind. Don't try to work out the date·from what you know. Trust your intuition about it, for it is basically unimportant later on. Describe to yourself what your house looks like. See yourself walking out of the house, heading toward your bicycle. Perhaps you see.yourself all dressed up. It doesn't make any sense to be dressed like that when you're just going out to play. Ask yourself why you're wearing what you're wearing. You may realize that you're about to take a trip to see your grandmother and you want to ride your bicycle one last time. See yourself climbing onto your bike, and review the accident. See the color of the car that takes you to the hospital and look at your parents' reactions. You may observe that they are both very concerned but they seem preoccupied. At last you may realize that this is the moment when Mother is leaving Daddy because they're very unhappy with each other. You may realize that falling off the bicycle was your attempt to divert them from their problems and bring them together again. Since you probably failed in your attempt and they did indeed separate from each other, you feel helpless and a failure. On an unconscious level, you feel it was your fault that they didn't remain together and that, generally speaking, you're a failure in life because you're ineffective in your actions. A review such as this can bring about a drastic change of perspective and, therefore, a change in the outer conditions of your life.

Treat your regression session as if you were making your own personal film. You are the screenwriter, the director and the actor. It doesn't matter if you don't "remember" the exact details of a particular scene. If you are describing an incident that happened when you were three years old, the probability of your "remembering" what you wore on that specific day is small. But if you trust your fantasy, it is possible to clothe that little boy or girl in whatever you choose. You can always change your mind and see yourself in another costume later in the scene. The choice of garments is not important; it only serves to exercise the muscles of the mind creatively.

Remember that you are aiming for the dropped stitch. The incidents along the way are not important enough for you to worry about making them accurate in every way. The emerging emotional reactions will be accurate and, when it emerges, you will feel so strongly about your new perception that any doubt will disappear. Trust your fantasy about what you suspect is correct. Learn to make a choice about an obscure memory or sensation. "Did this happen, or could that have happened?" Which choice seems more logical or probable in your life? Trust your gut reaction about which choice seems closer to the truth.

You may find your astrological chart an invaluable aid in pointing the way to areas of past trauma. In the chapter describing Saturn, I have listed the meanings of Saturn in difficult aspect to each planet. I have described what they mean in the light of the present life and how they describe your psychological programming and awareness now, but I have also described how that may have come into being from a past life. Look in your own astrological chart to see what difficult aspects Saturn makes to other planets and take them one at a time. If, for instance, you have Saturn squaring Venus and, indeed, you're aware of a less-than-fulfilling love in your own life, read my description of what that could mean, review the case history in the chapter on Saturn/Venus and ask yourself if a similar thing could have happened to you in a past life. Then allow your subconscious mind to veer away from someone else's example and allow the information about your own past to float to the surface.

But remember, the aspects are simply tools that can give you a clue about what to expect in your specific case. You don't have to learn astrology or use your astrological chart to have a regression session.

HOW TO CONDUCT YOUR REGRESSION SESSION

Find a comfortable place to sit, where you will not be disturbed for at least two hours. Put a tape recorder at your side so that you can turn it on at the beginning of your session and then forget that it is there.

Next, still your conscious mind by focusing on a beautiful rose.

See the color of the rose, notice how far it is open and how many petals it has. Next, see a beautiful, multifaceted jewel emerging from the center of that rose. It can be a ruby or a rose quartz, or even an emerald if you prefer. See the light of the jewel directed into the point between your eyes. That is the center that enables you to synchronize your left and right brains so that information can come to the surface. See the light of the jewel becoming deep blue, the color of indigo (it's also the color of that specific energy center or chakra) and affirm to yourself that you will release from your subconscious any information about the past that is necessary for review. Then trust that the information will emerge.

Next, as you feel energy rising through your body, picture a white light of protection around you—see yourself sitting inside a white cloud. Keep your posture very erect, but relax your body. Place cushions behind yourself, if necessary.

Finally, ask yourself for the information you need. Frame your questions *out loud*. Begin by asking, "What is the first moment of trauma in my life? What is a time when I am suffering?" Then wait for a picture, a thought, a sensation, a sound or a glimmer of some forgotten incident to unfold on your mental screen or in your thoughts. Investigate the situation in which you find yourself. Ask yourself how old you are, what you look like, what you are wearing, what the room looks like, who else is in the room, what happens, how you feel about it and how the others in the scene feel about it, too. Paint in all the details so that your right brain can come into play. Make the whole situation as real as possible and pay attention to minute details, such as how others are dressed. Allow yourself to see things you hadn't realized were there and to gain new insights to your behavior and the behavior of those around you. When you have found the act of omission or commission that started it all and reviewed it thoroughly, forgive yourself and any other person who was involved.

For example, perhaps you have experienced the death of a parent. Review the events of that death from the moment you hear of the passing, or from the time when you know the parent is ill and will not live. One of the most traumatic events we undergo is the passing of a parent or loved one. When we are experiencing the shock of the moment, we become dazed and may not allow ourselves to mourn the person. Be sure to do that now. Be sure to see the funeral and all the events surrounding it that may irritate or upset you.

Most important, be sure to examine any guilt you may have about your negligence or absence. It is essential to ask yourself if there was anything you left unsaid to the person. If there are things you wish you had expressed or clarified, take the time to put the person in front of you and express your feelings. Tell the person that you miss them and that you wish you had been more considerate or loving, or whatever you feel.

The guilts we carry with us from the past are the ones that can cause the most damage in our lives. If we acknowledge those guilts and ask for forgiveness from ourselves and from others, healing begins immediately. Try to understand that your thoughts are reaching people through the ethers, whether they are on the earth plane or not. You will be heard, even if only through the psychic connections you have with the individual.

After your regression session, it will be clear to you that we never lose anyone important in our lives. In fact, we never lose our enemies, either. So it is very important to make peace with those we love *and* those we hate. And because grieving prevents life from flowing on in a productive and smooth fashion, it is important to make peace with the person who died and with ourselves.

When you have finished reviewing a moment of trauma and have forgiven yourself and others for causing pain, move to an earlier traumatic event in your life. Repeat the same reviewing procedure, and continue moving back in time until you reach your very first moment of trauma in this lifetime—your birth.

What does it feel like coming down the birth canal? What is your mother doing and feeling? What is it like in the womb *before* you are born? Is there a doctor there when you come out? Nurses? What are they doing? How are they welcoming you? What do they do to comfort you or acknowledge you? And most importantly, what is your decision about how you're going to survive in life? This first birth survival decision precludes every other decision you make about survival in life.

Ask yourself what it could have been like. Several answers may come to you, like a multiple-choice exam at school. You may wonder, "Would it have been like this? Or like that?" Which answer seems closer to the truth? You will have a gut reaction to one of the answers, and that's the one you should explore further.

Now you are ready to move on to a previous life. Ask yourself to find a past life that will give an explanation of the trauma you have just uncovered. Or, if you are investigating a romantic situation that has ended badly, take this opportunity to find and review a previous connection. Take a look at the death of a relationship, even if there is no actual death involved. Ask yourself where you might have known that person before. Examine your fantasy about a past life and ask if you were guilty of omission or commission. The pain of severed relationships usually comes when the relationship was not a happy one. Look to see what caused the most grief and assure yourself that you deserve more happiness in the future. Forgive yourself, and forgive the other person. If you can release that person to have true happiness in his or her life, you'll clear the way for true happiness in your own life.

Acknowledge to yourself that from lifetime to lifetime, you've had many, many loves. If you are lonely, ask that the *right* person come to share your life. The trust that you've established in yourself during this process will lead to your participation in events in which you may have a chance to meet the person with whom you can share happiness.

You may have started your session with a question concerning a specific problem you're having at the moment. For instance, in the chapter on Saturn and Jupiter, I described a spontaneous past-life memory I had of being in the lion's den as a Christian martyr. That memory came from a question I posed to myself about having to give away my dearly loved cats due to terrible allergic reactions to them. I asked myself, "Where did my allergies to cats begin?" The answer became clear in a very short time.

You will know when you've reached the end of your session, for a particular insight will float into your mind that brings a feeling of "Aha!" At that point, your mind will take over in a different way, perhaps already beginning the process of assimilating the information into consciousness. Even if you do not reach a profound feeling of "Aha!"—if you are tired, give yourself a rest. Even only a start of a regressive look at the past will instigate a series of new awareness.

If you are able to do an entire regression session in two hours and you reach a past life that has meaning in your life now, you are to be congratulated. If you are not able to reveal very much to yourself, be loving and considerate of your inner mental process, for we all have different ways of getting the information we need in life, just as we all have different learning patterns in school. If one small new insight floats into your conscious mind, you've taken one small step to a new life. The process is like dripping water on a stone. If it takes many years, during which tiny bits of information float to the surface, you can feel happy about the process. I have had only one formal regression session. That was twenty years ago. Since that time, many tiny pieces of the puzzle have come together to bring out a more complete picture, and they are still emerging.

Once again, the questions that are most important to ask are about moments in your life when guilt, loss or trauma played an important role. But don't expect to have the kind of dialogue the people in the case histories had. Your information may come in its own unique fashion. Just trust that your higher consciousness will guide you to the pictures or sensations that are right for you at the moment.

Trust the information that comes to your conscious mind. If you do not receive a satisfactory answer, please avoid closing the door with a judgmental statement such as "I knew I wouldn't get anything." If you think you can, you can. If you think you can't, it is certain that you will be disappointed with the results. If you can suspend judgment, you may have asked yourself an important question in your meditative state that will bring no results at that moment. But one day when you are thinking about something else entirely, perhaps while you're driving a car and observing the traffic carefully, your subconscious mind can slip away from the judgmental left brain and give you a flash of inspiration that answers your question.

Last, I wish with all my heart that the information I have given you will help you attain even a tiny bit more comprehension about the meaning of life, and of your life in particular. Here's to continual growth. For the hundredth monkey theory indicates that if you have one tiny new awakening of consciousness, so will I and so will the rest of mankind.*

*In Southeast Asia, a phenomenon was observed in connection with monkeys. For centuries, monkeys dug up potatoes to eat and put them into their mouths unwashed. Suddenly one monkey took his potato to the riverbank and washed it off before eating it. Eventually, all the monkeys copied that monkey and began to wash their potatoes. Soon, on an island in the South Pacific, thousands of miles away, monkeys began washing their potatoes. This is called the hundredth monkey theory.

Dear Friends,

For some time, I have wanted to be able to share information that comes my way with my friends and clients. I have decided to write a monthly newsletter that will be a network for revealing new techniques and advances emerging around the globe. Reports from light centers springing up around the world will enable you to participate and share from a distance, and will tell you how to find these centers when you wish to visit them in person.

Perhaps most important of all, we will discuss current cycles described by astrology, so that you can understand the significance in your own life. We will look at the financial picture, for instance, and the situation connected to land and real estate, to be alert for changes in the coming times. You will be advised of monthly patterns that will indicate personal hot times for action, as well as times to lay low. Periodically, we will include articles by experts in the variety of fields connected to the healing profession: psychologists, psychiatrists, nutritionists, body therapists as well as financial analysts. Each issue will be jam packed with pertinent information.

Subscription price is $49.95 for one year. (You will receive two free issues if you subscribe for two years in advance.) Please send check or money order payable to Jupiter Pluto Communications, 204 E. 77th Street, New York, N.Y. 10021. First edition will commence in September 1987.

It will be my joy to be in touch with you on a continuing basis.

Yours truly,

Jeanne Avery

Detach and return this portion with payment.

Please send check or money order in the amount of $49.95 for a ☐ one year   ☐ two year subscription to Kaleidoscope, New Age Newsletter, payable to: Jupiter Pluto Communications, 204 E. 77 Street, New York, N.Y. 10021.

Name _____

Address _____

City _____ State _____ Zip _____

Birth date _____ Time _____ Place _____

☐ Please send gift subscription in my name.
☐ Please send price list of services.

For information about lectures and workshops for your group, and regarding annual conference, "Healing in the New Age" held in Ibiza, Spain, please contact me at 204 E. 77th Street, New York, N.Y. 10021. Telephone 212-371-4063.

Other books by Jeanne Avery:

The Rising Sign, Your Astrological Mask
Astrological Aspects, Your Inner Dialogues

To be published soon:

Astrology and Your Health, A Practical Guide to Physical, Mental and Spiritual Well-being.

_____

Jeanne Avery
Jupiter Pluto Communications
204 E. 77 Street
New York, N.Y. 10021